Performance Evaluation of Mutual Funds in India

Performance Evaluation of Mutual Funds in India

G.Y. Shitole
Gomathy Thyagarajan

ADHYAYAN

ADHYAYAN PUBLISHERS & DISTRIBUTORS
New Delhi-110002

Published by
ADHYAYAN PUBLISHERS & DISTRIBUTORS
4378/4B, 105, J.M.D. House, Murari Lal Street
Ansari Road Darya Ganj, New Delhi - 110002
Ph.: 011-23263018, 011-23277156, Fax: 23280028
Email: adhyayanpublishers@yahoo.com

Performance Evaluation of Mutual Funds in India

Edition 2012
ISBN 978-81-8435-306-8

Printed in India

Published by Harish Chandra Yadav for Adhyayan Publishers & Distributors, Delhi. Laser Typesetting at Jain Computers and Printed at Tarun Offset Printers, Delhi

Acknowledgement

The satisfaction that accompanies the successful completion of any task would be incomplete without the mention of people who made it possible, whose constant guidance and encouragement crown all the efforts with success.

We wish to place on record our sincere thanks to Dr. Sanjay S. Kapthan and Dr. Ram Sable for their encouragement and support in various ways. We owe our sincere thanks to Mr. J.C. Sharma, Retired Professor, Tata Institute of Social Sciences for his guidance in the application of statistical tools in the research work for analysis of the data.

We also take this opportunity to thank all the investors who spared their valuable time in contributing their ideas for the study and for sharing their knowledge and experiences. We would also like to thank all our respondents of primary data and employees of ICICI Prudential Mutual Fund, HDFC Mutual Fund and Franklin Templeton Mutual Fund for their valuable information. Our special thanks are extended to the distributors for enabling us to visit their offices to observe their daily operations and dealings with their clients. We are also indebted to our family for their beliefs; confidence, patience and support that made our efforts see the light of the day.

Throughout the development of this text, experienced instructors have provided critical feedback and suggestions for improvement. These individuals deserve special thanks for their valuable insights and contributions. Last but not the least, we express our sincere thanks to M/S Adhyayan Publications for the support and encouragement provided by them. We shall also look forward to and gratefully acknowledge all suggestions received for further improvement of the book.

Dr. G.Y. Shitole
Professor & Head,
Department of Commerce,
S.N.D.T. Women's University,
Mumbai.

Dr. Gomathy Thyagarajan,
Assistant Professor,
Thakur Institute of Management
Studies and Research,
Mumbai.

Preface

Mutual funds in India have emerged as a strong financial intermediary and have witnessed dramatic growth in terms of new fund openings, the number of mutual fund families, and in the total assets under management in recent years. The shift in the preferences of the mutual fund investors towards mutual funds can be attributed to many reasons like increase in returns from mutual fund investments, availability of solid products tailored to meet their financial needs, tax incentives offered by the government and a series of regulatory measures taken by SEBI.

Despite various attractions offered by mutual funds, The Indian mutual fund industry is still in an evolutionary phase. Many of the schemes announced during the last decade failed. The funds have not met their promises and asset manager specialization is still in a sprouting stage. The total net assets of mutual funds are very less as compared to other developed countries. In the product offering too, the Indian fund industry is not close to the developed countries. India's 32 member fund industry has to scale new heights to narrow the gap with the other developed countries. Besides, mutual funds can survive only if they perform well, protect the investor and satisfy the expectations of the investor community

As performance appraisal of mutual funds is a topic receiving much attention in the financial world, a sincere attempt has been made by the authors to examine the steady growth of the industry, the innovations and the developments that have taken place and to examine the performance of Indian mutual fund industry. This research on Mutual Fund industry will specifically focus on the following three companies viz: Franklin Templeton, HDFC and Prudential ICICI Mutual Funds for the period 2002-2007. The idea behind performance evaluation of these companies is to find out the risk adjusted return levels at which they are delivered in comparison to their benchmark indices.

The analysis of investor preferences has also been carried out considering all-important factors such as:

- Preferences among investments
- Preferences among mutual fund organisations
- Preference among scheme types etc

Similarly, the analysis of distributors has also been carried out in order to find out the role played by them in influencing an investor's investment decision. The authors' objective is to propose suggestions based on the analysis for the functional improvement of the fund industry that may trigger new ideas amongst fund managers and also to reshape the fault lines in the industry for the benefit of the investors.

List of Tables

List of Graphs

List of Figures

Abbreivations

AR	Absolute Returns
AMC	Asset Management Company
AMFI	Association of Mutual Funds in India
AUM	Assets Under Management
ATM	Automated Teller Machine
BOB	Bank of Baroda
BOI	Bank of India
CAGR	Compounded Annualized Growth Return
CRISIL	Credit Rating Information Services of India Ltd.
ELSS	Equity Linked Saving Schemes
ETF	Exchange Traded Funds
FII	Foreign Institutional Investors
GIC	General Insurance Company Ltd.
GETF	Gold Exchange-Traded Funds
HDFC	Housing Development Finance Corporation Ltd.
ICICI	Industrial Credit and Investment Corporation
IDBI	Industrial Development Bank of India
LIC	Life Insurance Corporation of India
M&A	Mergers and Acquisitions

MIP	Monthly Income Plan
MF	Mutual Funds
NAV	Net Asset Value
NFO	New Fund Offer
PNB	Punjab National Bank
RBI	Reserve Bank of India
SEBI	Securities Exchange Board of India
SBI	State Bank of India
SIP	Systematic Investment Plan
SD	Standard Deviation
SR	Sharpe Ratio
STP	Short Term Plan
ULIP	Unit Linked Insurance Plans
UTI	Unit Trust of India

Contents

1

Introduction to Mutual Funds

1.1 Introduction to Mutual Funds

The financial system is a set of institutional activities through which financial surpluses available in the economy are mobilized. A financial system, which is basically strong, functionally diverse and displays efficiency and flexibility, is vital in creating a market-driven, productive and competitive economy. A mature financial system has to gear up and undergo varied and comprehensive changes in order to achieve rapid economic development.

The financial sector reforms in India in the early nineties, resulted in explosive growth of the economy in the form of opening up of the Indian financial market to foreign and private Indian players, large inflow of foreign institutional investors, increased competition and better product offerings to consumers. One of the major developments of this decade has been the launch of mutual funds. A Mutual Fund is a special type of investment institution, which pools the savings of a number of investors who share a common financial goal and invests them in a well-diversified portfolio to obtain ***optimum return on investments*** with *least risk* to the investors.

Mutual funds have now emerged as a strong financial

intermediary and are the fastest growing segment of the financial services sector in India. It aims at promoting a diversified, efficient and competitive financial sector. It also aims at increasing the return on investment and accelerating the growth of the economy. It is a medium of investment suitable to the small investors, who are not able to invest in stock market directly.

Mutual funds now play a very significant role in channelising the savings of millions of individuals. The mutual fund industry in India over the years has seen remarkable changes in terms of quantity as well as quality of product and service offerings. The tremendous growth of Indian Mutual Fund industry is an indicator of India's efficient financial market and the trust which investors have on the regulatory environment. Millions of investors rely on mutual funds as their primary investments because they offer a convenient, cost-effective and easy way to invest in the financial markets. The Securities Exchange Board of India (SEBI) regulates this fast growing industry and it is the representative body of all mutual funds in the country.

Every mutual fund has a goal - either growing its assets (capital gains) and/or generating income (dividends) for its investors. Distribution in the form of capital gains (short-term and long-term) and dividends may be passed on (paid) to the shareholders as income or reinvested to purchase more shares.

A mutual fund is valued daily and reports a price known as a Net Asset Value (NAV) per share. In its simplest form, a NAV is the total value of all the securities held in a fund divided by the total number of shares owned by its shareholders. As the price of the NAV increases or decreases, the shareholder's value will increase or decrease.

1.2 Historical Perspective of Mutual Funds[1]

Tracing the history of mutual funds, worldwide, the mutual fund - unit trust as it is referred in some parts of the world, has a long and successful history.

The Beginning

The close-ended investment companies launched in the Netherlands in 1822 by King William I has been cited by historians as the first mutual fund. While some researchers point to a Dutch merchant named Adriaan van Ketwich whose investment trust was created in 1774 as the first fund. It is also believed that Van Ketwich developed the idea that diversification would increase the appeal of investments to smaller investors with minimal capital.

The next company "The Foreign and Colonial Government Trust", formed in London in 1868, resembled a mutual fund.[2] It promised the investors, modest returns by spreading the investment over a number of different stocks. They sold a fixed number of shares, the price of which was determined by supply and demand.

The idea of pooling resources and spreading risk using close-ended investments soon took root in Great Britain and France, making its way to the United States in the 1890s. The Boston Personal Property Trust, formed in 1893, was the first close-ended fund in the U.S. The creation of the Alexander Fund in Philadelphia, Pennsylvania, in 1907 was an important step in the evolution towards the modern mutual fund.

The Modern Fund[3]

The Massachusetts Investors' Trust[4] launched in Boston in 1924 is believed to be the first modern mutual fund. The fund went public in 1928; eventually it was named as Mutual Funds Investment Management. State Street Investors' Trust was the custodian of Massachusetts Investors' Trust and later, State Street Investors started its own fund in 1924 with Richard Paine. The year 1928 can be called as a significant year in the history of mutual funds, which also saw the launch of the Wellington Fund, which was the first mutual fund to include stocks and bonds, as opposed to direct merchant bank style of investments in business and trade.

There were 19 open-ended mutual funds by the end of

1929 competing with nearly 700 close-ended funds. With the stock market crash of 1929, the dynamics began to change as highly-leveraged close-ended funds were wiped out and small open-ended funds managed to survive.

1.3 Regulation and Expansion

The industry exploded at a rapid rate opening up new markets around the world. The creation of the Securities and Exchange Commission (SEC), the passing of the Securities Act of 1933 and the enactment of the Securities Exchange Act of 1934 safeguarded the interests of the investors. Mutual funds were also required to register with the SEC and to provide disclosure in the form of a prospectus. Additional regulations came in to force when the Investment Company Act of 1940 required more disclosures and sought to minimize grievances of investors of different categories.

The mutual fund industry expanded aggressively and by 1950s, the number of open-ended funds topped 100[5]. Thus the global growth of mutual funds was fuelled not only by globalisation but also by the investor's expectations of high and long-term returns.

1.4 Current Global Scenario of Mutual Funds

The complexion and size of the mutual fund industry dramatically changed across the world as new products and services were added. The number of mutual funds worldwide has grown rapidly and most of the mutual funds are based in the United States, UK, Japan and France. The industry has made significant strides in terms of its variety, sophistication and regulation.

Mutual funds found increasing acceptance in the developed countries when compared to the developing countries in the early and mid 90's but gradually it found its place even in the developing countries because of its advantages. Gradually the number of mutual funds increased significantly world wide and many developed countries started designing country specific funds to match the trend prevailing in other developed countries. The following table gives us the figures of total number of funds for all the countries for the period 2002-2007.

Table 1.1 shows that the number of mutual funds worldwide stood at 66,350 at the end of the fourth quarter of 2007. By type of fund, 41 percent were equity funds, 20 percent were bond funds, 21 percent were balanced/mixed funds, and 5 percent were money market funds. It is evident from these figures that equity funds are the most popular funds worldwide and next in line is the balanced funds. Infact, the total number of money market funds during the year 2002 stood at 4,394 which decreased to 3,480 during the year 2007.

Table 1.1
Total Number of Funds World Wide for the period 2002-2007

S. No.	*Details*	*2002*	*2003*	*2004*	*2005*	*2006*	*2007*	*%*
1.	Equity	22,974	22,688	22,362	23,264	25,698	26,950	41
2.	Bond	11,619	11,886	13,309	13,231	13,571	13,446	20
3.	Money Market	4,394	4,974	3,623	3,536	3,409	3,480	5
4.	Balanced/ Mixed	11,228	11,465	11,603	11,393	12,530	13,963	21
5.	Other	1,310	1,578	1,997	3,317	4,116	5,6131	3
	Total **All Countries**	**53,996**	**54,569**	**54,982**	**56,868**	**61,855**	**66,350**	**100**

Source: National Mutual Fund Associations and European Fund and Asset Management Association (EFAMA)

Now let us observe the following graph that shows the mutual fund assets by region.

Graph 1.1
Worldwide Mutual Fund Assets by Region, 2007

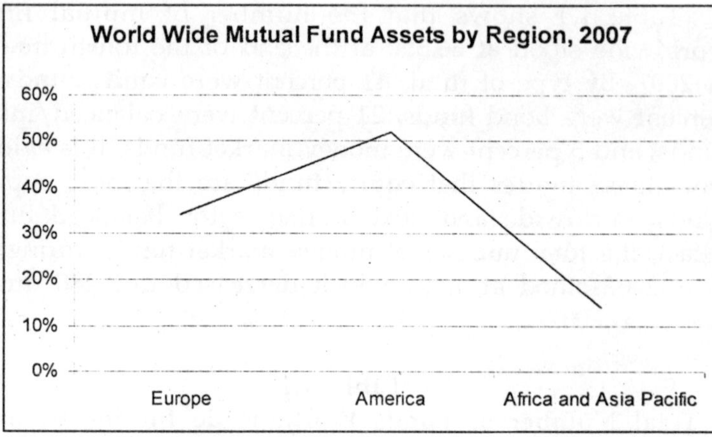

Source: ICI Statistics and Research, Worldwide Mutual Fund Assets and Flows, Fourth Quarter 2007

Graph 1.2 shows that by region, 51 percent of worldwide assets were in America in the fourth quarter of 2007, 34 percent were in Europe and 14 percent in Africa and Asia/ Pacific. Mutual fund assets worldwide increased from 1.6 percent to $26.20 trillion at the end of the fourth quarter of 2007[6]. For the year as a whole, assets grew at a rate of 20.1 percent. Net cash flow to all funds worldwide stood at $383 billion in the fourth quarter of 2007, an increase of $316 billion in the third quarter of 2007. On an annual basis, net cash flow of all funds was $1.54 trillion in 2007, an increase of 18.5 percent from 2006[7]. It is evident from the above table and graph that the mutual funds have grown tremendously and in developed countries like the U.S.A there are funds to satisfy everybody's requirement.

1.5 Evolution of Mutual Fund Industry in India

The mutual fund wave that swept the other countries

bypassed India also. The formation of Unit Trust of India marked the evolution of the Indian mutual fund industry in the year 1963. The primary objective of setting up mutual fund at that time was to attract the small investors. This was achieved through the combined efforts of the Government of India and the Reserve Bank of India.

UTI commenced its operations from July 1964 in order to encourage savings and investment. UTI Act's different provisions laid down the structure of management, scope of business, powers and functions of the trust as well as accounting, disclosures and regulatory requirements for the trust. The mutual fund industry took off very slowly in the beginning. But it accelerated when the public sector and private sector mutual funds entered the market after the year 1987.

The mobilization of funds and the number of players operating in the industry reached new peaks, as investors started showing more interest in mutual funds. The interests of the investors were protected by SEBI. The Government offered tax benefits to the investors in order to encourage them. SEBI also introduced SEBI (Mutual Funds) Regulations, 1996 and set uniform standards for all mutual funds in India. Various Investor Awareness Programs were launched during this phase by SEBI to educate investors and make them informed about the mutual fund industry.

The industry also witnessed several mergers and acquisitions. Some of them are: acquisition of schemes of Alliance Mutual Fund by Birla Sun Life, Sun F&C Mutual Fund and PNB Mutual Fund by Principal Mutual Fund. Simultaneously, more international mutual fund players also entered India like Fidelity, Franklin Templeton Mutual Fund etc. There were 32 funds as on December 2007. This phase thus became a continuing phase of growth and consolidation for the industry.

The following table shows a brief synopsis of the history of mutual funds in India.

Table 1.2
Synopsis of the History of Mutual Funds in India

S.No.	Year	Details
1	1963	Launch of India's first mutual fund - UTI
2	1964	Launch of US-64
3	1987	In 1987, the Industry was opened to other Public Sector Banks & Financial Institutions. 7 such funds commenced.
4	1993	In 1993 SEBI notified 'Mutual Fund Regulations'.
5	1993	Private Sector players were permitted to enter the industry.
6	1994	Morgan Stanley is the first foreign player
7	1996	SEBI's mutual fund regulations comes in to effect
8	1998	India's first index fund-UTI Master Index Fund launched
9	1999	First Take over - Zurich Mutual fund takes over 20th century AMC
10	2000	The Assets under Management crosses Rs.1,00,000 crore
11	2001	US 64 scam leads to UTI overhaul
12	2002	UTI bifurcation comes under SEBI preview
13	2003	In 2003 the UTI Act was repealed. UTI mutual fund came into being.
14	2004	Securities transaction costs introduced
15	2005	The industry's AUM crosses 2,00,000 crore
16	2006	The industry's AUM crosses 3,00,000 crore
17	2007	Mutual funds launch Gold ETFs that will invest in overseas securities
18	2007	The industry's AUM crosses 5,00,000 crore

Source: Outlook Money, 2nd edition, The Layman's guide to mutual funds, 2007.

1.6 Geneses of the Problem

The Indian Mutual Fund Industry is one of the fastest growing segments of the Indian economy. During the last ten year period the industry has grown at nearly 22[8] percent CAGR. India ranks 19th[9] and is one of the fastest growing, among the countries of the world. But when compared with the United States of America, the AUM in the US is more than 200[10] times than the Indian counterpart. In the product offering too, the Indian fund industry is not close to the US. Even though the total net assets of mutual fund has grown by 366.85[11] percent in India between 1998-2005 as compared to 85.22 percent growth worldwide, the total net assets of mutual funds during the same period is very less as compared to other developed countries.

From the above discussion, it is evident that the Indian mutual fund industry is still in an evolutionary phase. The Indian fund industry has to scale new heights to narrow the gap with the other developed countries. On an average, even if it is able to reach at least 20 per cent levels of a country like Brazil without taking in to consideration the US or the UK, Indian mutual funds will be able to secure a better position world-wide.

To achieve this, focused advertising, better customer service, newer distribution channels, consistent returns, new product offerings catering to the needs of the investment community and asset manager specialization is important at this point of time. As the industry moves from the growth to the maturity phase, competition has become fierce. To stand out from the clutter, a strong brand image has to be developed by the fund managers. The distribution channels in India also have to improve substantially as the funds have so far not been able to reach the smaller towns. Besides, mutual funds can survive only if they satisfy the expectations of the investors so it is important on the part of the fund managers and mutual fund product designers to combine various elements of liquidity, return and security in making mutual fund products the best possible alternative for the small investors in the Indian market.

The industry needs to collaborate with other sectors of the economy such as banking and telecommunications. The mutual fund industry also faces some major challenges in terms of manpower crunch, diminishing talent pool of fund managers, pressure of consolidation, innovation and product differentiation as increasing responsibility is being placed on the trustees to ensure that the funds are managed to the full benefit of the unit holders.

From the above discussion it is very obvious that India's 32 member mutual fund industry is struggling to reshape the fault lines in the industry and to reshape the market dynamics. It is essential to make this Industry the strongest and the most preferred instrument in Indian capital market for the coming years. In this context, the authors have made an attempt to study the performance of Indian mutual fund industry to find out whether the factors discussed above have been achieved already by this industry or whether there is still a long way to go for the industry. A sincere attempt has also been made by the authors to evaluate the performance of ICICI Prudential mutual fund, Franklin Templeton mutual fund and HDFC Mutual fund for the period 2002-2007.

1.7 Scope

This book deals with the Indian mutual fund industry and the main focus of this book is to examine and evaluate the Indian fund industry. An attempt has been made to examine the steady growth of the industry, the innovations and the development that has taken place in India. An in-depth analysis of the performance of Franklin Templeton, HDFC and ICICI Prudential mutual funds has been carried out in this book for five-year period starting from January 2002 to December 2007. This book consists of a detailed examination about the sample companies' products, descriptions and various charts and tables that depicts the performance of the companies. The idea behind performance evaluation of these companies is to find out the risk adjusted return levels at which they are delivered in comparison to their benchmark indices. An examination of these companies gives us an actual insight in to the performance of these companies.

The analysis of investor preferences has also been carried out considering all-important factors such as their perceptions, behaviour, preferences among mutual fund organisations and preferences among scheme types etc with regard to ICICI Prudential mutual fund, HDFC mutual fund and Franklin Templeton mutual fund.

Similarly, the analysis of distributors has also been carried out in order to find out the role played by them in influencing an investor's investment decision. This aspect is especially very important in order to find out the strategies used by the distributors, which affects the investor's choice of mutual fund organisation.

Based on the analysis, inferences have been drawn and suggestions have been made for the benefit of both the industry players as well as the investors. The book aims at generating fresh ideas about the fund industry and presenting suggestions not only for the functional improvement of the fund industry but also to create awareness about the conceptual and technical aspects of the mutual funds. This book is relevant to all the parties associated with the fund industry like the policy makers, the fund managers, distributors and the investors and helps them to rectify their respective areas of weaknesses.

1.8 Objectives

Against this background, the following objectives have been framed by the authors:

1. To study the organisation, management and regulation of mutual funds in India

This objective focuses on the basic understanding of the concepts, structure, management, regulation and working pattern of Indian mutual funds. This objective is important from the authors' point of view because conceptual awareness, overall understanding and the knowledge of various regulations in effect is required for a subject of this nature before the actual research work is carried out.

2. To study the services offered by mutual funds

Mutual fund services have been undergoing a sea change

in the Indian market place and the asset management companies are finding their niche in delivering unique products and service offerings. An attempt has been made to list out the benefits and the services offered by the mutual funds to the unit holders because information about the products and services offered by the mutual fund companies gives a glossary about the queries that exists in the minds of individual investors.

3. To examine the growth and development of Indian mutual funds in terms of resource mobilisation and assets under management

The book attempts to provide an in-sight in to the industry. It discusses in detail the growth and development of the Indian mutual fund industry in terms of resource mobilization and assets under management since the inception of UTI, the first mutual fund of the country. The challenges faced by the industry will also be analysed to highlight the areas where improvement is required.

4. To understand the inception, growth and performance of Franklin Templeton, HDFC and ICICI Prudential Asset management companies

Since this book mainly focuses on Franklin Templeton, HDFC and ICICI Prudential Asset management companies, it is necessary to first understand the background, the products offered and the working pattern of these companies. The sample schemes of these companies taken up for the purpose of the study will be analysed in terms of CAGR returns in comparison against their benchmarks for the period 2002-2007.

5. To evaluate the performance of the sample schemes of Franklin Templeton, HDFC and ICICI Prudential mutual funds and to measure the risk/volatility in order to arrive at the appropriate risk-adjusted rate of return using W.F. Sharpe's method.

This is an important objective as the hypothesis is drawn based on this objective. In order to test the hypothetical statement an attempt is made by the authors to evaluate the performance of the sample schemes by using the Sharpe's ratio which measures the excess return per unit of total risk. Sharpe's ratio represents the trade off between risks and returns. The main advantage of the Sharpe ratio is that it brings different schemes on an even level, and it helps the authors to find out whether the excess returns earned are due to smart investment decisions, or due to excess risk undertaken by the fund manager.

The following aspects will also be examined by the authors.

1. To identify the preferred investment avenues among individual investors.
2. To identify the investment objectives of the investors.
3. To find out the investors risk perceptions of mutual funds.
4. To identify the product qualities that affects the selection of mutual funds and specific schemes.
5. To identify the most popular mutual fund among the three selected companies from both the distributors and investors perception.
6. To identify scheme preferences of investors among the three selected companies.
7. To find out the investors image of the three companies chosen for the study.
8. To find out whether the investors are satisfied with the performance of the three mutual fund companies selected for the purpose of the study.
9. To assess the influence of distributors in fund / scheme selection of the investors.
10. To identify investor related services offered by the distributors.
11. To find out whether the distributors recommend the funds chosen for the purpose of the study to the investors.
12. To ascertain investor preferences of schemes and funds from the distributor.

13. To find out whether the funds chosen for the purpose of the study are better performers than other private, public and foreign players.
14. To ascertain the views of the mutual fund investors and distributors about the current and the future state of mutual fund industry.
15. To highlight the challenges faced by the Indian mutual funds.
16. To offer suggestions to rectify the weak lines of the system.
17. To offer appropriate suggestions and recommendations based on the findings of the study.

1.9 Research Design/Methodology

Research design is highly essential as it is the blueprint for collection, measurement and analysis of data in order to obtain answers to research questions to solve the research problem. The study is both descriptive and analytical. The systematic method adopted to carry out to solve the research problem is called as the methodology. The research design has been classified into four subsections they are:

1. Research hypotheses
2. Sampling size, composition and procedure
3. Method of data collection
4. Technique of analysis

1. Research Hypotheses

Keeping in mind the objectives of the book, the authors have framed the following hypotheses.

(1) The Sharpe ratios of the sample schemes have outperformed the Sharpe ratios of their respective benchmarks.

(2) The individual investor's selection of mutual funds is based on his perception about the funds in terms of brand image.

2. Sampling Size, Composition and Procedure

(i) Mutual fund companies

Based on the non-probability method of purposive or judgement sampling, three big and active players in the market were selected. They are Franklin Templeton, HDFC and ICICI Prudential Mutual Funds. The procedure adopted in selection of schemes is described below:

First, before deciding on the title of the book the authors did an extensive research to find out some of the best performing companies. For this, the authors had to depend on the secondary sources namely reports like SEBI Bulletin, SEBI's Hand book of statistics, mutual fund updates, leading mutual fund magazines like Mutual Fund Insight , Outlook Money, Dalal Street, Capital Market and Internet sites like Value Research online, Mutualfundindia.com etc. Based on the toppers and laggards at that point of time these sample companies were selected. The total number of schemes including options of these sample companies as on December 31, 2007 is as follows:

- ICICI Prudential AMC - 374
- HDFC AMC - 287
- Franklin Templeton AMC - 213

The sample schemes selected for the purpose of the study is shown below in the following figure.

As mentioned earlier, the emphasis of the study is to specifically examine the performance of the above companies. Taking in to consideration the limitations in a research and since it is practically not possible to examine all the schemes of these companies, the authors first classified all the schemes as equity, debt, and balanced. The next step was to filter the schemes which had no common parameters to form a basis of comparison among the three companies. Next, four debt funds, four equity funds and one balanced fund from each of the category along with their plans and options for

Figure 1.1
Sample Schemes of the Study

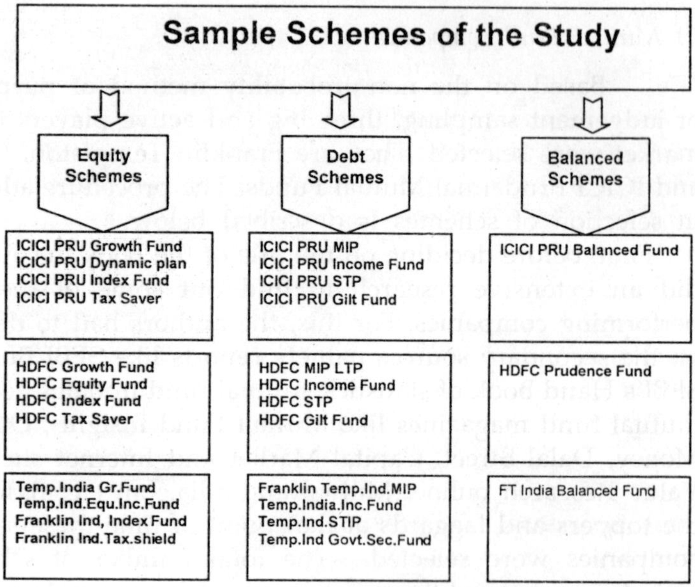

each of the company was selected. Only growth options are considered in this study. The objective-wise classification was made to facilitate peer group comparison. The selection criterion of the schemes is based on common parameters which can be used to compare the same class of the schemes across different companies. But from a broader perspective comparison of the parameters based on all categories is not possible because the objectives of the schemes may be common between one scheme and another say for example monthly income plan of one company and another company but the period or the sub clauses differ which leads to inappropriate comparison. So the authors have selected the above schemes.

As regards the analysis, the performance of the schemes were measured by observing the risk-adjusted rates of return they were able to earn during the duration of the test period (five years) using the Sharpe's performance measure in order to arrive at a conclusion. This reward to variability ratio measures the excess return per unit of total risk (Standard Deviation).

(ii) Mutual fund individual investors and distributors

As investors respond differently to fund performance across fund types, it is important for a study of this nature to find out the perceptions of investors also. Besides the perceptions of the distributor's who are responsible in influencing the investor's decision making has also be examined in this book. Therefore by using the random sampling method, the pre-tested questionnaires were administered on individual mutual fund investors and AMFI registered mutual fund distributors.

As regards the sample size, the main sample in the survey covered 50 distributors geographically spread across Mumbai city and 125 educated individual investors. In the case of investors, they were screened and the inclusion was purely based on their knowledge about mutual funds. This was necessary, because the questionnaire presumed awareness of some basic terminology about mutual funds. The investors sample also covered a wide range of income groups, age groups and occupation groups. The personal income and investments of investors were not enquired in the questionnaires because of the confidential nature of information. This careful selection of sample is not only due to the time and financial constraints but also to pick up only the investors who have invested in these three companies. The criterion that was kept in mind during the process of selection was - the investor should have invested at any point of time in all the above three sample companies or at least a minimum of two.

The survey was based on direct personal interviews with the investors using the interview schedule method. The survey was conducted during the period December 2007 to January 2008. The questionnaires had close-ended questions. The following figure shows the sample size of both the mutual fund investors and the distributors.

Figure 1.2
Sample Size of the Study

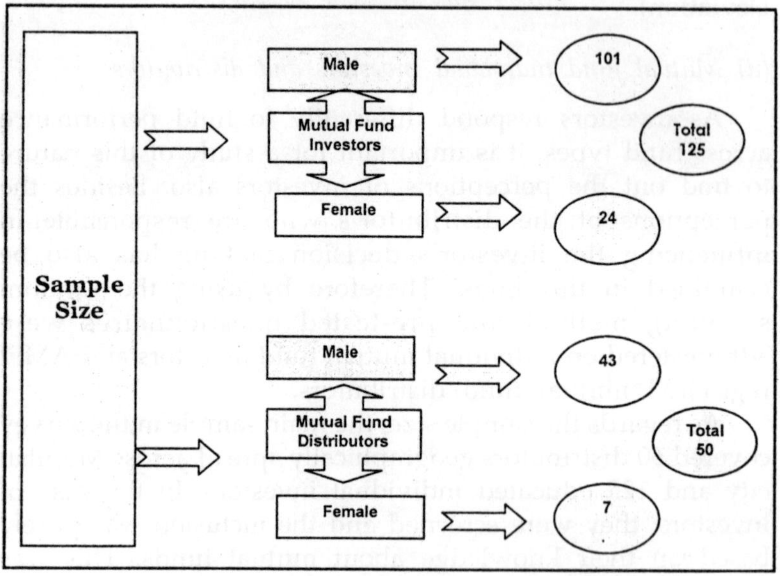

Thus from the above figure it can be observed that out of 125 mutual fund investors, 101 were male investors and 24 were female investors. The distributor sample covered 43 male distributors and 7 female distributors.

3. Method of Data Collection

The data for this study is gathered both from the primary and secondary sources. Generally, data can be collected in different ways for the subject of study. One method is to observe subjects on certain parameters, which is called observation studies and the other method is the questionnaire method. The authors have selected the second method in this book.

1. Primary data collection

The survey method was used for primary data collection in this study. Two surveys were conducted for which two sets of questionnaires were prepared. One set for the mutual fund individual investor and the second one for the mutual fund distributors. The unit of observation and analysis of survey was only among individual investors whose definition is "An individual who has currently invested in any mutual funds and this does not include institutional investors" and in case of distributors, AMFI registered distributors.

The questionnaires had close-ended questions. Both the questionnaires were partially overlapping and administered by different means for accuracy. Both the sets of questionnaires were then pre-tested. The pre-tested questionnaires were then administered on the sample. The methodology for both the surveys was similar. They were based on direct personal interviews with distributors and investors using the interview schedule method. The survey was conducted during the period December 2007 to January 2008.

Some of the objectives of the survey were:

- To identify and understand the perceptions, behaviour, preferences among mutual fund organisations and preference among scheme types etc with regard to ICICI Prudential mutual fund, HDFC mutual fund and Franklin Templeton mutual fund.
- To identify and understand the distributor's perceptions, strategies and the influence they have on the investor's decision making which also enables us to understand the distributor's views on investor's perception regarding the sample companies and their performance chosen for the purpose of the study.

2. *Secondary data collection*

Since the primary objective of the study is to evaluate the performance of the sample schemes for the period January 2002 to December 2007 of selected mutual funds, the CAGR returns along with the index value of the benchmark indices were obtained from the following sources:

1. Reference books, journals.
2. Annual Reports and offer documents of Various Mutual Funds
3. SEBI's Handbook of Statistics, Reports.
4. Memorandum & Articles of Association.
5. AMFI updates and Reports
6. News letters and Monthly fact sheets of ICICI Prudential mutual fund, HDFC and Templeton AMC's.
7. Internet sites

Further, the finance journals, magazines, newspapers, market reports, fund fact sheets and the annual reports of other mutual fund companies were also scrutinised. The data thus collected were analysed with the help of statistical tools.

4. Technique of Analysis

The performance of the funds were measured by observing the rates of return they were able to earn during the duration of the test period **(five years)** using the **Sharpe's Ratio method of performance evaluation.** This method utilizes a risk-adjusted return measurement and it is considered to be the most popular technique to measure portfolio performance. Sharpe Ratio is computed using the formulae:

Sharpe ratio of the mutual fund scheme = (Rp-Rf)/SDp
The benchmark comparison is = (Rm-Rf)/SDm

- Where Rp is the average return of the mutual fund scheme portfolio
- Where Rm is the average return of the benchmark portfolio
- Rf is the average risk free rate
- SDp, SDm is the standard deviation of the portfolio.

The investors and the distributors' responses were analysed using statistical methods.

1.10 Limitations of the study

The major limitations of the study are as follows:

1. Secondary data was collected only from the investors and distributors residing in Mumbai region. Due to geographical constraints the investors and the distributors from other parts of the country could not be covered.
2. Another major limitation of the book is, there are other popular performance measures for evaluating the performance of mutual funds but only one technique has been used in this book to evaluate the schemes selected for the purpose of the study.
3. Another limitation of the book is the sample size of the mutual fund companies. Only three big companies have been selected due to the general limitations of a research work like for e.g. time, availability of resources, period of study and geographical limitations. The underlying assumption here is by examining the profile of these three companies, an understanding of the industry in general is attained.
4. Since it is very difficult to evaluate all the schemes of the sample companies, only few schemes have been selected.

1.11 Conclusion

The Indian Mutual fund industry has started opening up many exciting investment opportunities for Indian investors. The industry has started witnessing the phenomenon of savings now being entrusted to the funds rather than in banks alone. The scenario is changing slowly and mutual funds have now become one of the most appropriate investment vehicles for most investors. As financial markets have become more sophisticated and complex, there is more scope for research. Keeping in mind the above factors and the objectives of the study, this book will try to examine various aspects such as the regulation, overview of the industry and the profile of the sample companies chosen for the purpose of the study.

References

1. McWhinney James E., A Brief History of the Mutual Fund, Investopedia.
2. Bansal Lalit K., Mutual funds Management and Working, New Delhi, Deep and Deep publications, 1996.
3. McWhinney James E., A Brief History of the Mutual Fund, Investopedia.
4. Jayadev M., Investment Policy and Performance of Mutual Funds, New Delhi, Kanishka publications, 1998.
5. McWhinney James E., A Brief History of the Mutual Fund, Investopedia.
6. ICI Statistics and Research, Worldwide Mutual Fund Assets and Flows, Fourth Quarter, 2007.
7. ICI Statistics and Research, Worldwide Mutual Fund Assets and Flows, Fourth Quarter, 2007.
8. The Evolution of India's Mutual Fund Industry, XXII IIFA Conference Montreal, Canada, October 6-9, 2008.
9. The Evolution of India's Mutual Fund Industry, XXII IIFA Conference Montreal, Canada, October 6-9, 2008
10. ICI Statistics and Research, Worldwide Mutual Fund Assets And Flows, 2007.
11. ICI Statistics and Research, Worldwide Mutual Fund Assets And Flows, 2007.

2

Review of Literature on Mutual Funds

2.1 Introduction

A critical literature review within a specific field or interest of research is one of the most essential, but also complex activities in the process of research. The purpose is to gain an insight of knowledge and ideas that have been established on a topic. This chapter will draw from such a pool of professionally shared knowledge and will undoubtedly contribute further to the traditional understandings in this field.

In this chapter, the available literature on the different aspects of this topic and the host of factors that has contributed to the phenomenal growth of the industry will be reviewed. The objective of this literature review is to understand the following aspects of the study:

- ➢ Conceptual awareness
- ➢ Regulatory issues
- ➢ Associated risk and returns
- ➢ Performance evaluation

For better understanding, the review of literature has been further divided under two broad classifications.

- Review of Literature on Mutual Funds in India
- Review of Literature on Mutual Funds in Other Countries

2.2 Review of Literature on Mutual Funds in India

The number of researches in this area is low in India as compared to other developed nations. Since 1986, a number of articles and brief studies have been published in financial dailies, periodicals, professional and research journals, explaining the basic concept of Mutual Funds and highlight their importance in the Indian capital market environment. They touch upon varied aspects like Regulation of Mutual Funds, Investor expectations, Investor protection, Trend in growth of Mutual Funds and some are critical views on the performance and functioning of Mutual Funds. The literature review begins with the books that are available in India in this aspect of the study.

Sadhak H.[1] in his book discusses in detail the growth of Indian mutual fund industry over a period of time. Dr. Sadhak clearly explains the characteristics of mutual funds, and the benefits/risks of investing in them. In addition, he describes recent changes in regulatory practices, marketing strategies, investment management, products, distribution, and service delivery systems. Several improvements in the strategic and operational practices of mutual funds are suggested keeping in mind the mechanisms used by fund managers in developed economies. Thus this revised edition provides fund managers and investors a meticulous analysis of mutual funds.

Vaid Seema[2] in this book has dealt with the conceptual and the regulatory framework and the growth of mutual funds. This book is very comprehensive and it explains the basic concepts in a very simple manner. The regulations and other aspects related to the regulatory frame work have been covered extensively. The different types of schemes, their classifications, their characteristics and their relevance have been dealt with by this author in a very precise manner. The growth of mutual funds in India has been examined by the author very critically. In short, this book is a guideline for researchers and readers interested in this area of study.

Raju Venkatapathi[3] in his book offers detailed description about various kinds of mutual fund products matching to the investor's expectations and objectives. A comparative picture has been drawn to explain the pros and cons of each instrument so that the investor is able to choose the right one. The book also attempts to provide information to assist the investor to assess their risk-return profile and accordingly choose the right product. The author in this book has put enormous efforts to understand and analyse motivations of the mutual fund investors.

Gupta Amitabh[4] in his book evaluates in detail the performance of mutual funds during the five-year period from April 1, 1994 to march 31, 1999. The study also investigates the market timing abilities of Indian mutual fund managers. It also examines the structural changes arising in the Indian mutual fund industry during the period 1987 to September 30, 2001. The book also examines the regulatory frame work of mutual funds, the growth of mutual fund industry in India and it also attempts to test the market timing abilities of fund managers. The book, thus, attempts to find whether the risk-return characteristics of mutual fund schemes are in conformity with their stated objectives, whether the Indian mutual funds been able to achieve benefits of diversification, whether mutual fund managers posses superior stock selection skills, whether the fund managers have been able to beat the market and whether the legal framework within which mutual funds operate is sufficient for the healthy growth of the industry.

Bansal Lalit K.[5] has portrayed a vivid picture of the concept of mutual funds, the constitution of mutual funds and the regulation of mutual funds. The author has also made an attempt to explain the accounting and disclosure practices followed by the mutual fund schemes. The different mutual fund schemes existing in India have been discussed in a separate chapter and he concludes the book by presenting the challenges of the mutual fund industry.

Gupta L.C and Choudhary Utpal K.[6] in their book have examined the perception and attitude of investors towards mutual funds. This book gives valuable insight into the functioning of mutual funds in India. It brings out how the investors perceive mutual funds in relation to various types of investments. This study that was undertaken by the Society for Capital Market Research and Development and later published in book form, brings out the fact that competition in the mutual fund industry has grown and become vibrant in India and it also exposes the myth of investors' loyalty and malpractices of mutual funds. The study also highlights the crisis, which UTI, the oldest financial institution, experienced due to substantial net outflows i.e. redemption and repurchases exceeding sales.

Gupta L.C. [7] made a Household Investor Survey in April 1992. The main objective of the mutual fund survey was to provide data on the investor preferences on mutual funds and other financial assets. The findings of the study provide a clear picture of the perceptions of the investors and their preferences for different savings instruments with emphasis on safety, risk and return. The findings of the study are more appropriate to the policy makers and mutual funds to design the financial products for the future.

Bhalla V.K.[8] in this book has unfolded the topics in to related chapters covering specific areas of Investment environment, Alternative Investment outlets for funds, Security analysis, Portfolio analysis and management, financial derivatives and International financial flows. The book in detail also describes techniques, vehicles and strategies for planning, implementing, and overseeing the optimal allocation of the funds of an investor or an institution in the changing environment.

Sahadevan and Raju[9] focused on data presentation on expenses and other related aspects, which are generally covered in annual reports of the mutual funds without going into the details of financial performance evaluation of the funds. The authors have very beautifully presented the different forms of expenses incurred by a fund and how the expenses are shown in the company annual reports. A bird's eye view of financial performance evaluation is given but the author have very carefully ignored the details in this regard. This book will be of great help to readers from accounting and management areas.

Sundar Sankaran[10] describes the significance of mutual funds as a suitable investment avenue which caters to varied needs of investors. This book gives insights into how mutual funds work the types of mutual funds and their investment strategies and portfolio compositions. The legal structure and the expenses of the mutual fund are discussed in a comprehensive manner. The lesson to the investor given by the author is a very good guide for the investors.

Baid Rachna's[11] book is a fine exposition on the mutual fund industry, its products and services. This book covers the topics such as concept, role, formation and organisation of mutual funds, besides touching upon accounting and valuation, investment management, development of model portfolios and the unit holders' protection. This book provides comprehensive information on a wide range of financial planning areas. This book provides, in a detailed yet concise format, the information that the uninitiated investor requires to enter the world of mutual fund investing and asset allocation recommendations.

Sisodiya Amit Singh[12] highlights the journey of the mutual fund industry in the country, the various phases it went through in its over four decades of existence, and how increased deregulation paved the way for a healthy competition which benefited both the investors and the industry players. This book attempts to offer incisive insights into the Indian mutual fund industry. The book comprises of three sections namely, 'Indian Mutual Fund Industry-An Overview', 'Product Innovation-Enabling Greater Penetration', and, 'Issues and Challenges' which is briefly discussed in the following paragraphs.

Sisodiya Amit Singh, Reddy Aala Santosh and Zaheer Feroz[13], highlights the emergence of the mutual fund industry as a major force in Indian financial markets. The article observes that with the total Assets Under Management (AUM) increasing from Rs.1,01,565cr in January 2000 to Rs.1,75,918cr by July 31,2005, the industry's growth has been nothing but exceptional. Further the article says that a slew of factors have contributed to a surge in the industry's growth. According to the author, a buoyant domestic economy coupled with a booming stock market has been one of the major drivers of growth in recent times, particularly in the last five years. Another significant factor facilitating this growth has been a comprehensive regulatory regime. Besides, increased focus on product and distribution innovations has also fuelled the growth of the industry.

Kumar Shishir and Sisodiya Amit Singh[14] highlights the growing need for a strong distribution network and models for the mutual fund industry in India to serve the huge untapped market in the country. The authors observe that the intensifying competition and the need to attain economies of scale are forcing industry players to increase their reach in non-metro cities and small towns, where the potential is high, but, penetration is low. This is resulting in fund houses exploring innovative distribution channels like Depository and Distributor models along with the traditional ones like Collection Centre model. Further, increasing commoditization and growing needs of the customers are forcing players to shift to solution-based models from the product-based ones. In both the models, the role of the distribution channel remains critical.as it helps face competition by maintaining relationships, providing advisory services and customizing need-based solutions.

Jain Abhinav[15] in his article highlights that, in the long run, economies of scale will determine the survival of the players and consolidation is the way to gain that. He adds that the rush to merge has also been necessitated owing to several other factors. For instance, the mutual fund industry has until recently been very sluggish which made existence economically unviable for small players. Besides, some foreign players opted to pull out of the country owing to restructuring and realignment of their focus at the global level (for example,

Newton Asset Management) and for some of them the small size of their asset under management simply made it unviable to commit time and investment (for example, Alliance Capital). The author concludes by saying that for many domestic, especially PSU fund houses, the lack of expertise necessitated their exit from the industry.

Rajeshwer and Jutur Sharat[16], suggests that the introduction of Gold ETFs in India heralds a new era in the market for gold. Historically, gold has been the best hedge against inflation. According to the authors, the purchasing power of gold has remained unchanged since ages and it is said that today by selling an ounce of gold, one can purchase the same quantity of goods as was the case some centuries ago. The authors feel that GETFs are going to open a new dimension in the industry.

Kumaraswamy Naidu G. and Sravana Kumar B.[17] highlights the risk and benefits of Investing in gold. Gold ETFs, like any share, can be traded and bought by the investors through their stockbrokers. They can be used for speculating in the short-term for betting on the price of gold, or it can be used for long-term investing. Gold ETFs, being liquid make investment in goldattractive. Further, the authors feel that Gold ETFs will eliminate counterparty risk and maintenance cost.

Sisodiya Amit Singh and Bala Bharathi Y.[18], discusses another new breed of funds called arbitrage funds in India. Arbitrage funds exploit the pricing differences between the cash and futures markets, hence enabling investors to benefit from such opportunities at lower costs than the stock market investors. The idea is that stock prices in cash/spot market always differ from those in the derivatives market. The arbitrageur (in this case, the mutual fund) will simultaneously purchase and sell the underlying security to gain risk-free profits from the transactions. These funds are effectively insulated from the market fluctuations to provide market neutral returns.

Bansal Manish[19], details an eight-step strategy for the Indian mutual fund industry so as to achieve greater penetration and hence fuel its growth. Some of the major recommendations of the article are -

- Migrate from 'industry' to 'opportunity zone'
- Revisit mutual funds' core competence
- Rebuild investors' confidence
- Manage risks through derivatives
- Treat investors like customers.

Madhusudhan and Jambodekar V.,[20] conducted a study to assess the awareness of MFs among investors, to identify the information sources influencing the buying decision and the factors influencing the choice of a particular fund. The study reveals among other things that Income Schemes and Open Ended Schemes are more preferred than Growth Schemes and Close Ended Schemes during the then prevalent market conditions. Investors look for safety of Principal, Liquidity and Capital appreciation in the order of importance; Newspapers and Magazines are the first source of information through which investors get to know about MFs/Schemes and investor service is a major differentiating factor in the selection of Mutual Fund Schemes.

Sarkar Jaideep and Majumdar Sudip[21] evaluated the performance of five growth oriented schemes for the period February 1991 to August 1993. They have employed the CAPM and Jensen measuring to evaluate the performance. They have also evaluated the boom period performance. They have used the Jensen measure to evaluate the performance of the scheme during the first quarter of 1992 by employing Jensen (adjusted) model. They conclude that the selected mutual fund schemes have not offered superior returns during the study period than the market in general. However, they conclude that in the boom period the funds performed well.

Raychaudhuri Arjun[22] studies about persistence in mutual fund performance in India, from 2001-04. The study uses several tests from the literature to conclude that there is persistence in the mutual fund market. It is found by the author that performance measures that are constructed using large lags of data are better predictors of future performance. In addition, the predictions of performance for longer future periods are superior to predictions made for short-run future periods. Finally, it is found that auto-regression tests for persistence may fail despite the presence of persistence

Barua[23] made a pioneering attempt to evaluate the performance of Master Share, scheme of UTI from the investor point of view with others. They employed the Capital Asset Pricing Model (CAPM), and computed the risk of the 'master Share' Scheme (For the period 1987-1991). The risk adjusted performance is measured by using Sharpe, Jensen and Treynor ratios. Here the bench-mark selected is the 'Economic Times Ordinary Share price Index. The study concludes that, 'master Share' has performed better in systematic risk, but not in terms of total risk.

Shah Ajay and Thomas Susan[24] chose 11 mutual fund schemes and studied the performance evaluation of these schemes, on the basis of market price data. The returns were computed for these schemes on weekly basis since their commencement. Jensen and Sharpe measures were used to evaluate the performance of the schemes. They concluded that except UGS 2000 of UTI, none of the schemes earned superiors returns than the market in general. The risk of these schemes was very high and funds might be inadequately diversified.

Sujit Sikidar and Amrit Pal Singh [25] carried out a survey with an objective to understand the behavioural aspects of the investors of the North Eastern region towards equity and mutual funds investment portfolio. The survey revealed that the salaried and self employed formed the major investors in mutural fund primarily due to tax concessions. UTI and SBI schemes were popular in that part of the country then and other funds had not proved to be a big hit during the time when survey was done.

Sunder Syama[26] conducted a survey to get an insight into the mutual fund operations of private institutions with special reference to Kothari Pioneer. The survey revealed that awareness about Mutual Fund concept was poor during that time in small cities like Visakapatnam. Agents play a vital role in spreading the Mutual Fund culture; open-end schemes were much preferred then; age and income are the two important determinants in the selection of the fund/ scheme; brand image and return are the prime considerations while investing in any Mutual Fund.

Kaura and Jayadev[27](1995) evaluated the performance of five growth oriented schemes in the year 1993-94, by employing the Sharpe, Treynor and Jensen measures. According to them, 'Mastergain 91', Can bonus' and 'IndSagar' have performed better than the market in terms of systematic but not in terms of total risk. However, the methodology would have been more appropriate had the study period been longer.

Shukla Sharad ,[28] **Mulraj. J**[29] **and Vikraman, Shaji**[30] in their articles that appeared in the Financial dailies (The Economic Times, Financial Express, Business Standard) and the periodicals (Dalal Street, Business Toady, etc.) have discussed in their articles about the evaluation of mutual fund schemes by comparing the changes in NAV indices However, these analyses were purely for a short period and ignored the concept of risk.

Sarkar J. and Majumdar S.[31] evaluated financial performance of five close-ended growth funds for the period February 1991 to August 1993 and concluded that the performance was below average in terms of alpha values (all negative and statistically not significant) and funds possessed high risk. No reference was provided about the timing parameters in their study. The criterion used for the selection of these five close ended schemes by the author has not been clearly depicted. But the results of the analysis indicate the performance of the close ended schemes on a generic basis has been found to be inconsistent.

Gupta and Sehgal[32] evaluated mutual fund performance over a four year period, 1992-96. The sample consisted of 80 mutual fund schemes. They concluded that mutual fund industry performed well during the period of study. The performance was evaluated in terms of benchmark comparison, performance from one period to the next and their risk-return characteristics. This study is very interesting because when it comes to performance evaluation, there are different techniques of performance evaluation. The authors have selected the method of benchmark comparison and the sample schemes selected for the purpose of study

Sondhi[3] Sondhi, H., 2004, Financial Performance of Indian Mutual Funds, an unpublished doctoral dissertation, IIT, New Delhi. Studied the financial performance evaluation of equity oriented mutual funds on the basis of type, size and ownership of mutual funds using the measures of absolute rate of return, comparison with benchmarks (BSE100) and the return on 364 days T-bills and risk adjusted performance measures (Sharpe, Treynor, Jensen's Alpha and Fama). This method of performance evaluation is more appropriate and the researcher has very beautifully presented the facts and figures. The methodology adopted in this study is very systematic and the results are shown as per the different methods according to the required parameters.

Jayadev M.[34] evaluated the performance of 62 mutual funds schemes using NAV data for varying period between 1987 and 1995. He reported superior performance for bulk (30 out of 44) of the sample schemes when total risk was considered. However, in terms of systematic risk only 24 out of 44 schemes outperformed the benchmark portfolio. He also found that Indian mutual funds were not properly diversified. Further, in terms of Fama's measure, he did not find selectivity ability of the fund manager.

Dave S.A.[35] in his paper discusses the performance of mutual fund industry and has reviewed the performance of individual funds. According to him, the Indian economy has shown an unparalled performance. The GDP growth rate has been very good, the savings rate has increased and the corporate earnings have improved during the period of study. But he feels that the mutual fund industry' performance has not been very satisfactory inspite of the improved fundamentals. He has also mentioned that wrong investments and agency conflicts are responsible for the poor performance of the industry. He feels that the mutual fund industry must try to restore its image as early as possible by individual and collective acts to restore the faith of investors in the mutual fund industry.

Thomas Susan[36] in her paper has examined the performance of Indian mutual funds. According to her performance evaluation of fund manager consists of asking whether he has significantly added value as compared with a passive benchmark which replicate his level of risk. She also discusses how to measure risk and has examined the concept of performance evaluation using Jensen's measure and Sharpe's measure for Mastershare and MSGF for the period 1994-95 using market prices and NAV respectively. Her results are very interesting. The results show a slight difference in alpha. This statistical imprecision is the major weakness of performance evaluation procedures when they are applied with short data series and the length of the series steadily grows as time passes thus enhancing the value of performance evaluation.

Kulkarni Vivek[37], in his article provided basic answers to the questions related to the performance evaluation. The article explains framework for good performance evaluation, criteria for selection of benchmark, methodology of CRISIL's in measuring risk in evaluating portfolio performance and influence of fund management fees in a performance evaluation etc. According to him, the benchmark must facilitate a fair comparison in a risk return frame work. He has very vividly explained how CRISIL measures risk in evaluating fund performance. He also feels that the fund managers do not have access to liquid and cheap sources of funds because our repo market is too small in contrast to the US market. Some of the other factors according to him which is very important are the services that the investor gets from the mutual funds, the repurchase facility and redemption schemes.

Hudson Julie[38] the article provides idea about selection of benchmark, using Sharpe and Treynor's measure for evaluation of portfolio performance, method of calculation of tracking Error etc. The study concludes that the most important need for the progress of the mutual fund industry in India is a well-established reporting standard. The author feels that fund holder who takes the risk and pays the fund management fees has the right to basic information which allows a reasonable assessment of risk and return. The author further concludes by saying that the progress of the mutual fund industry in India is a well established reporting standard.

Chakrabarti and Harsha Rungta[39] in their study attempts to identify and evaluate the performance of mutual funds with focus on private sector equity funds. The authors study the risk-return characteristics of selected major equity based private mutual funds companies. The inference of the study reveals that there is no one-to-one correspondence between performance by return and performance by risk-adjusted returns.

Narasimhan M.S. and Vijayalakshmi S.[40], made an empirical evaluation of diversification and timing performance of 76 mutual fund schemes of around 25 fund houses. The study employed two alternative methods to examine this issue. In the first case, the portfolio return and risk and correlation between the stocks in the portfolio of each scheme can be computed and compared with each other. The second methodology is to examine the correlation between the frequently appearing stocks in the portfolio. The study then compared the average returns, standard deviation and co-efficient of variation of these stocks, it is found that in almost all cases the risk level is high compared to the returns. The study also examines the fund managers ability to identify and invest in stocks that are expected to perform both currently as well as in near future. These portfolios of funds are compared with the top 100 performers of the relevant period for this purpose. The results show that there is a general shift in the investment strategy of holding a diversified portfolio and in optimizing the risk-return of investments to investing in predictive winners of the period.

Turan M.S., Bodla B.S., and Mehta Sushil Kumar [41] analyzed the performance of 54 listed schemes of mutual funds on the basis of weekly data on NAVs. For this purpose, besides risk and return analysis, the risk adjusted performance measures have been employed. The study consisted sample schemes from different sectors and the measure of risk was calculated. The study reveals that a considerably low level of risk is associated with the selected schemes, irrespective of the sector concerned.

Biswadeep Mishra[42] in his research paper attempts to evaluate the timing and selectivity skills of mutual funds. It also tries to test the non-stationary of mutual fund betas and finds out the causes of non-stationary beta. The study utilizes the Chen and Stockum (1986) model that uses a generalized varying parameters regression procedure to examine mutual fund's selectivity, beta instability, and timing skills simultaneously. Since the model removes the limitations of traditionally utilized Jensen's measure, it has been applied to Indian mutual funds to find out beta instability and their selectivity and timing skills. It was concluded that the selected mutual fund schemes had no timing ability, even though at individual level some of the schemes had timing skills. The generalized varying parameter (GVP) estimates also revealed that the systematic risk of Indian mutual funds did not remain stable over time.

Ramesh Chander[43] , in his study appraised the performance of mutual funds in India as suggested by Sharpe, Treynor and Jenson. The study also examined the portfolio management practices of mutual fund managers with respect to portfolio construction, portfolio management, portfolio evaluation and disclosure. This study is very comprehensive and interesting as it covers all important areas of constructing a portfolio and management. The evaluation procedure and the disclosure methods are very clearly explained.

Social Audit Committee[44] was constituted by UTI in 1984 under the chairmanship of Justice M.H. Kania (former Chief Justice of India). The social audit committee evaluated the performance of UTI from various dimensions, such as return, investor services and satisfaction of employees and agents of UTI. The main findings of the committee report are as follows:

- Unit Scheme 64 (US64) and various other monthly Income schemes have consistently yielded more than interest rate on bank deposits. The 'Mastershare' scheme has higher return than the BSE SENSEX and National Index during 1988 to 1991. However, after 1922, the performance was poor and the units were quoted much below their NAV in the market.
- From the investor's point of view, UTI is regarded as a progressive financial institution managing the funds most efficiently with low expense ratio. However, some of the investors have deteriorated. Further, UTI does not have enough transparency in respect of its investments, particularly regarding the US'64 as neither the NAV of that scheme nor its full investment list is made public.

From the above review, it can be stated that research covering large number of funds for a long-term, has not yet commenced. There are some important areas where research is necessary.

Value Research India Pvt. Ltd[45] carried a survey during the period June 30, 2000 to 31December, 2001. The mutual fund schemes were examined and the study reveals out of 83 schemes 15 schemes gave negative returns. Out of these 15 schemes 13 were growth schemes. One important observation of the study was none of the income or income-cum-growth schemes gave returns above 20 per cent. The risk adjusted returns of these schemes out performed the index even in bear phase. The study concluded that on the whole Indian mutual funds are safe on the whole for investment purpose.

Fernandes Kshama,[46] evaluated index fund implementation in India. In this paper, tracking error of index funds in India is measured .The consistency and level of tracking errors obtained by some well-run index fund suggests that it is possible to attain low levels of tracking error under Indian conditions. At the same time, there do seem to be periods where certain index funds appear to depart from the discipline of indexation.

Ranganathan Kavitha[47] has about the behavioural finance. The realization that this is a serious subject is, however, barely dawning. Analysts seem to treat financial markets as an aggregate of statistical observations, technical and fundamental analysis. A rich view of research waits this sophisticated understanding of how financial markets are also affected by the 'financial behaviour' of investors. With the reforms of industrial policy, public sector, financial sector and the many developments in the Indian money market and capital market, Mutual Funds which has become an important portal for the small investors, is also influenced by their financial behaviour. Thus the author in this study has made an attempt to examine the related aspects of the fund selection behaviour of individual investors towards Mutual funds, in the city of Mumbai. From the researchers and academicians point of view, such a study will help in developing and expanding knowledge in this field.

Roy Bijan[48], conducted an empirical study on conditional performance of Indian Mutual funds. This paper uses a technique called conditional performance evaluation on a sample of eighty-nine Indian mutual fund schemes. This paper measures the performance of various mutual funds with both unconditional and conditional form of CAPM, Treynor- Mazuy model and Henriksson-Merton model. The effect of incorporating lagged information variables into the evaluation of mutual fund managers' performance is examined in the Indian context. The results suggest that the use of conditioning lagged information variables improves the performance of mutual fund schemes, causing alphas to shift towards right and reducing the number of negative timing coefficients.

Sehgal Sanjay and Manoj Jhanwar[49] in their article examine if there is any short-term persistence in mutual funds performance in the Indian context. It is found that no evidence confirms persistence using monthly data. Using daily data, it has been observed by the researchers that for fund schemes sorted on prior period four-factor abnormal returns, the winner's portfolio does provide gross abnormal returns of 10per cent per annum on post-formation basis. The economic feasibility of zero-investment trading strategies that involve buying past winners and selling past losers is however in doubt. This is owing to the fact that these strategies generate low gross returns and that the winner's portfolios involve higher investment costs than losers portfolios, thus destroying a major portion of extra-normal returns. The empirical findings are consistent with the efficient market hypothesis and have implications for hedge funds and other managed portfolios that rely on innovative investment styles, including the fund of funds trading strategies that implicitly assume short-term persistence.

Panwar Sharad and Madhumathi R.[50] in their study used sample of public-sector sponsored & private-sector sponsored mutual funds of varied net assets to investigate the differences in characteristics of assets held, portfolio diversification, and variable effects of diversification on investment performance for the period May, 2002 to May, 2005. The study found that public-sector sponsored funds do not differ significantly from private-sector sponsored funds in terms of mean returns per cent. However, there was a significant difference between public-sector sponsored mutual funds and private-sector sponsored mutual funds in terms of average standard deviation, average variance and average coefficient of variation(COV).The study also found that there was a statistical difference between sponsorship classes in terms of e SDAR(excess standard deviation adjusted returns)as a performance measure. When residual variance (RV) is used as the measure of mutual fund portfolio diversification characteristic, there is a statistical difference between public-sector sponsored mutual funds and private-sector sponsored mutual funds for the study period. The model built on testing the impact of diversification on fund performance and found a statistical difference among sponsorship classes when residual variance is used as a measure of portfolio diversification and excess standard deviation adjusted returns as a performance measure.

Ferruz Luis and Ortiz Cristina[51] in their article investigate the mutual fund market in India and verify whether or not the fund classification obtained from the name given to identify them corresponds to that which would be obtained were prior management to be taken into account. This industry has undergone spectacular growth in recent years, making this study one of extreme interest, not least because institutional control could be less in times of expansion. The methodologies employed in the study were factor analysis and cluster analysis. The former determines that risk would clearly identify two groups of funds in the same manner as public classification of the funds; cluster analysis, on the other hand, identifies funds that are, in fact, very close to one another, when for the bulk of investors they are not.

2.3 Review of literature on Mutual funds in Other Countries

In the US, the Mutual Funds have a long history of more than 50 years. The advanced research of mutual fund performance evaluation contributed a lot to the wealth of knowledge, a brief review of which follows.

Sharpe W.F[52] has done pioneering work on the performance evaluation of mutual funds and has developed a composite measure that considers return and risk- which is popularly known as Sharpe's reward to variability ratio that considers both risk and return. He evaluated the performance of 34 open-ended mutual funds during the period 1944-63 by the measures developed by him. He concluded that the average mutual fund performance was distinctly inferior to an investment in the DJIA. It was also revealed in his study that good performance was associated with low expense ratio and only low relationship was discovered between fund size and performance.

Sharpe[53] in his article classified the range of mutual fund investment styles into two broad categories:

1. The characteristics-based style analysis (such as value, growth, small-cap, large-cap, income, balanced etc.), which is based on portfolio's and benchmark's current and/or historical holdings and its security weights and is considered to be the e most powerful and comprehensive approach.
2. The returns-based style analysis is a statistical technique that was originally proposed by William F. Sharpe under the name of effective asset mix and attribution analysis. The approach is based on a multi-index model, which suggests that a portfolio's return is related linearly to the return on a series of factors.

Treynor J.L. and Mazuy K.K.[54] in their study developed a model that tested the mutual funds historical success while anticipating returns. They also tested this model on 57 open ended funds during the ten year period and found no statistical evidence that investment manager of 57 funds were not able to guess the market movements in advance. This study suggests that an investor in mutual funds was totally dependent on fluctuations in the general market. The study revealed that the improvement in rate of return was due to the fund managers' ability to identify under priced shares in the market.

Jensen M.C.[55] developed an absolute measure of performance that is based on CAPM. In this model the excess returns of the fund were were regressed upon the excess returns of the market to estimate the characteristic line of regression. He also evaluated the ability of the fund managers in selecting the undervalued securities. He concludes that for the sample 115 mutual funds, the fund managers were not able to forecast security prices well enough to recover research expenses and fees.

E. Fama[56] developed a methodology for evaluating investment performance of managed portfolios. He suggested that the over all performance of managed portfolios could be broken down into several components. He argued that the observed return of a fund could be due to ability of fund managers to pick up the best securities at a given level of risk (their selectivity ability). Some portion of this return could also arise due to the prediction of general market price movements (their timing ability). Fama suggested that return on a portfolio could be subdivided into two parts. The return for security selection and return for bearing risk. Various finer subdivisions of both selectivity and risk were also suggested. The model developed by him combined concepts from modern theories of portfolio selection and capital market equilibrium with those of traditional concepts of what constitute good portfolio management.

McDonald J.G. [57] evaluated performance in terms of Sharpe and Treynor's index as also in terms of Jensen's alpha. The study revealed that 54 per cent of the funds had positive alphas. Mean alpha for the sample was found to be 0.052. Statistical significance was not reported in his study.

Kon S.F.[58] evaluated performance in terms of selectivity and timing parameters over a period, January 1960 to June 1976. The sample had 37 funds. The study concluded that individually few funds have shown positive selectivity and timing skills but collectively mutual funds failed to perform satisfactorily.

Henriksson R.D.[59] evaluated performance in terms of market timing abilities with sample of 116 open-ended investment schemes during the period, February 1968 – June 1980. The empirical results obtained indicated unsatisfactory timing skills of the fund managers.

Chang, et al[60] tested stock selectivity abilities and market timing abilities of 67 mutual funds over a performance period January 1971 to December 1979. They used parametric statistical tool to test the presence of either of the two skills in these mutual funds. They concluded that the fund managers are unable to outperform a passive investment strategy.

Blake, Elton, and Gruber[61] have examined two samples of bond funds—one sample designed to eliminate survivorship bias and a second much larger sample using linear and nonlinear models. Overall and for subcategories of bond funds, they find that bond funds under perform relevant indexes post expenses. The authors' results are robust across a wide choice of models. They find that, on average, a percentage-point increase in expenses leads to a percentage-point decrease in performance. The nonlinear model weights closely match actual composition weights. The authors find no evidence of predictability using past performance to predict future performance for their unbiased sample.

Malkeil[62] in his article has analysed several studies which suggest that equity mutual fund managers achieve superior returns and that considerable persistence in performance exists. His study utilises a unique data set including returns from all equity mutual funds existing each year. These data enable the reader more precisely to examine performance and the extent of survivorship bias.

Jain and Wu[63] examines a sample of 294 mutual funds that are advertised in Barron's and Money magazine and they found out that the pre advertisement performance of these funds is significantly higher than that of the benchmarks. They also tested whether the sponsors select funds to signal continued superior performance or they use the past superior performance to attract more money into the funds. Their analysis shows that there is no superior performance in the post advertisement period. Thus, the results do not support the signalling hypothesis. On the other hand, they also found out that the advertised funds attract significantly more money in comparison with a group of control funds.

Wermers[64] used a new database to perform a comprehensive analysis of the mutual fund industry. They found that funds hold stocks that outperform the market by 1.3 percent per year, but their net returns under perform by one percent. Of the 2.3 percent difference between these results, 0.7 percent is due to the underperformance of non stock holdings, whereas 1.6 percent is due to expenses and transactions costs. Thus, funds pick stocks well enough to cover their costs. Also, high-turnover funds beat the Vanguard Index 500 fund on a net return basis. Their evidence supports the value of active mutual fund management.

Zheng[65] has used a large sample of equity funds, to find evidence that funds that receive more money subsequently perform significantly better than those that lose money. This effect is short-lived and is largely but not completely explained by a strategy of betting on winners. In the aggregate, there is no significant evidence that funds that receive more money subsequently beat the market.

Statman[66] in his article tries to separate facts from beliefs because he feels that conversations about socially responsible investing are difficult because they combine facts with beliefs. Proponents of socially responsible investing believe that combining social goals with investments do good. Opponents believe that such combinations are unwise or even illegitimate. After careful examination he reports that the Domini Social Index, an index of socially responsible stocks, did better than the S&P 500 Index and those socially responsible mutual funds did better than conventional mutual funds over the 1990-98 period but the differences between their risk-adjusted returns are not statistically significant. Both groups of mutual funds trailed the S&P 500 Index.

Chalmers, Edelen and Kadlec[67] estimated trading costs for a sample of equity mutual funds and found that these costs average 0.78 per cent of fund assets per year. They also found that the cross-sectional variation in trading costs is greater than that implied by turnover, and trading costs have more explanatory power for fund returns and they concluded by saying that turnover is an important factor in assessing mutual fund trading costs.

Malhotra and McLeod[68] in their paper conduct an empirical analysis of mutual fund expenses. The results of their analysis of equity funds suggest that expense-conscious investors should look at the fund size, age, turnover ratio, and cash ratio as key determinants of expenses. Their analysis of bond funds suggests that the key factors are the fund's sales charge, weighted average maturity and size.

Grinblatt, Titman, Wermers and Daniel[69] develops and applies new measures of portfolio performance which use benchmarks based on the characteristics of stocks held by the portfolios that are evaluated. Specifically, the benchmarks are constructed from the returns of 125 passive portfolios that are matched with stocks held in the evaluated portfolio on the basis of the market capitalization, book-to-market, and prior-year return characteristics of those stocks. Based on these benchmarks, "Characteristic Timing" and "Characteristic Selectivity" measures are developed that detect, respectively, whether portfolio managers successfully time their portfolio weightings on these characteristics and whether managers can select stocks that outperform the average stock having the same characteristics. The authors apply these measures to a new database of mutual fund holdings covering over 2500 equity funds from 1975 to 1994. Their results show that mutual funds, particularly aggressive-growth funds, exhibit some selectivity ability, but that funds exhibit no characteristic timing ability.

Chevalier and Ellison[70] examine whether mutual fund performance is related to characteristics of fund managers that may indicate ability, knowledge, or effort. In particular, they study the relationship between performance and the manager's age, the average composite SAT score at the manager's undergraduate institution, and whether the manager has an MBA. Although the raw data suggest striking return differences between managers with different characteristics, most of these can be explained by behavioural differences between managers and by selection biases. After adjusting for these, some performance differences remain. In particular, managers who attended higher-SAT undergraduate institutions have systematically higher risk-adjusted excess returns.

Blake, Elton and Gruber[71] examines predictability for stock mutual funds using risk-adjusted returns. They find that past performance is predictive of future risk-adjusted performance. Applying modern portfolio theory techniques to past data improves selection and allows the authors to construct a portfolio of funds that significantly outperforms a rule based on past rank alone. In addition, they can form a combination of actively managed portfolios with the same risk as a portfolio of index funds but with higher mean return. The portfolios selected have small but statistically significant positive risk-adjusted returns during a period where mutual funds in general had negative risk-adjusted returns.

Markowitz[72] in this paper first considers the view that the investor does (or should) maximize discounted expected, or anticipated, returns. This rule is rejected both as a hypothesis to explain, and as a maximum to guide investment behaviour. He next considers the rule that the investor does (or should) consider expected return a desirable thing and variance of return an undesirable thing. This rule has many sound points, both as a maxim for, and hypothesis about, investment behaviour. He also illustrates geometrical relations between beliefs and choice of portfolio according to the "expected returns - variance of returns" rule.

David Logan Scott[73] analyzes the role that mutual funds play in achieving a balanced portfolio. In addition to explaining how shares in mutual funds are bought and sold, this book guides the investors how to assess a fund's investment objective in light of their own goals, how to choose from among stock, bond, and money market funds, how to evaluate the three different kinds of income associated with mutual funds, dividends, capital gains, and market appreciation and how to save on fees when buying and redeeming mutual fund shares.

Rowland Mary[74] in her book gives details of various funds, schemes, fund managers and also the views of well-known investment advisers in America. The author explains that every investor should set specific goals for investment and choose the right type of funds to achieve the goal. The author also lays lot of importance on the role of fund managers. In parts two, three and four she explains and elucidates the concepts and principles of investment.

Philip Davis E. and Benn Steil[75]in their book provides a comprehensive economic assessment of institutional investment. It charts the development and performance of the asset management industry and analyzes the implications of rising institutionalized saving for the development of the securities trading industry, the financial sector as a whole, and the wider economy. The book draws extensively on international experience, particularly in the United States, Western Europe, and Japan.

Graciela Kaminsky L., Richard Lyons K. and Sergio Schmukler L.[76] **in their article** provides an overview of mutual fund activity in emerging markets. It describes their size, asset allocation, and country allocation and then focuses on their behaviour during crises in emerging markets in the 1990s. It analyzes data at both the fund-manager and fund-investor levels. Due to large redemptions and injections, funds' flows are not stable. Withdrawals from emerging markets during recent crises were large, which is consistent with the evidence on financial contagion.

Michael C. Jensen[77] derived a risk-adjusted measure of portfolio performance (Jensen's alpha) that estimates how much a manager's forecasting ability contributes to fund's returns.

Wenchi Kao G., Louis Cheng T. W., Kam Chan C.[78] in their article examines the selectivity and market-timing ability of international mutual fund managers. Ninety-seven international mutual funds with a minimum of five-year return history selected from the Morningstar database have been analyzed. The findings of this study suggest that managers of international mutual funds possess good selectivity and overall performance. This study also finds weak evidence of poor market-timing ability. Finally, this study concludes saying that managers for European funds show poorer performance than those managing the other three international fund groups.

Russ Wermers[79] analyses the trading activity of the mutual fund industry from 1975 through 1994 to determine whether funds "herd" when they trade stocks and to investigate the impact of herding on stock prices. Although the authors find little herding by mutual funds in the average stock, they find much higher levels in trades of small stocks and in trading by growth-oriented funds. Stocks that herds buy outperform stocks that they sell by 4 percent during the following six months; this return difference is much more pronounced among small stocks. Their results are consistent with mutual fund herding speeding the price-adjustment process.

Haslem John A.[80] provides summaries of existing research with practical guidelines for mutual fund analysis. The book cover a broad range of topics, including understanding the advantages and disadvantages of mutual funds and long and short-term investing, evaluating stock/bond allocations within fund portfolios, assessing fund diversification risk, measuring fund returns and risk, and making fund buy/sell decisions.

Ronald Rutherford K.[81] uniquely in his book covers the statistical and non-statistical issues involved in selecting and managing a balanced portfolio of mutual funds. He explains investment policy development techniques, explores all asset classes of mutual funds, and covers the critical issues of style analysis, data interpretation and style management.

Seth Anderson C and Parvez Ahmed[82] have designed their book for the academic researchers interested in the various issues surrounding mutual funds and for the practitioners interested in funds for investment purposes. The author briefly trace the historical evolution of funds, presents important aspects of the Investment Company Act of 1940, and then summarises a substantial portion of the academic literature which has been written over the past five decades.

Baks, Klaas, Metrick, Andrew1, Wachter and Jessica[83] analyses mutual-fund performance from an investor's perspective. The portfolio-choice problem for a mean-variance investor choosing among a risk-free asset, index funds, and actively managed mutual funds has been analyzed. To solve this problem, the authors have employed a Bayesian method of performance evaluation; a key innovation in this approach is the development of a flexible set of prior beliefs about managerial skill. The researchers have then applied this methodology to a sample of 1,437 mutual funds and have found out some extremely skeptical prior beliefs nevertheless lead to economically significant allocations to active managers.To conclude, the literature survey reveals that, on an average mutual fund managers are not able to offer higher returns than the unmanaged portfolios. The implication of these studies is that the markets are reasonably efficient.

Pendaraki K.[84] studied construction of mutual fund portfolios, developed a multi-criteria methodology and applied it to the Greek market of equity mutual funds. The methodology is based on the combination of discrete and continuous multi-criteria decision aid methods for mutual fund selection and composition. UTADIS multi-criteria decision aid method is employed in order to develop mutual fund's performance models. Goal programming model is employed to determine proportion of selected mutual funds in the final portfolios.

Zakri Bello Y.[85] matched a sample of socially responsible stock mutual funds matched to randomly select conventional funds of similar net assets to investigate differences in characteristics of assets held, degree of portfolio diversification and variable effects of diversification on investment performance. The study found that socially responsible funds do not differ significantly from conventional funds in terms of any of these attributes. Moreover, the effect of diversification on investment performance is not different between the two groups. Both groups underperformed the Domini 400 Social Index and S & P 500 during the study period.

2.4 Conclusion

From the above review it can be inferred that mutual fund as an investment vehicle is capturing the attention of various segments of the society, like academicians, industrialists, financial intermediaries, investors and regulators for varied reasons and deserves an in depth study. The authors of traditional reviews, who may be experts in their field, have used informal, unsystematic and subjective methods for collecting and interpreting information. . An advantage of these reviews is that they are often conducted by experts who have a thorough knowledge of the research field; however, a disadvantage lies in the authors possibly having preconceived notions or biases leading them to overestimate the value of some studies. Even though some of the studies conducted so far are subject to some criticisms on the ground that relatively small sample size, short time period, scope limited to either open ended or closed ended or listed schemes, the literature survey reveals that there is still further scope for advanced research in this area.

References

1. Sadhak H., Mutual Funds in India -Marketing Strategies and Investment Practices, New Delhi, Response Books, 2003.
2. Vaid Seema, Mutual Fund Operations in India, Varanasi, Rishi Publications, 1994.
3. Raju Venkatapathi, Mutual funds in India-Investor's perceptions, New Delhi, Quality publishing company, 2000.
4. Gupta Amitabh, A Study of Investment Management, New Delhi, Anmol Publications, 2002.
5. Bansal Lalit K., Mutual Funds - Management and Working, New Delhi, Deep and Deep Publications, 1997.
6. Gupta L.C and Choudhary Utpal K., How good are mutual funds, New Delhi, Society for Capital Market Research and Development.
7. Gupta, L.C., Mutual Funds and Asset Preference Household Investors Survey, New Delhi, Society for Capital Market Research and Development, 1994.
8. Bhalla V.K.., Investment Management-Security analysis and portfolio management, New Delhi, S. Chand and co publishers, 2005.
9. Sahadevan and Raju, M.T., Mutual Funds, Data, Interpretation and Analysis', New Delhi, Prentice Hall of India Pvt. Ltd.,1996.
10. Sankaran Sundar, Indian Mutual Funds Handbook, New Delhi, Vision Books,2003.
11. Baid Rachna, Mutual Funds Products and Services, New Delhi, TaxMann Publications (P.) Ltd.,2007.

12. Sisodiya Amit Singh, Mutual Fund Industry in India-An Introduction, ICFAI university press.
13. Sisodiya Amit Singh, Reddy Aala Santosh and Zaheer Feroz, "On a Growth Trail", Mutual Fund Industry in India-An Introduction, ICFAI university press.
14. Kumar Shishir and Sisodiya Amit Singh, "Evolving Distribution Models", Mutual Fund Industry in India-An Introduction, ICFAI university press.
15. Jain Abhinav, "The Consolidation Spree", Mutual Fund Industry in India-An Introduction, ICFAI university press.
16. Rajeshwer and Jutur Sharat, "Gold Exchange Traded Funds-Enter India", Mutual Fund Industry in India-An Introduction, ICFAI university press(publication division).
17. Kumaraswamy Naidu G. and Sravana Kumar B., "The Gold ETFs-The Nitty Gritty", Mutual Fund Industry in India-An Introduction, ICFAI university press(publication division).
18. Sisodiya Amit Singh and Bala Bharathi Y., "Arbitrage Funds in India: Leveraging the Derivatives Markets", Mutual Fund Industry in India-An Introduction, ICFAI university press.
19. Bansal Manish, "Mutual Funds-Eight Steps to Nirvana", Mutual Fund Industry in India-An Introduction, ICFAI university press.
20. Madhusudan Jambodekar V, "Marketing Strategies of Mutual Funds -- Current Practices and Future Directions", Working Paper, UTI – IIMB Centre for Capital Markets Education and Research, Bangalore,1996.
21. Sarkar Jaideep and Majumdar Sudip, "Performance Evaluation of Mutual Funds in India", NMIS Management Review, Vol. VI, No. 2, July-December 1994, pp. 64-78.
22. Raychaudhuri Arjun," Persistence in the Indian Mutual Fund Market", The ICFAI Journal of Financial Economics, Vol. III, Issue 1, 2005, pp 6-25.
23. Barua Samir K, "A Regulatory Framework for Mutual Funds", Economic and Political Weekly, May 25, 1991, pp. 55-59.
24. Shah Ajay and Susan Thomas," Performance Evaluation of Professional Portfolio Management in India", A paper prepared by CMIE, 10 April, 1994.
25. Sujit Sikidar and Amrit Pal Singh, " Financial Services : Investment in Equity and Mutual Funds – A Behavioural

Study, in Bhatia B.S., and Batra G.S., ed., Management of Financial Services, New Delhi, Deep and Deep Publications, 1996.

26. Sunder Syama, "Growth Prospects of Mutual Funds and Investor perception with special reference to Kothari Pioneer Mutual Fund", Project Report, Sri Srinivas Vidya Parishad, Andhra University, Visakhapatnam,1998.
27. Kaura and JayaDev, "Performance of Growth Oriented Mutual Funds: An Evaluation", The ICFAI Journal of Applied Finance, Vol. 1, No.1, January 1995, pp. 1-14.
28. Shukla, Sharad, "Mutual Funds: Past Performance is no Indicator of the Future", The Economic Times, June 1, 1992.
29. Mulraj, J., "Master Shares : A Critical Evaluation", The Economic Times, September 28, 1992.
30. Vikraman, Shaji, "Mutual Funds performance : The Criterion", Business line, February 13, 1994.
31. Sarkar, J. and Mazumdar S., "Weak Form of Efficient Market Hill Publishing Company Ltd.,1997, pp. 1-41.
32. Gupta, O.P. and Sehgal, S., "Investment Performance of Mutual Funds - The Indian Experience", "Indian Capital Market - Trends and Dimensions", Tata McGraw Hill Publishing Company Ltd.,1997, pp. 1-41.
33. Sondhi, H., 2004, Financial Performance of Indian Mutual Funds, an unpublished doctoral dissertation, IIT, New Delhi.
34. Jayadev M., "Mutual Fund Performance: An Analysis of Monthly Returns" Finance India Vol. X, No. 1, March 1996, pp.73-84.
35. Dave S.A., "The Challenges of the Mutual Fund Industry" (Edited volume 'The Future of Fund Management in India' Editor Tushar Waghmare), Tata McGraw Hill Publishing Company Ltd.,New Delhi, 1998 pp.15-17.
36. Thomas Susan, "Performance evaluation of Indian Funds" (Edited volume 'The Future of Fund Management in India' Editor Tushar Waghmare), Tata McGraw Hill Publishing Company Ltd., New Delhi 1998, pp. 23-31.
37. Kulkarni Vivek, "Fund Evaluation at CRISIL" (Edited volume 'The Future of Fund Management in India ' Editor Tushar Waghmare), Tata McGraw Hill Publishing Company Ltd., New Delhi, 1998, pp. 33-35.

39. Anjan Chakrabarti and Harsha Rungta "Mutual Funds Industry in India: An In-depth Look into the Problems of Credibility, Risk and Brand" The ICFAI Journal of Applied Finance, Volume 6, No. 2, April 2000, pp. 26-46.

40. M.S. Narasimhan and Vijayalakshmi S., "Performance Analysis of Mutual Funds in India" Finance India Vol XV No. 1, March 2001, pp. 155-174.

41. Turan M.S., Bodla B.S., and Mehta Sushil Kumar,"Performance Evaluation of Listed Schemes of Mutual Funds" Management Researcher, Vol. VIII, No. 1 & 2 July-December 2001, pp. 38-66.

42. Biswadeep Mishra "Selectivity and Timing Skills of Mutual Funds in India: An Empirical Analysis",The ICFAI Journal of Applied Finance, Volume 8, No. 5, September 2002, pp. 5-16.

43. Ramesh Chandra, "Performance Appraisal of Mutual Funds in India" Excel Books, New Delhi, 2002, pp. 79-110.

44. Report of the Social Audit Committee, Unit Trust of India, 1998.

45. Value Research India Pvt. Ltd., "Mutual Fund Survey-2000-2001", New Delhi, 2001.

46. Fernandes Kshama, "Evaluating index fund implementation in India", Working paper, http://www.nse-india.com/content/research/Paper66.pdf.

47. Ranganathan Kavitha," A Study of Fund Selection Behaviour of Individual Investors Towards Mutual Funds - with Reference to Mumbai City", Indian Institute of Capital Markets 9th Capital Markets Conference Paper, 2006.

48. Roy Bijan, Saiket Sovan Deb, "The conditional performance of Indian mutual funds: an empirical study", Working paper, http://papers.ssrn.com/sol3/papers.cfm?abstract_id=593723

49. Sehgal Sanjay and Manoj Jhanwar, "Short-Term Persistence in Mutual Funds Performance: Evidence from India", 10th Capital Markets Conference, Indian Institute of Capital Markets, WWW.SSRN.com.

50. Panwar Sharad and Madhumathi R.,"Characteristics and performance evaluation of selected mutual funds in India", Indian Institute of Capital Markets 9th Capital Markets Conference Paper, 2006.

51. Ferruz Luis and Ortiz Cristina ," Does Mutual Fund Management in India Correspond to It's Investment Objective Classification?",WWW.SSRN.com.
52. Sharpe. William.F., "Mutual Fund Performance" Journal of Business, 39, 1966, 119-138.
53. Sharpe, W.F., "Determining a Fund's Effective Asset Mix," Investment Management Review, December 1988, pp. 59-69.
54. Treynor J.L. and Mazuy K.K., "Can Mutual Funds outguess the Market" Harvard Business Review, 44, 1966, pp. 131-13.
55. Jensen M. C., "The performance of Mutual Funds in the period 1945 - 1964" Journal of Finance, Vol. 23, No 2, 1968 pp. 389–416.
56. Fama E., "Efficient Capital Market: A Review of theory and Empirical work" Journal of Finance, Vol.25, No. 5, 1970.
57. McDonald, J.G., "Objectives and Performance of Mutual Funds: 1960-67", Journal of Financial and Quantitative Analysis, June 1974, pp. 311-333.
58. Kon, S.F., "The Market Timing Performance of Mutual Fund Managers", Journal of Business, July 1983, pp. 323-347.
59. Henriksson, R.D., "Market Timings and Mutual Funds Performance: An Empirical Investigation", Journal of Business, January 1984, pp.73-96.
60. Chang, E.C. and Lewellen W., (1984), 'Market Timing and Mutual Fund Investment Performance', Journal of Business, January 1984, pp.57-72.
61. Blake, Elton and Gruber, "The Performance of Bond Mutual Funds", Journal of Business, 1993.
62. Malkiel, "Returns from Investing in Equity Mutual Funds 1971 to 1991",Journal of Finance 1995.
63. Jain and Wu, "Truth in Mutual Fund Advertising: Evidence on Future Performance and Fund Flows", Journal of Finance, 2000.
64. Wermers, "Mutual Fund Performance: An Empirical Decomposition into Stock-Picking Talent, Style, Transactions Costs, and Expenses", Journal of Finance, 2000.
65. Zheng, "Is Money Smart? A Study of Mutual Fund Investors' Fund Selection Ability", Journal of Finance, 1999.

66. Statman, "Socially Responsible Mutual Funds", Financial Analysts Journal, 2000.

67. Chalmers, Edelen and Kadlec, "Mutual fund trading costs", Rodney L. White Center for Financial Research Working Papers, 1999.

68. Malhotra and McLeod: "An Empirical Analysis of Mutual Fund Expenses", Journal of Financial Research, 1997.

69. Grinblatt, Titman, Wermers and Daniel, "Measuring Mutual Fund Performance with Characteristic-Based Benchmarks", Journal of Finance, 1997.

70. Chevalier and Ellison, "Are Some Mutual Fund Managers Better Than Others? Cross-Sectional Patterns in Behaviour and Performance", Journal of Finance, 1999.

71. Blake, Elton and Gruber, "The Persistence of Risk-Adjusted Mutual Fund Performance", Journal of Business, 1996.

72. Markowitz, "Portfolio Selection", Journal of Finance, 1952.

73. David Logan Scott, "David Scott's Guide to Investing in Mutual Funds", Houghton Mifflin, 2004.

74. Rowland Mary, The new commonsense guide to mutual funds, New Delhi, Vision Books.

75. Philip Davis E. and Benn Steil," Institutional Investors", MIT Press, 2001.

76. Graciela Kaminsky L., Richard Lyons K. and Sergio Schmukler L., "Mutual Fund Investment in Emerging Markets : An Overview", The World Bank Economic Review, Vol. 15, No. 2, 315-340,2001.

77. Michael C. Jensen," The Performance of Mutual Funds in the period 1945-1964", Journal of Finance, Vol. 23, No. 2,1967, 389-416.

78. Wenchi Kao G., Louis Cheng T. W., Kam Chan C., "International mutual fund selectivity and market timing during up and down market conditions", The Financial Review, Volume 33 Issue 2, May 1998, Page 127.

79. Russ Wermers, "Mutual Fund Herding and the Impact on Stock Prices", The Journal of Finance,Volume 54 Issue 2, April 1999, pg. 581.

80. Haslem John A., "Mutual Funds - risk and performance analysis for decision making", Blackwell Publishing, 2003.

81. Ronald K. Rutherford, "The Complete Guide to Managing A Portfolio of Mutual Funds", Tata McGraw-Hill Publishing Ltd., 1998.

82. Seth Anderson C. and Parvez Ahmed," Mutual Funds: Fifty Years of Research Findings", Springer 2005, Vol. 16,2005, IX, 165 p., Hardcover,ISBN: 978-0-387-25307-7.

83. Baks, Klaas, Metrick, Andrew, Wachter and Jessica, "Should Investors Avoid All Actively Managed Mutual Funds? A Study in Bayesian Performance Evaluation", Journal of finance, Vol 56, no.1,Feb 2001, pp-45-85.

84. Pendaraki, K., "On the construction of mutual fund portfolios: A Multi- criteria methodology and an application to the Greek market of equity mutual funds", European Journal of Operational Research, Vol. 163, June 2005.

85. Zakri Bello Y.,"Socially Responsible Investing and Portfolio Diversification", The Journal of Financial, Research, Vol. XXVIII, No. 1, 2005, pp.41-57.

3

Conceptual and Structural Framework of Indian Mutual Fund Industry

3.1 Introduction

Mutual funds have opened new avenues to millions of small investors. An average investor is generally inexperienced and clueless as to how the stock market functions. The risks associated with it can endanger the hard-earned money of the investor. The other options that are available are the bank rates but the bank rates have fallen down and are generally below the inflation rate. When the bank rates fall down, the value of money also decreases over a period of time which in turn affects the returns of the investor. This is where Mutual Funds come into picture because returns in the mutual funds are generally better than any other option in any other avenue over a reasonable period of time. Mutual funds make savings and investing simple, accessible, and affordable. Mutual funds are an alternative to investing directly. So in order to understand the concept of mutual funds, this chapter provides an overview of the basics of mutual fund, the products that are available and the major transformation and structural changes witnessed in the last two decades.

3.2 Conceptual Background of Mutual Funds

A Mutual Fund is a professionally managed investment vehicle which allows a group of investors to pool their money together with a clear common financial goal. It consists of a wide collection of stocks and/or bonds, which is managed by professionals called fund managers. Each investor holds shares, which forms a portion of the holdings and the returns are divided in proportion of their holdings. Thus, a mutual fund investor can enjoy the benefits of high return from investment in shares and other instruments, and at the same time minimize the risk associated with it.

The Securities Exchange Board of India (Mutual Funds) Regulations, 1996 defines a mutual fund as a "a fund established in the form of a trust to raise money through the sale of units to the public or a section of the public under one or more schemes for investing in securities, including money market instruments." Thus mutual fund is a special type of institution that pools the savings of a number of investors who share a common financial goal and invests them in a well-diversified portfolio to obtain optimum return on investments.

3.3 Return on Mutual Funds

An investor in mutual fund earns return from two sources:

- Income from dividend paid by the mutual fund.
- Capital gains arising out of selling the units at a price higher than the acquisition price.

The figure given below shows the working pattern of mutual funds and the parties directly and indirectly associated with it.

The working pattern of the fund is very simple. First, Mutual funds are designed to meet the needs of large, medium and small investors with the objective of either growing its assets (capital gains) and/or generating income (dividends) for its investors. These investors buy units of

Figure 3.1
Working of Mutual Funds

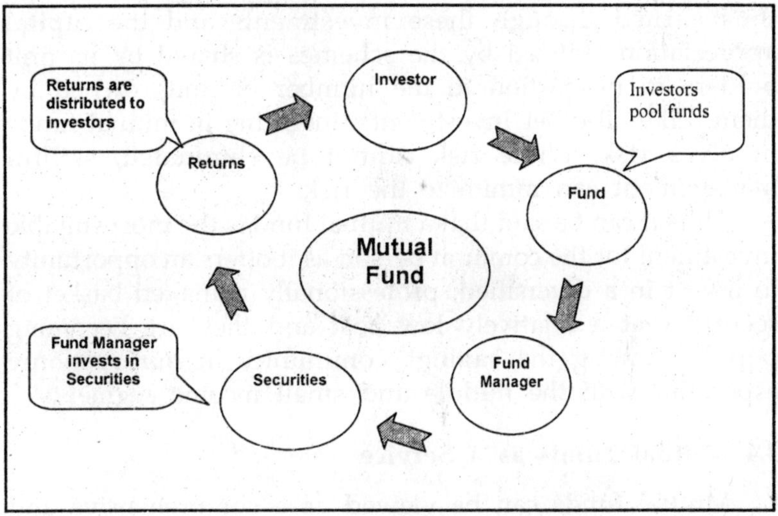

a particular mutual fund scheme that has a defined investment objective and strategy. The money thus collected is managed by professional fund managers who in turn invest them in diversified securities. Each fund is divided into a small fraction called "units" of equal value. Each unit holder is allocated units in the proportion to the size of his investment. Thus, every investor, whether big or small, will have a stake in the fund and can enjoy the wide portfolio of the investment held by the fund. Their investments provide the money for a mutual fund to buy securities such as stocks and bonds. Distributions in the form of capital gains (short-term and long-term) and dividends may be passed on (paid) to shareholders as income or reinvested to purchase more shares.

A mutual fund is valued daily and reports a price known as a net asset value (NAV) per share in its simplest form; a NAV is the total value of all the securities held in a fund divided by the total number of shares owned by its shareholders. As the price of the NAV increases or decreases, the shareholder's value will increase or decrease. The income thus earned through these investments and the capital appreciation realized by the schemes is shared by its unit holders in proportion to the number of units owned by them. Like all other investments, investing in mutual funds involves risk. While risk cannot be eliminated, skillful management can minimize the risk.

Thus it can be said that a mutual fund is the most suitable investment for the common person as it offers an opportunity to invest in a diversified, professionally managed basket of securities at a relatively low cost and they are becoming popular among the savings community in our economy especially with the middle and small income segments.

3.4 Mutual Funds as a Service

Mutual funds can be viewed as a comprehensive and versatile instrument as they have greater characteristics of a service rather than a product. Services offered by mutual funds vary across funds. To name a few, the service of organizing the funds, pooling of resources, and managing assets and investments of the investors. Some mutual funds are more investor friendly than others, and offer information at regular intervals. For instance, some funds disclose the expense ratios, an important criterion for fund selection, once a year, some disclose it once every 3 months, while a few disclose it every month.

The most important service offered by mutual funds is **(PMS)** - Portfolio management service. PMS is a type of professional service offered by portfolio managers to their client to help them in managing their money in less time. Portfolio managers manage the stocks, bonds, and mutual funds of clients considering their personal investment goals and risk preferences. In addition to money, the portfolio managers manage the portfolio of stocks, bonds, and mutual funds and at the same time take care of administrative issues

The other services provided by the mutual funds are:

1. Portfolio diversification
2. Marketability
3. Redemption of units within 24-48 hours
4. Switching between accounts/plans and options
5. Toll-free telephone numbers
6. Check-writing privileges
7. Automatic investment programs
8. Demat form of holding mutual funds
9. Buying/Selling and Redeeming units through net
10. Reporting performance to the investors through monthly fund fact sheets
11. Communication of financials
12. Easy accessibility through distributors, ATM and Post offices

3.5 Advantages of Mutual Funds

Mutual funds offer several advantages that make them an appropriate wealth creation medium. Mutual funds also act as a gateway to enter into big companies that were previously inaccessible to an ordinary investor with his small investment. More specifically, some of the important advantages of mutual funds are listed below.

1. Well regulated

Mutual funds are regulated by Securities and Exchange Board of India (SEBI). The rules and regulations framed and enforced by SEBI protects the interests of the investors and ensures that a transparency is maintained by keeping a strict vigilance on the mutual funds. SEBI also demands the disclosure of portfolios periodically to keep a track whether the investment in mutual fund is in line with the objective or not.

2. Well diversified

The element of pooling funds and investing across different securities like bonds, securities, real estate, government securities etc. offers investors the benefit of diversification. This kind of diversification adds to the stability of the investor's returns and the investment risk is limited by reducing the effect of a possible decline in the value of any one security. Mutual fund unit-holders can now benefit widely from diversification techniques that were initially available only to investors wealthy enough to buy significant positions in different stocks.

3. *Choice of schemes*

Mutual funds provide investors with a wide choice of fund schemes across different asset classes (equity/debt) and open ended/close ended schemes. Investors have the option of investing in a scheme that matches their investment objective to achieve their financial goals. These schemes further have different plans/options. Debt schemes are designed to offer security to the investors while equity funds are considered risky like the stock markets. Money market funds on the other hand offer liquidity to those who target surplus funds for very short-term periods.

4. *Professional management*

Professionally qualified and experienced fund managers with better investment management skills who seek to maximize returns and minimize risk monitor investor's money. As they deal in large volumes, the transaction costs will be very low. The earnings of the fund in the form of capital appreciation and revenue income are distributed to the investors after deducting the expenses.

5. *Low transaction costs*

Mutual funds pay lesser transaction cost due to the benefits of scale in brokerage, custodial and other fees. These benefits are then passed on to the investors. Even a small investor can get started on mutual funds as it has nominal investment requirements.

6. Transparency

Mutual funds are very transparent and all facts and updates are disclosed to the investors as required by the regulators. The performances of the funds are also reviewed by various rating agencies, making it easy for investors to decide on their investment.

7. Liquidity

Mutual funds have more liquidity than most investments like shares, deposits and bonds. Moreover, the process is standardized, making it quick and efficient so that the investors can get their cash on hand at the earliest. Open ended schemes are more popular as they have the option of withdrawing or redeeming the investor's money at any point of time at the current NAV.

3.6 Disadvantages of Mutual Funds

Some of the important disadvantages of mutual funds are listed below:

1. Costs

Mutual funds charge the investors for the fund's management expenses, operating fees and redemption fees. If the fund is purchased in a taxable account, taxes may also have to be paid on capital gains. The transaction costs also add up significantly at times when some funds buy and trade shares frequently.

2. Risks associated with mutual funds

Like any business, mutual funds have risks associated with returns. Risk refers to the possibility of loosing principal and any earnings or failure to make returns on an investment. Risk and potential return are always related with each other. This is called as risk/return trade-off. Some of the risks associated with mutual fund investing are listed below.

- **Principal risk**: The risk of investment falling down

from its original value or invested amount.

- **Income risk**: The possibility of falling overall interest rates that can affect fixed-income fund's dividends.
- **Fund manager risk**: The risk of failure on the fund manager's part to execute the fund's investment strategy effectively resulting in the failure of stated objectives.
- **Market risk**: The possibility of decline in overall prices of the stock fund or bond fund.
- **Country risk**: The possibility of a weak economy that can arise due to political events, financial problems, or natural disasters which has a direct effect on the investments in that country.
- **Industry risk**: The probability that a group of stocks in a single industry will decline in price due to developments and other related factors in that industry.
- **Inflation risk**: The chances that high cost of living will reduce or eliminate a fund's real inflation-adjusted returns.

3.7 Structure of Mutual Funds in India

Mutual funds as discussed before is a very simple concept, the risk of investment is reduced by spreading the investment across multiple entities, which is done by pooling a number of small investments systematically in to a well designed and structured medium. The structure of mutual funds in India is regulated by SEBI (Mutual Fund) Regulations, 1996. This regulation necessitates a fund to be established in the form of a trust under the Indian Trust Act 1882. The following paragraph describes the four-tier structure of Indian mutual funds.

1. Sponsor

A sponsor is an entity that sets up the mutual fund. SEBI regulations defines sponsor as any person who either by itself or in association with another body corporate establishes

Figure 3.2
Structure of Mutual Funds in India

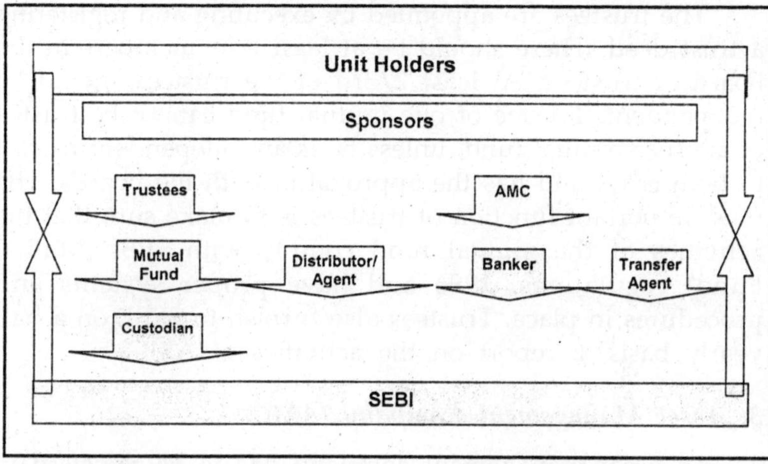

a mutual fund. A sponsor is an entity that sets up the mutual fund. Sponsor does the following important activities:

- Sponsor creates a Public Trust under the Indian Trust Act, 1882
- Sponsor appoints trustees to manage the trust with the approval of SEBI.
- Sponsor creates an Asset Management Company under the Companies Act, 1956.
- Sponsor appoints and registers the trust as a mutual fund with SEBI.

2. ***Trust/trustee***

The Trustees manage a trust. Trustees can be formed in either of the following two ways:

- As governed by the provisions of Indian Trust Act, 1882 trustees can be formed by appointing board of trustees and
- As governed by the provisions of Indian Trust Act, 1882 and Companies Act, 1956 trustees can be formed

by setting up a trustee company.

The trustees are appointed by executing and registering a trust deed. There should be at least four members in the board of trustees. At least 2/3rd of the trustees should be independent. Trustee of one mutual fund cannot be trustee of another mutual fund, unless he is an independent trustee in both cases and has the approval of both the boards. The most important function of trustees is to make sure that the activities of the mutual fund comply with SEBI (Mutual Fund) regulations, 1996 and have proper systems and procedures in place. Trustees also furnish to SEBI, on a half yearly basis, a report on the activities of AMC.

3. *Asset Management Company (AMC)*

An asset management company has to be registerd in the form of a company under the Companies Act, 1956. Sponsor creates The asset management company created by the sponsor is the entity, that manages the funds of the mutual fund (trust) for which a small fee is paid to the AMC for management of its fund. The AMC acts under the supervision of trustees and is subject to the regulations of SEBI too. At present there are 33 AMC's in India.

4. *Custodian*

The portfolio which is in the form of securities, are kept in safe custody with custodian. Custodians ensure that delivery has been taken of the securities, which are bought, and that they are transferred in the name of mutual fund. They keep the investment account of the mutual fund. They collect and account for the dividends and interest receivables on mutual fund investments. They also keep track of various activities of the company like bonus issue, rights issue, and stock split, buy back offers, open offers etc.

3.8 Regulations of Mutual Funds

SEBI (Securities and Exchange Board of India) regulates

the Indian mutual fund industry. SEBI has framed the SEBI (Mutual Funds) Regulations, 1996, (referred as SEBI Regulations) provides the scope of the regulations of mutual fund in India.

SEBI regulations provide for the following points:

- The structure and formation of mutual funds.
- Appointment of key functionaries.
- Operations of mutual fund.
- Rights and obligations of functionaries and investors.
- The restriction imposed on investment.
- The compliance to be fulfilled and the penalties imposed on non fulfilment of the same.'

3.9 The Association of Mutual Funds in India

Association of Mutual Funds in India (AMFI), an apex body of all Asset Management Companies (AMC) was incorporated on 22nd August, 1995. AMFI is registered with SEBI and functions as a non-profit organization. Till date all the AMC's that have launched mutual fund schemes are its members. It functions under the supervision and guidelines of its board of directors. Association of Mutual Funds India has made the Indian mutual fund industry a professional industry. It protects and promotes the interests of mutual funds as well as their unit holders. Some of the important objectives of AMFI[1] are:

- To maintain a high professional and ethical standard in all areas of operation of the industry.
- To interact with SEBI and work according to SEBI's guidelines in the mutual fund industry.
- To represent the Government of India, the Reserve Bank of India and other related bodies on matters relating to the mutual fund industry.
- To recommend and promote the top class business practices and code of conduct for the different parties associated with the mutual fund industry.

- To develop a team of well qualified and trained agent distributors.
- To conduct awareness programme for investors in order to promote proper understanding of the concept and working of mutual funds.
- To undertake studies and research either directly or in association with other bodies.

3.10 Products

Mutual funds offer a wide variety of schemes to suit the various needs of investors. Firstly, funds are usually classified as close-ended or open-ended. The peculiarity depends upon whether they give the investors the option to redeem and buy units at any time from the fund itself (open-ended) or whether the investors have to wait for a given maturity period before they can redeem their units to the fund (close-ended).

Funds can also be grouped in terms of whether they collect from investors any charges at the time of entry or exit or both, thus reducing the investible amount or the redemption proceeds. Funds that make these charges are classified as load funds, and funds that do not make any of these charges are termed no-load funds.

Finally, funds can also be classified as being tax-exempt or non-exempt, depending on whether they invest in securities that give tax-exempt returns or not. Let us observe the following figure to understand the classification of mutual funds.

Under each broad classification, we may then distinguish between several types of funds on the basis of the nature of their portfolios, meaning whether they invest in equities or fixed income securities or some combination of both. Every type of fund has a unique risk-profile that is determined by its portfolio, for which reason, funds are often separated into more or less risk-bearing. Now let us have a look at the classification of mutual funds.

Figure 3.3
Classification of Mutual Funds in India

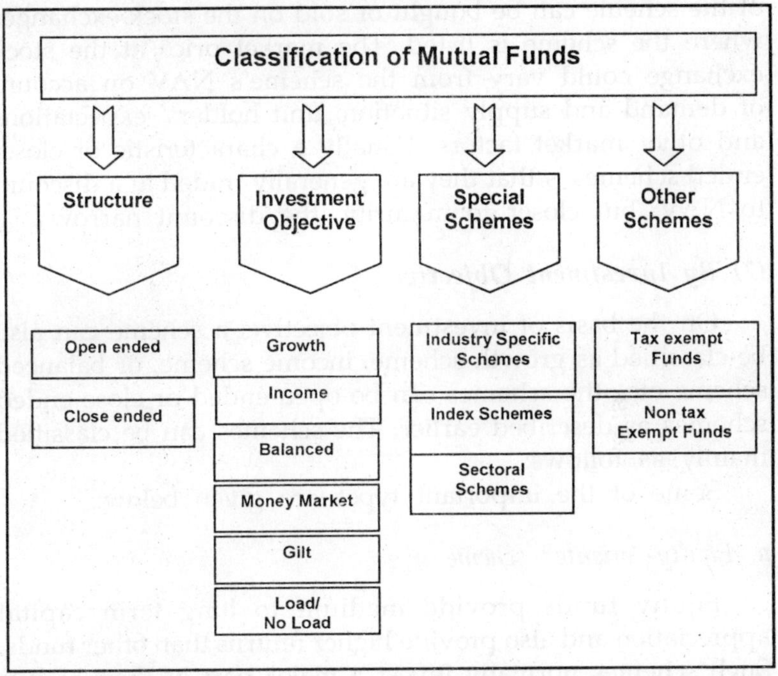

(1) By Structure

a. Open-ended fund/ scheme

Open-ended schemes usually do not have a fixed maturity period and are available for subscription and redemption on an ongoing basis. The units can be bought and sold any time during the life of the scheme at NAV related prices which are declared on a daily basis. The key feature of open-end schemes is liquidity.

b. Close-ended fund/ scheme

Close-ended mutual fund schemes have a stipulated maturity period wherein the investor can invest directly in the scheme at the time of the initial issue and thereafter units of the scheme can be bought or sold on the stock exchanges where the scheme is listed. The market price at the stock exchange could vary from the scheme's NAV on account of demand and supply situation, unit holders' expectations and other market factors. Usually a characteristic of close-ended schemes is that they are generally traded at a discount to NAV; but closer to maturity, the discount narrows.

(2) By Investment Objective

On the basis of investment objective, a scheme can also be classified as growth scheme, income scheme, or balanced scheme etc., the schemes can be open-ended or close-ended schemes as described earlier. The schemes can be classified mainly as follows:

Some of the important types are given below:

a. Equity- oriented scheme

Equity funds provide medium to long term capital appreciation and also provide higher returns than other funds. Such schemes normally invest a major part of their corpus in equities. Such funds have comparatively high risks. These schemes provide different options to the investors like dividend option, capital appreciation, etc. and the investors may choose an option depending on their preferences. Some of the Equity schemes are:

- Aggressive Growth Funds
- Growth Funds
- Speciality Funds
- Sector Funds
- Foreign Securities Funds
- Mid-Cap or Small-Cap Funds
- Option Income Funds
- Diversified Equity Funds
- Equity Index Funds
- Value Funds
- Equity Income or Dividend Yield Funds

b. Debt- oriented scheme

Income funds invest in medium to long-term debt instruments issued by private companies, banks, financial institutions, governments and other entities belonging to various sectors. The objective of these funds is to provide regular and steady income to investors. Such schemes generally invest in fixed income securities such as bonds, corporate debentures, Government securities and money market instruments. Such funds are less risky compared to equity schemes. Although debt securities are generally less risky than equities, they are subject to credit risk by the issuer at the time of interest or principal payment. Some of the Debt schemes are:

- o Diversified Debt
- o Focused Debt Funds
- o High Yield Debt funds
- o Assured Return Funds
- o Fixed Term Plan Series

c. Balanced fund

Balanced fund is a type of mutual fund that buys a combination of common stock, preferred stock, bonds, and short-term bonds, to provide both income and capital appreciation while avoiding excessive risk.

Balanced funds provide investors with an option of single mutual fund that combines both growth and income objectives, by investing in both stocks (for growth) and bonds (for income). Such diversified holdings ensure that these funds will manage downturns in the stock market without too much of a loss. But on the flip side, balanced funds will usually increase less than an all-stock fund during a bull market. These funds are appropriate for investors looking for moderate growth.

d. Money market or liquid fund

These funds are also income funds and their aim is to

provide easy liquidity, preservation of capital and moderate income. These schemes invest exclusively in safer short-term instruments such as treasury bills, certificates of deposit, commercial paper and inter-bank call money, government securities, etc. Returns on these schemes fluctuate much less compared to other funds. These funds are appropriate for corporate and individual investors as a means to park their surplus funds for short periods.

e. Gilt fund

Also known as Government Securities in India, Gilt Funds invest in government papers (named dated securities) having medium to long term maturity period. Issued by the Government of India, these investments have little credit risk and provide safety of principal to the investors. However, like all debt funds, gilt funds too are exposed to interest rate risk. Interest rates and prices of debt securities are inversely related and any change in the interest rates results in a change in the NAV of debt/gilt funds in an opposite direction.

f. Index fund

Index Funds replicate the portfolio of a particular index such as the BSE Sensitive index, S&P NSE 50 index (Nifty), etc. These schemes invest in the securities in the same weightage comprising of an index. NAVs of such schemes would rise or fall in accordance with the rise or fall in the index, though not exactly by the same percentage due to some factors known as "tracking error" in technical terms. Necessary disclosures in this regard are made in the offer document of the mutual fund scheme. There are also exchange traded index funds launched by the mutual funds which are traded on the stock exchanges.

g. Load funds/No-load funds

Mutual Funds incur various expenses on marketing, distribution, advertising, portfolio churning, fund manager's salary etc. Many funds recover these expenses from the investors in the form of entry load, exit load, deferred load etc. These funds are known as Load Funds. All those funds that do not charge any of the above mentioned loads are known as No-load Funds.

(3) *Special Schemes*

The special schemes are given below:

- Industry specific schemes

Industry Specific Schemes invest only in the industries specified in the offer document. The investment of these funds is limited to specific industries like InfoTech, FMCG and Pharmaceuticals etc.

- Index schemes

Index Funds try to replicate the performance of a particular index such as the BSE Sensex or the NSE 50.

- Sectoral schemes

Sectoral Funds are those, which invest exclusively in a specified industry or a group of industries or various segments such as 'A' Group shares or initial public offerings.

(4) *Other schemes*

Tax-exempt funds / Non-Tax-exempt funds

Funds that invest in securities free from tax are known as Tax-exempt Funds. All open-ended equity oriented funds are exempt from distribution tax (tax for distributing income to investors). Long term capital gains and dividend income in the hands of investors are tax-free.

Funds that invest in taxable securities are known as Non-Tax-exempt Funds. In India, all funds, except open-ended equity oriented funds are liable to pay tax on distribution income. Profits arising out of sale of units by an investor within 12 months of purchase are categorized as short-term capital gains, which are taxable. Sale of units of an equity oriented fund is subject to Securities Transaction Tax (STT). STT is deducted from the redemption proceeds to an investor.

3.11 Benchmarking a Fund

All mutual funds schemes have different objectives and therefore their performance also varies. Schemes are usually benchmarked against commonly followed market indexes like the BSE Sensex, Nifty, BSE 200, CNX 500. The relevant index can be chosen after taking into consideration the asset class of the scheme. The fund's performance can be tracked against the benchmark index. For example BSE Sensex can be used as a benchmark for an equity scheme.

3.12 Fees associated with Mutual Funds

All mutual funds in India charge a fee from the investors. These fees have been enumerated as under:

1. Load - Load is more like a sales commission that is charged as a percentage at the time of purchasing shares in various mutual funds.
2. Management and Expense fees- Mutual funds charge a fee to manage the investments, that is, the money collected from various investors. The management and expense fee is charged as a percentage of the fund's assets on a yearly basis.
3. Redemption fees- When shares are sold in a mutual fund, a redemption fee is charged.
4. Back end loads- The back end loads are charged while withdrawing the money from the fund. This fee is charged in order to bring down the frequency of money withdrawal from the funds.

The mutual funds have distinct revenue streams and expenses. The following table reflects the AMC's recurring expenses.

It is evident from table 3.1; the expenses of the AMC typically comprise of fund management expenses, marketing fees and audit fees among other expenses. The recurring expenses are indicative and the actual expense could be different. There are well-defined expenses and guidelines formulated by SEBI. These guidelines set limits as to what the AMC can charge the fund at a particular net asset level.

Table 3.1
AMC's Recurring Expenses

Sr.No.	*Expense*	*Percent of weekly Net Assets*
1.	Fund management fees	1.25
2.	Marketing/Selling Expenses	0.80
3.	Audit Fees	0.15
4.	Registrar Fees	0.12
5.	Trustee Fees	0.11
6.	Custodian Fees	0.07
7.	Total Recurring Exp.	2.50

Source: www.personalfn.com

3.13 Distribution in the Mutual Fund Industry

A mutual fund distributor is an entity responsible for marketing and selling the shares of a mutual fund company. These mutual fund distributors are also known as underwriters for the fund. The distributor is responsible for the following:

- Creating prospectus for the mutual fund
- Develop extensive marketing campaigns (television, internet, magazine)
- Sell the shares directly to the public
- Provide a wholesale market to reach a larger number of investors

Today the scenario in our industry is an exponential rise of distributors. Numbers are set to rule the world of mutual fund distribution in more ways than one. The number of distributors registered with AMFI, the association formed by mutual funds, has touched 1, 00,000[2].

In India, AMC's work with five distinct distribution channels, they are direct, banking, retail, corporate and individual financial advisor. The following figure gives us an idea about the distribution structure of Indian mutual funds.

The Direct channel

The investors invest directly in the schemes through the Asset Management companies and the companies in general do not give any advice for investment. Some of the tools of direct investment are:

- Monthly A/C statement
- Processing of transaction
- Maintenance of records
- Websites
- Telephonic Services

The Banking channel

As banks have a large customer base, the mutual fund companies have entered in to an agreement with the public, private and foreign banks distribution of funds and servicing. This channel of distribution is believed to be the most vital distribution channel for fund companies as there are many advantages like long time relationship with the customers etc.

The Retail channel

The distribution companies sell the schemes of several fund houses simultaneously and brokerage is paid by the respective AMC's for their funds sold. The retail channel offers the benefits of specialist knowledge and established client contact and, therefore private fund houses generally prefer this channel.

The Corporate channel

Corporates can either invest directly in mutual funds,

or through an intermediary such as a distribution house or a bank. The Corporate Channel includes a variety of institutions that invest in shares on the company's name. These are businesses, trusts, and even state and local governments.

Individual Financial advisors- Distributors/Agents

An agent acts as an intermediary between the customer and the fund house. There are also several sub-brokers working under one main broker. The huge network of sub-brokers, thus ensure larger market penetration and geographic coverage. In order to be an agent or a sub-broker, an individual should clear the test for certification conducted by AMFI. As per AMFI, as at the end of December 2007, the number of candidates who successfully cleared the test across 79 cities conducted by AMFI stood at 1, 14,004.

3.14 Conclusion

This chapter gives us conceptual clarity about the mutual funds and their benefits. The present chapter gives us also a clear idea about the regulatory framework, structure, products and the distribution channels that are available in the country. The regulatory framework is very comprehensive and matches with the best in terms of standards, practices and procedures. It is also observed that there is a wide innovation in the different categories of mutual funds in India. Thus it can be concluded that all this has resulted in healthy growth of the industry. The regulatory framework is very comprehensive and matches with the best in terms of standards, practices and procedures.

References

1. Source : AMFI website
2. Source: AMFI website

4

An Overview of the Mutual Fund Industry in India

4.1 Introduction

This book observes that the mutual fund industry is a fast growing sector of the Indian financial markets and have become a major vehicle for mobilization of savings, especially from the small and household savers for investment in the capital market. The driving force of mutual funds is the guarantee that is given for the safety of the principal in addition to the advantage of capital appreciation together with the income earned in the form of interest or dividend.

The conceptual frame work of mutual funds in India and its working pattern were examined in the previous chapter. The authors observed that mutual fund industry in India has not only emerged strongly but has also witnessed dynamic transformation in terms of its size, products and resources mobilized. Therefore, it is important to examine the performance of the industry in the changed environment. In this context, this chapter examines the phenomenal growth of the industry in terms of assets under management and resources mobilized by the industry over the last few years.

4.2 Growth of Mutual Fund Industry in India

The origin of Indian mutual fund industry can be traced back to the year 1963 with the setting up of the Unit Trust of India (UTI) by the Government of India. The entry of private and foreign asset management companies and increased awareness about the benefits of mutual funds coupled with qualitative and quantitative deliverables by the fund management companies has spurred the Indian mutual fund industry and consequently the Indian mutual funds business is witnessing rapid growth. Initially the growth of this industry was very slow but with the entry of private and foreign players the industry witnessed an explosive growth. This explosive growth of mutual funds in our country can also be attributed to the capital market development (reflecting investor confidence in market integrity, liquidity and efficiency) and financial system orientation.

Tracing the history of Indian mutual funds, the industry has actually passed through four different phases.[1] The following paragraphs gives us a better understanding of the journey of the industry.

1. *First Phase (1963–1987)*

UTI the first mutual fund of India was created in 1963, by an act of parliament. It was set up by the Reserve Bank of India and functioned under the control of the Reserve Bank of India. UTI's first scheme US-64 was officially launched in July 1964. It was operating under special enactment i.e. Unit Trust of India Act (1963). Later UTI was de-linked from RBI and the Industrial Development Bank of India (IDBI) took over the regulatory and administrative control in place of RBI. UTI started diversifying its activities and provided attractive investment opportunity in order to face the challenges. The following table gives us a clear picture of the different events that took place during this phase.

Table 4.1
Events of UTI

Sr.No.	*Year*	*Events of UTI*
1	1964	UTI launched US-64
2	1967	UTI launched re-investment plan
3	1971	UTI launched ULIP-1971
4	1978	UTI was de-linked from RBI
5	1986	UTI launched Children's Gift Growth Fund
6	1986	UTI launched India's first offshore fund(India Fund) in August
7	1986	UTI launched India's first close ended scheme Master Share in October

Source: Compiled from UTI's Annual Reports

The net resources mobilized by UTI stood at Rs. 18 crores during the year 1971. This figure marginally rose to Rs. 167 crores during 1983 and stood at Rs. 1,261 crores in 1987 which marked the end of first phase. This long 23 year period of UTI's monopoly gave the investors an opportunity to invest only in eight different schemes. It can be rightly said that UTI paved the way for the formation of a vibrant mutual fund industry in our country.

2. *Second Phase (1987-1992)*

The second phase started during the year 1987 and this year marked the entry of non UTI mutual funds. During the year 1986, public sector banks and financial institutions were given permission to establish mutual funds and the domination of UTI was broken. SBI mutual fund, the first non-UTI fund was launched in the country by the State Bank of India in the year 1987. This was followed by Canbank Mutual Fund (Dec 87), Punjab National Bank Mutual Fund (Aug 89), Indian Bank Mutual Fund (Nov 89), Bank of India Mutual Fund (June 90), Bank of Baroda Mutual Fund (October 92), LIC Mutual Fund (1989) and GIC Mutual Fund (1990). Suddenly the mutual fund investors were flooded with choices during this phase. The Indian Trust Act[2] was formed during this phase only.. An examination of the following graph clearly reflects the drastic increase in the resources mobilised during this phase.

Graph 4.1
Net Resources Mobilised by Public Sector during Phase II

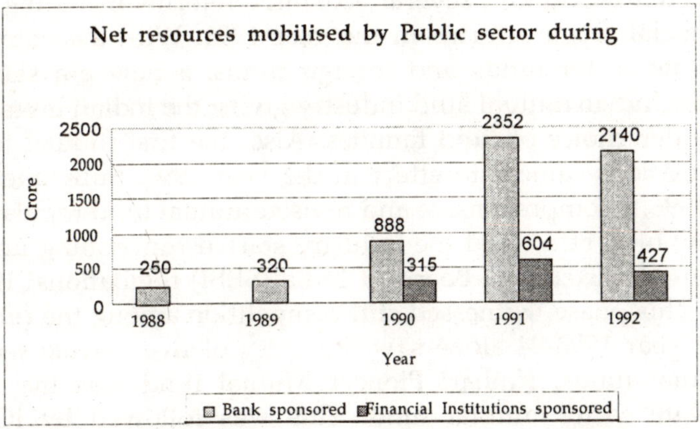

Source: SEBI's Hand book of Statistics

It can be seen from the above table, that the funds raised by the bank sponsored mutual funds stood at Rs. 250 crores in 1988 and within 3 years reached Rs. 2,352 crores in 1991. The subsequent year saw a marginal decline where the funds mobilised stood at Rs. 2140 crores in 1992.

The mutual funds sponsored by the financial institutions stood at Rs. 315 crores in 1990 and sharply increased to Rs. 604 crores in 1991 but due to the various factors that influenced the market and the reforms that were initiated during that period, the funds mobilised fell down to Rs. 427 crores in 1992.

Despite competition, UTI continued to enjoy monopoly and was considered a dominant player in the industry. The total number of schemes that were available to the investors also increased from 10 in 1986-87 to 116 by the end of 1992.[3]

3. *Third Phase (1993-2003)*

This phase is considered as the most important phase not only from the Indian financial sector's angle but also from the economic angle of the country. The government of India introduced several economic reforms including the financial sector reforms in the year 1991. With the entry of private sector funds and foreign funds, a new era started in the Indian mutual fund industry giving the Indian investors a wider choice of fund families. Also, the first mutual fund regulations came into effect in the year 1993. Subsequently in 1996, a comprehensive and revised mutual fund regulation came in to effect and the industry started functioning under Securities Exchange Board of India (SEBI) regulations, 1996.

This phase, witnessed stiff competition among the funds. The year 1993-94 alone saw the entry of five private sector mutual funds. Kothari Pioneer Mutual fund was the first private sector mutual fund. This was followed by ICICI Mutual fund, 20th Century Mutual fund, Morgan Stanley mutual fund and Taurus mutual fund. The subsequent year 1994-95 witnessed the entry of six mutual funds. Thus the number of funds started increasing steadily in the country and the assets under management stood at Rs. 1,40,095 crores as on December 2003. The graph below shows the Gross mobilisation of mutual funds during this period.

From the above graph it is evident that, from the time of its entry, the Private Sector mutual funds have literally captured the market. The Gross mobilisation of Private Sector mutual funds stood at Rs. 2, 84,095 crores during 2002-03. The total funds mobilised during this period was Rs. 3,14,706 crores and the total assets under management as on March 2003 was Rs. 1,09,299 crores. This sharp difference in gross mobilisation by the private sector mutual funds is due to the innovative methods adopted by the fund managers in designing the schemes in order to attract the investoRs.

Graph 4.2
Gross mobilisation of Mutual Funds – Phase III

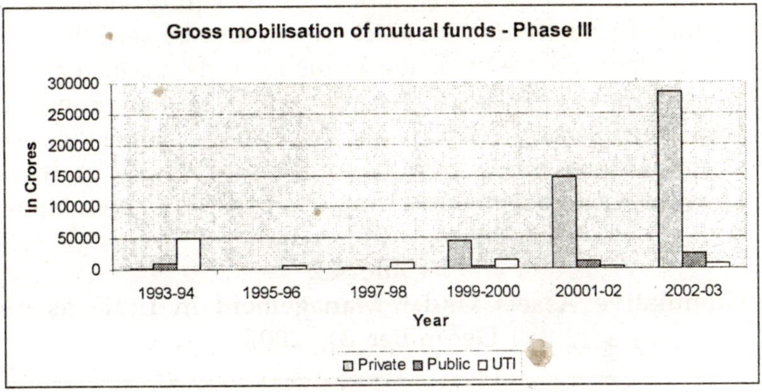

Source: SEBI Bulletin, Vol. 2, No.24, 2004

4. *Fourth Phase (2003-2007)- Growth and Consolidation*

The Unit Trust of India Act 1963 was repealed in February 2003, resulting in UTI being split into two different entities. One is the Specified Undertaking of the Unit Trust of India with AUM of Rs. 29,835[4] crores (as on January 2003). The Specified Undertaking of Unit Trust of India does not come under the purview of the Mutual Fund Regulations. It functions under the rules framed by Government of India. The second is the UTI Mutual Fund Ltd, sponsored by SBI, PNB, BOB and LIC. It functions under the mutual fund regulations and is registered with SEBI.

The industry has also witnessed several mergers and acquisitions during this phase. Some of them are the mergers and acquisitions initiated by Templeton, HDFC, Fidelity, and Sahara. Other examples are Alliance Mutual Fund by Birla Sun Life, Sun F&C Mutual Fund and PNB Mutual Fund by Principal Mutual Fund. This split up of UTI, along with mergers and acquisitions within India's mutual fund industry propelled the industry into a new era of growth and restructuring. During this period, the industry witnessed sea change activities. Thus the Mutual Fund scenario has been undergoing significant changes in recent times in terms of growth and restructuring. Some of the reasons for the success of this industry are awareness and interest shown by the investors in mutual funds, inflow in the equity market and continued growth of companies. It can also be said that this current growing trend of the industry is the result of keen efforts of the regulators, Association of Mutual Funds of India and industry participants. According to data released by industry body Association of Mutual Funds of India, assets under management during this phase are given below:

Table 4.2
Cumulative Assets Under Management in India as on December 31, 2007

Sr.No.	*Period*	*Assets at the end of the period(Rs. In Crores)*
1	2002-2003	1,09,299
2	2003-2004	1,39,616
3	2004-2005	1,49,600
4	2005-2006	2,31,862
5	2006-2007	3,23,598
6	November 2007	5,37,943
	As on Dec 31,2007	5,49,936

Source: Compiled from AMFI data

The table given above shows the cumulative assets under management in India for the study period 2002 to 2007. The journey of the industry has been nothing less than spectacular, particularly in the last 5 years. The AUM which stood at Rs. 1,09,299 crores during the period 2002-2003 steadily rose to Rs. 5,49,936 crores as on december 2007. An interesting observation from the above table is, during the year 2007 alone; there has been a sharp rise in the AUM. The Assets Under Management as on december 31, 2007 stood at Rs. 5,49,936 crores as against Rs. 3,23,597 crores as at the end of the previous year, registering an increase of 70 percent.

The market value of cumulative assets under management of all mutual funds increased by 2 percent from Rs. 5,37,943 crores as on November 31, 2007 to Rs. 5,49,936 crores as on December 31, 2007. Thus it can be said that the Indian mutual funds business is expected to grow significantly in the coming years due to a high degree of transparency and disclosure standards comparable to anywhere in the world. The size of the mutual funds industry is expected to be worth Rs. 4 lakh crores by 2010 from its current level.[5]

During this period, the industry has also grown manifold in terms of Asset Management Companies, total number of schemes and resources mobilised as can be seen from the following paragraphs.

4.3 Asset Management Companies

Now, let us have a look at the Asset Management Companies operating in the country. In India, there are mutual funds sponsored by public sector banks, institutions, private sector (including wholly foreign owned) and joint sector with foreign participation.

The broad three categories are:

1. Bank Sponsored
2. Institutions
3. Private Sector

All mutual funds whether promoted by public sector or private sector entities including those promoted by foreign entities are governed by the same set of regulations. There is no distinction in regulatory requirements for these mutual funds and all are subject to monitoring and inspections by SEBI.

The following table gives us the list of Asset Management Companies operating in India and their Assets Under Management as on December 31, 2007.[6]

Table 4.3
List of Asset Management Companies and their AUM as on December 31, 2007

Name of the Asset Management Company	*AUM*	*Total*
A. BANK SPONSORED		
(i) JT. VENTURES - PRED.INDIAN		
(1) Canara Robeco AMC.	2703	
(2) SBI Funds Mgt. Private	29241	
Total	31944	
(ii) OTHERS		
(1) BOB Asset Management Co. Ltd.	105	
(2) UTI AMC	56853	
Total	56958	
TOTAL A (i+ii)		88,902
B. INSTITUTIONS		
(1) LIC Mutual Fund AMC	13859	13859
C. PRIVATE SECTOR		
(i) INDIAN		
(1) Benchmark AMC	6901	
(2) DBS Cholamandalam AMC	3283	
(3) Deutsche AMC	11207	
(4) Escorts Asset Management Ltd.	196	
(5) J.M. Financial AMC	12555	
(6) Kotak Mahindra AMC	20428	
(7) Quantum AMC	68	
(8) Reliance Capital AMC	80780	
(9) Sahara AMC	228	
(10) Tata Asset Management Ltd.	23518	
(11) Taurus Asset Management Co.	457	
TOTAL C (i)	159621	
(ii) FOREIGN		
(1) AIG Global AMC	2852	
(2) Franklin Templeton	31175	
TOTAL C (ii)	34027	

(contd.)

JOINT VENTURES - PRED. INDIAN'			
	(1) Birla Sun Life AMC.	31819	
	(2) DSP Merrill Lynch Fund Managers Ltd.	21029	
	(3) HDFC Asset Management Co. Ltd.	48561	
	(4) ICICI Prudential Asset Management Co. Ltd.	56773	
	(5) Sundaram BNP Paribas Asset Management Company Ltd.	11887	
	TOTAL C (iii)	170069	
(iii)	JT. VENT. - PRED. FOREIGN - C (iv)	83458	
TOTAL C (i+ii+iii+iv)			447175
TOTAL (A+B+C)			549936

Source: RBI Hand Book of Statistics on Indian Economy, 2007-2008

The above table gives data on Assets Under Management for each of the Asset Management Companies. At the end of December 2007, there were 32 funds which managed assets of Rs. 5,49,936 crores under 839 schemes as compared to assets worth Rs. 47,000 crores under management in March 1993. Out of 32 companies, 4 companies were bank sponsored. The total assets of the bank sponsored mutual funds stood at Rs. 88,902 crores. LIC Mutual fund is the only fund that is an institution sponsored fund and the assets of this company as on December, 2007 was Rs. 13,859 crores. During the same period, there were 11 Indian Private Sector sponsored mutual funds with Rs. 1,59,621 crores of assets under their management. and 2 foreign mutual funds with Rs. 34,027crores of assets under their management. There were 5 joint venture funds which were predominantly Indian and 9 joint venture funds which were predominantly foreign with assets under management of Rs. 1,70,069 crores and Rs. 83,458 crores respectively.

An interesting observation of table- 4.3 shows that Reliance Capital Asset Management Ltd. is the largest Asset management company in our country which manages

Rs. 80,780 crores as on December 31, 2007. Thus, it can be said that with a strong regulatory framework, clear guidelines and the talent to back it up, the Indian mutual fund industry has emerged strongly during this phase. Besides, factors like low interest rates, tax holidays on some schemes, excellent performance of the stock market in the last couple of years have tremendously contributed to the growth of this industry.

The following table shows the total existing schemes as on December 2007.

Graph 4.3
Total Existing Schemes as on December 31, 2007

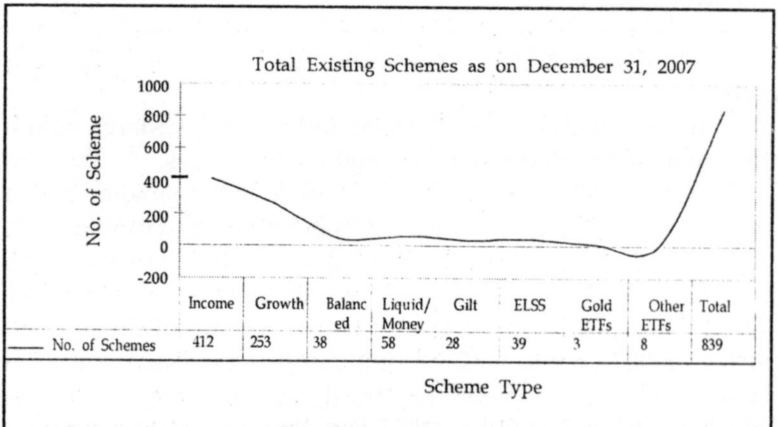

Source: RRI Hand Book of Statistics on Indian Economy, 2007-2008

An examination of the total existing schemes, as on December 2007 shows that there were 839 schemes in total as at the end of the year December 2007. The maximum number of schemes was in the Income category with 412 schemes followed by the Growth schemes with 253 schemes. The scorching pace of growth, which draws strength from factors such as the current state of liquidity and a general absence of negative news, is reflected in maximum number of income schemes. The balanced, Gilt and Liquid stood at 38, 28 and 58 schemes respectively as on December 31, 2007. There were 39 ELSS schemes and 3 Gold ETFs schemes during the same period. A brief note about the history of the products in India is given below:

- The industry initially picked up with traditional products like equity, debt and balanced.
- The industry then gradually launched Liquid / Money Market funds, Sector specific funds, Index funds, Gilt funds, Capital Protection Oriented Schemes, Fund of Funds, Special Category funds, Children funds, Education Funds, Insurance linked funds and Exchange traded funds.
- A major break through is the launch of Gold ETFs, introduced in 2007.
- Real Estate Mutual Funds (REMFs) guidelines were also issued by the Regulators.

4.4 Category - Wise Assets Under Management

After observing the total schemes and the scheme types, it is important to examine the assets managed under each category as on December 31, 2007.

From the above table, it can be seen that the performance of income funds is a major talking point at the moment. The mutual funds have traditionally been the active participants in the debt segment of Indian stock market. The net asset values (NAVs) of income funds have moved up sharply to 36 percent of the total assets that are managed in the country.

For the MF industry, income funds' have shown that a lot of money belonging to the investor community is chasing income funds right now. There is a surge of interest in income fund. The broad performance trend is being clearly felt across the income fund spectrum.

Very close in the race is the growth funds with 35 percent of assets under their management. Growth schemes which aim at consistent growth and preservation of capital are

Table 4.4
Category-Wise Assets Under Management as on December 31, 2007

Sr. No.	Scheme Type	Open Ended Rs. In	Close Ended Crores)	Total	Percent Total
1	Income	1,23,875	73,467	1,97,342	**36**
2	Growth	1,57,128	35,001	1,92,129	**35**
3	Balanced	16,182	3,755	19,937	**4**
4	Liquid/Money Market	1,12,349	-	1,12,349	**20**
5	Gilt	1,975	-	1,975	**Less than 1 percent**
6	ELSS	16,466	2,597	19,063	**4**
7	Gold ETFs	467	-	467	**Less than 1 percent**
8	Other ETFs	6,674	-	6,674	-
	Total	4,35,116	1,14,820	5,49,936	100

Source: RRI Hand Book of Statistics on Indian Economy, 2007-2008

generally the most preferred among the middle class investors. The performance of growth funds in general, has reached new heights with more and more investors opting for these schemes. A growth mutual fund is more risky to be invested, compared to an ordinary mutual fund but the premium or dividend that is derived is much higher than what is obtained from a normal mutual fund. It's performance is proportional to the performance of the stock market. That is, when the stock market undergoes losses the value and price of the fund falls rapidly compared to other funds and similarly when the market hits a high, the price of the fund shoots up. People basically invest in growth funds keeping in mind long term goals. The reason, the logic behind the investment is that the companies, firms or organizations invested upon will grow in value, thereby allowing the fund to reap the benefits of large capital gains.

The Liquid/ Money market funds which purely falls under open ended category manages 20 percent of the total assets and the value stood at Rs. 1,12,349 crores as on December 2007. Money market funds are generally the safest and most secure of mutual fund investments. The goal of a money-market fund is to preserve principal while yielding a modest return. Money-market mutual fund is similar to a high-yield bank account but is not entirely risk free. Thus, from the present study it can be seen that the Income schemes are the most popular schemes among the investors followed by the growth schemes. One interesting observation here is, even though balanced scheme has the objective of both debt and equity, the assets managed by this particular category stands only at 4 percent.

4.5 Resource Mobilisation

Mutual Funds are going to be the future wealth creators of the country following the initiatives taken by government and the liberalization of tax treatment of incomes earned through mutual funds. These measures were taken to make mutual funds the key instrument for long-term saving. The more the variety offered, the more will be the choice for the investors. As a result of the measures taken by the government, the mutual funds have now emerged as an important channel which mobilizes savings of millions of individuals/households from different parts of the country into investment in both equity and debt instruments. Therefore, in order to understand the growth and performance of the fund industry in India, it is not sufficient if the assets under management alone are examined. The resources mobilized by the industry over different periods explains the pattern of mobilization of funds. It also helps us to understand the pace of growth. Table 4.6 shows the Net resources mobilized by mutual funds.

Table 4.5
Net Resources Mobilised by Mutual Funds

(Rs. In crores)

Year	*UTI*	*Bank-sponsored Funds*	*FI-sponsored Funds*	*Private Sector Funds*	*Total (1 to 4)*
1970-71	18	-	-	-	**18**
1985-86	892	-	-	-	**892**
1992-93	11057	1204	760	-	**13021**
1996-97	-3043	6	137	864	**-2037**
1997-98	2875	237	203	749	**4064**
1998-99	170	-88	547	2067	**2695**
1999-00	4548	336	296	16937	**22117**
2000-01	322	248	1273	9292	**11135**
2001-02	-7284	863	407	16134	**10120**
2002-03	-9434	1033	862	12122	**4583**
2003-04	1050	4526	787	41510	**47873**
2004-05	-2467	707	-3384	7933	**2789**
2005-06	3424	5365	2112	41581	**52482**
2006-07	7326	3032	4226	79477	**94062**

Source: RRI Hand Book of Statistics on Indian Economy, 2007-2008

The above table shows that the Indian mutual fund industry has certainly stepped on the accelerator. The performance of mutual funds in India in the initial phase was not satisfactory. During the year 1970-71, the net resources mobilized by UTI was only Rs. 18 crores and the funds mobilized stood at Rs. 892 crores during 1985-86. But gradually the industry picked up and the industry managed to raise Rs. 13021 crores during 1992-93. The net resources mobilized by mutual funds in India started to decline when the prices of the stocks declined in the year 1992. An observation of the table given above shows that from the year 1993 the funds mobilized declined substantially and stood at Rs. -2037 crores during 96-97. The main reason for this decline was due to SEBI's prohibition of mutual funds from launching new schemes with assured return.

During that period, the market regulations did not allow portfolio shifts into other financial investments that were available and the investors were left with no choice apart from holding the cash or to further continue investing in shares. As a result, the performance of mutual funds in India suffered qualitatively. The 1992 stock market scandal, the losses by disinvestments and of course the lack of transparent rules rocked the confidence among the investors. Since the market conditions did not improve, the supervisory authority adopted a set of measures to create a transparent and competitive environment in mutual funds.

With the entry of private sector mutual funds also there was no change in the scenario. Table 4.6 shows that UTI mobilized Rs. 9,297 crores and the private sector mutual funds mobilized Rs. 1,560 crores during 1993-94.

The industry gradually took its shape. The companies launched more and more innovative schemes and the assets under management grew steadily and there was a sharp rise in the resources mobilized by the industry. The net resource mobilization improved dramatically with massive inflow of funds and the total funds mobilized stood at Rs. 22,117 crores during 1999-2000. The share of private sector mutual funds in the total funds mobilized reached its peak during this period with Rs. 16,937 crores. Within the Bank sponsored and the FI- sponsored funds, SBI Mutual funds mobilized maximum of Rs. 659 crores (refer table 4.6).

After this period, the share of UTI in the total funds mobilized started declining gradually. UTI failed to maintain its growth rates and market share in the industry. Competition forced industry players to focus on product innovation, market penetration, identifying new channels of distribution and last but not the least improving investors' service. Mutual funds saw record resource mobilisation as investors lined up to take advantage of the stock market boom. All these measures helped the industry grow significantly. The following table shows the break-up of bank-sponsored and FI-sponsored mutual funds.

Table 4.6
Net Resources Mobilized by Bank-Sponsored and FI-Sponsored Mutual Funds

Year	*Bank-Sponsored*						*FI-Sponsored*			*Total*
	SBI MF	*Can.bk MF*	*Id.Bk MF*	*BOI MF*	*PN MF*	*BOB MF*	*GIC MF*	*LIC MF*	*IDBI MF*	*(1 to 9)*
					Rs. in Crores					
2000-01	252	-5	-	-	2	0	-43	566	750	**1521**
2001-02	614	140	-	-	50	59	-56	640	-178	**1270**
2002-03	686	237	-	-	14	96	-97	578	380	**1895**
2003-04	1927	495	-	-	1841	263	-147	934	-	**5313**
2004-05	1024	-11	-	-	-	-307	-33	-3351	-	**2678**
2005-06	5280	56	-	-	-	29	-	2112	-	7477
2006-07	3208	-96	-	-	-	-79	-	4226	-	7258

Source: RRI Hand Book of Statistics on Indian Economy, 2007-2008

An interesting observation made from the above table with regards to funds mobilized is during the period 2004-05. The funds mobilized by this category were Rs. 2,678 crores. This result has been due to LIC mutual fund's under performance. But this category managed to pick up and the funds mobilized reached a maximum of Rs. 7,477 crores during 2005-2006. Overall 2005-06 has been very good.

A closer examination of some of the best funds in this category reveals that with over 20 years of rich experience in fund management, SBI MF has brought forward its expertise in consistently delivering value to its investors. Investors in SBI mutual fund have been richly rewarded by the outstanding performance of several funds in 2005. The strategy adopted by them to capture the position of a reliable fund in this category were : 1) The ability to identify a small number of ideas that could pay off and back them completely without sacrificing the requirement of a diversified portfolio and 2) the ability to pick less fancied stocks ahead of most other investors, ensuring an early entry.

Table 4.7 shows the net resources mobilized by private sector mutual funds from the year 2001-02 to 2006-07. The private sector mutual funds began to grow enormously at the cost of UTI and Public sector mutual funds. The private asset management companies currently holds over 80[7] percent share of AUM with resource mobilization at Rs. 79,477.4 crores as on December 31, 2007. The private sector mutual funds tried to capture the investor's attention and went on high marketing pitch to create awareness among the investors about the advantages of investing. The bulk of resource mobilisation was by the private sector mutual funds.

Reliance Mutual Fund has emerged as the largest private sector fund house in the country, as of March 2007, overtaking Prudential ICICI which had been holding that position for many years. The resource mobilization of Reliance Mutual Fund stood at Rs. 22,581 crores as on December 31, 2007. Reliance Fund is the most popular fund in the country currently and is believed to be one of the best managed funds by trade experts. Reliance Mutual has a history of

Table 4.7

Net Resources Mobilised by Private Sector Mutual Funds

	Mutual Fund / Year	*2001-02*	*2002-03*	*2003-04*	*2004-05*	*2005-06*	*2006-07*
1.	ICICI Prudential MF	1404.8	2000.6	4385.0	170.3	5634.6	13785
2.	Morgan Stanley MF	-24.1	-27.9	-14.9	-	-	0
3.	Taurus Mutual Fund	-6.7	-14.2	-3.2	-45.2	-43.4	31.3
4.	JM Financial MF	1177.3	1290.4	965.9	386.2	-1464.7	453.3
5.	Birla Sun Life MF	608.3	976.2	3108.1	1115.3	2067.2	4202.7
6.	Tata Mutual Fund	-17.4	89.4	2772.4	2387.5	1379.0	2290.8
7.	Reliance Mutual Fund	710.5	1305.2	3967.9	1849.7	15033.9	22581
8.	Franklin Templeton MF	2301.8	1146.7	4719.0	-966.5	-1828.3	4333.5
9.	DBS Chola Mutual Fund	177.2	-13.2	339.2	-138.7	876.7	148.8
10.	Sundaram BNP Paribus MF	150.6	458.0	1456.1	-180.1	587.8	4417.6
11.	Escorts Mutual Fund	-1.7	-35.0	46.8	-4.2	11.2	-
12.	DSP Merril Lynch MF	607.2	160.0	2522.3	104.7	4409.2	1424.8
13.	Kotak Mahindra MF	854.9	943.7	1914.7	1066.1	2432.0	1238.0
14.	ING Vysya Mutual Fund	46.0	168.1	880.4	-391.8	665.9	761.6
15.	HDFC Mutual Fund	3716.8	2122.4	4657.7	-54.9	3334.7	7140.4

	Mutual Fund / Year	*2001-02*	*2002-03*	*2003-04*	*2004-05*	*2005-06*	*2006-07*
16.	Standard Chartered MF	2039.9	861.9	2358.6	-256.5	1646.3	1547.2
17.	Benchmark Mutual Fund	5.8	4.1	54.3	377.4	236.8	2565.5
18.	Deutsche Mutual Fund	-	312.5	1670.2	-293.7	648.5	3184.7
19.	HSBC Mutual Fund	0	735.9	3576.8	1281.5	1800.4	1953.7
20.	Principal Mutual Fund	-	-	1841.1	1894.6	143.8	2862.4
21.	ABN AMRO Mutual Fund	-	-	-	847.8	1552.5	2039.9
22.	Sahara Mutual Fund	-	-	-	-	6.9	-110.7
23.	Quantum Mutual Fund	-	-	-	-	11.3	45.7
24.	Fidelity Mutual Fund	-	-	-	-	2438.7	1413.0
25.	Lotus Mutual Fund	-	-	-	-	0	1167.2
	Total	16134.0	12122.2	41509.8	7933.1	41581	79477.4

Source: RRI Hand Book of Statistics on Indian Economy, 2007-2008.

letting its funds get bloated in terms of its assets under management. The firm's culture places a premium on running a big fund. Ever since it started in 1995, it has rapidly increased its AUM. From being India's largest private sector mutual fund in 2006, it became the largest mutual fund by 2007.

The above tables clearly show how the fund industry has grown steadily. The large number of new fund offerings, the sharp rally in the equity markets and liquid fund inflow drove these levels of resource mobilization. This is an indication of the fact that investors have confidence in the Indian financial system and the regulation of the mutual fund industry. Also, all the schemes are launched with an aim of differentiating themselves from the others and the Indian mutual fund industry experienced unprecedented growth. The economic climate is also conducive for growth and mutual funds today have better infrastructure and innovative product ranges that cater to various client needs. As the industry moves from the growth to the maturity phase, competition has also become fierce with mergers and takeovers. Brand building exercise has just taken off. Recent advertisement campaign and new product offerings suggest that it is moving in that direction.

Some of the important factors that have contributed to the growth of this industry are highlighted below:

- Large market potential - high savings rate
- Comprehensive regulatory framework
- Favourable tax policies
- Introduction of new products
- Role of distributors
- Investor education campaign
- Performance record

Out of the above factors when we observe the performance records of the fund houses in general, most funds have provided market related returns. Many have out performed benchmark indices. There are also several independent research and rating agencies that evaluate performance and publish performance and ranking of mutual funds – CRISIL, ICRA, Value Research, etc. Thus, this book observes that the economic climate is conducive for growth of mutual funds.

4.6 Emerging Trends and Innovations[8]

The industry has seen interesting twists and turns during the past few decades. The most important trend in the mutual fund industry is consolidation and aggressive expansion of the foreign owned mutual fund companies and the decline of the companies floated by nationalized banks and smaller private sector players. Some companies have sold out to foreign owned companies, some have merged with others and there is a general restructuring going on.

The credit can be given to the private players for introducing new practices such as new product innovation, intelligent improvement in service standards and disclosure, usage of technology, broker education and support etc. In fact, they have forced the industry to improve itself and service levels of organizations like UTI that has enhanced dramatically in the last few years. Some of the innovations witnessed by the mutual fund industry during the last two years are as follows:

- Fund houses launched Gold ETFs and every fund house now looks eager to launch a Gold ETF, even those who don't even have the basic mutual fund offerings in place.
- Another long-standing innovation - global funds, debuted in the industry. Fund houses adopted different strategies. Some invested directly in global equities; others opted for the Fund of Funds (FOF) route by investing in global funds.
- Infrastructure funds were introduced and these funds also became popular among the public.
- A new feature in the form of limited cheque-writing facility has been introduced.

- To enhance service to investors, fund houses have has instituted toll-free inquiry facility enabling investors to access information about the fund without any charges.
- The industry also witnessed the launch of sector funds, targeting sectors such as information technology, pharmaceutical, brand value and fast moving consumer goods.
- Out-and-out gilt funds envisaging 100 percent investment in government securities were launched making the gilt market accessible to small investors.
- Another innovative product was to invest solely in dematerialized securities and exchange of any security in dematerialized segment, instead of cash, for the units of the scheme.
- Every fund house carries out education campaigns through investor meets seminars etc.
- There are several independent research and rating agencies that evaluate performance and publish performance and ranking of mutual funds like CRISIL, ICRA, Value Research etc.
- Nation wide Advertisement Campaign through print & electronic media is also carried out by fund houses.
- Another important trend is, various trade bodies and stock exchanges regularly conduct investor awareness programmes across the country.

4.7 Challenges of Indian Mutual Fund Industry

The Indian mutual fund industry is expected to grow significantly in the coming years, due to a high degree of transparency and disclosure standards comparable to anywhere in the world. Despite good growth, there are many challenges that need to be addressed. Following are some of the important challenges faced by the industry.

- One of the biggest challenges for the mutual fund industry in the near future, is to bring investors into equity funds.

- Another area that requires to be addressed seriously, is to spread to rural and semi-urban areas of the country.
- To innovate new products to tap the growth potential offered by the rural markets.
- To join hands with banking and telecommunications to tackle the challenge faced due to the lack of appropriate technological infrastructure in rural areas.
- The expectations of investors have touched the sky with respect to profitability factor. So the sector now has to meet the expectations of investors and integrate with the rest of the world.
- The product differentiation and quality standards are the key factors to attract an investor. Hence more research is required in this area. Mutual Funds need to offer products, which are affordable as well as competitive against low risk assured returns like post office saving deposits.
- A major challenge before the mutual fund industry would be the entry of new global players which is expected to go up further in the Indian Mutual Fund industry. It may lead to a new wave of consolidation by way of mergers and acquisitions (M&A) among the fund houses.
- Another challenge faced by the mutual fund industry is to deal with the retreating talent pool of the fund managers, pressures on restrictions and consolidations, innovation and product differentiation and meeting the issues of governance. Immense pressure is also put on the trustees to ensure that the operations of the funds are managed to the full benefit of the unit holders.

4.8 Factors affecting the Growth of Mutual Fund Industry

- ➢ Retail and urban investors' lack of awareness and knowledge about mutual funds.

- Investors unwillingness to undertake even minimal risk.
- Inadequate reach of funds.
- Competition from assured return products from Government like Government Of India Bonds,Post Office Monthly Income Schemes, Senior Citizen Savings Schemes, National Savings Certificates etc.
- Lack of systematic redressal system.
- Excess expenses being loaded on the investors.
- Lack of proper training for the distributors about the products.
- Lack of performance indicators.
- Lack of fund managers for every fund
- Lack of monitoring by regulators and strict punishment for defaulters.
- Lack of an effective mutual fund governance.

4.9 Future of Mutual Funds in India

New avenues have been opened up for the Indian mutual fund industry. The industry is not only witnessing unpredictable growth but also a transition to a better future. The authors believe that future is bright not only for the industry as such but also for the players. Following are some of the changes the industry is likely to witness.

1. More investors are likely to enter this industry and there will be a drastic increase in the number of schemes offered with new ideas and innovations.
2. The recurring expenses will drop with increased competition.
3. Only skilful players will sustain and operate in the industry.
4. More and more regulations will come in to force to check the activities of the players.
5. For the long term benefit of all the players in the industry, it is likely to join hands with other sectors of the economy such as banking and telecommunications.

6. Excess expenses being loaded on to the schemes will be driven away by the free market principle
7. The industry will become more Tech-savvy and investor friendly.
8. The distributor's role will become enormous.
9. With more and more players acquiring licenses, competition will be very intense.
10. A number of commodity mutual funds will be introduced in the future. The SEBI (Securities Exchange Board of India) has granted the permission for the same.
11. More emphasis will be put on the effective mutual funds governance.
12. Financial planners will play a major role in the mutual funds market.
13. Technological innovations could be leveraged for deeper penetration in Tier II and Tier III cities to eventually increase the overall mutual fund investment pie.
14. Schemes targeted at NRI's will gain importance.
15. The mounting cost of operations will be bought under control by the regulators.
16. With the diversified range of products on offer today, the thrust on investor education will gain importance.
17. The internet revolution in our country will penetrate to the grass root levels.

4.10 Conclusion

It can be observed from this chapter that the Indian mutual fund industry has grown remarkably. Some of the factors that add to this explosive growth of the industry are:

- Due to stiff competition, industry players have focused more on product innovation. This has not only helped the industry players to tap the needs of the investors, but also enabled them to spread out across all markets.

- Also, more and more investors, including retail investors, have begun to look at mutual funds as a suitable investment avenue.
- The need for greater market penetration has forced industry players to develop innovative channels of delivery to gain and strengthen their market share.
- Tax incentives have also helped mutual funds gain popularity with investors.
- Finally, the regulatory measures taken by SEBI have played a crucial role in instilling confidence among investors, especially retail investors.

Thus with growing risk appetite, rising income, high savings rate, comprehensive regulatory framework, favourable tax policies, savvy products, role of distributors, investor education and increasing awareness, mutual funds are indeed a favoured destination.

References

1. AMFI known as Association of Mutual Funds of India is an apex body of all Asset Management Companies registered with SEBI.
2. Mutual Funds Products and Services-Indian Institute of Banking and Finance.
3. Mutual funds in India by Amitabh Gupta,Anmol publications, New Delhi, 2002.
4. Jitendra Gala, Ankit Gala.,Guide to Indian Mutual Funds,Mumbai,Buzzing Stock Publishing house, 2007.
5. According to a study conducted by the Associated Chambers of Commerce and Industry of India (Assocham).
6. RBI Hand Book of Statistics on Indian Economy,2007-2008.
7. Computed from AMFI data.
8. SEBI Page.

5

Profile of ICICI Prudential Asset Management Company

5.1 Introduction

The previous chapter deals with the history of Indian mutual fund industry, the innovations and the developments that have taken place in India in terms of resource mobilisation and assets under management. But the main objective of the study is to specifically examine the three big and active players of the market namely ICICI Prudential Asset Management Company, HDFC Mutual Fund, Franklin Templeton Mutual Fund. The following three chapters will focus on the profile of these three companies. A study of the profile of these organizations will help us to understand the different schemes, their performances and other relevant aspects that gives a broad idea about the functioning of these funds.

This chapter begins with a brief note on the profile of ICICI Prudential Asset Management Company, its products, services and then the performances of sample schemes will be examined for the five year study period. The performances of the schemes are shown on the basis of compounded annualized growth returns (CAGR) against their respective benchmarks. As mentioned earlier in chapter one, it is difficult to examine all 374 schemes of this fund so only the sample schemes and their performances will be critically examined in the framework of Five year -Average Rate of return using the average of CAGR returns in comparison with its respective benchmark returns for the study period 2002 to 2007.

5.2 Profile of ICICI Prudential Asset Management Company

ICICI Prudential Asset Management Company (formerly known as Prudential ICICI Mutual Fund) is a joint venture between Prudential Plc, one of UK's largest players in the financial services sectors and ICICI Bank, India's premier financial institution[1]. ICICI Prudential Mutual Fund was set up as a Trust by the Settlers, ICICI Bank Ltd. and Prudential Plc. with the approval of Reserve Bank of India. ICICI Prudential Trust Limited is the Trustee to the Fund and ICICI Prudential Asset Management Company Ltd. is the Investment Manager to the Fund. Prudential ICICI Asset Management Company Limited was incorporated with a capital of Rs 65 crores. This represents a strategic long-term commitment, on the part of both partners, to the rapidly expanding financial services sector in India.

5.3 Brief Background of Sponsors, Trust, Trustee Company and Asset Management Company

The details of the sponsors and the other important parties associated with the company (refer figure 5.1) is briefly presented in the following paragraphs.

5.3.1 Sponsors - ICICI Bank Ltd.

ICICI Bank is India's largest private sector bank and the second largest bank with an asset base of $121 billion as on March 31, 2008. ICICI Bank provides a broad spectrum of financial services to individuals and companies. This includes mortgages, car and personal loans, credit and debit cards, and corporate and agricultural finance. ICICI Bank services a growing customer base of more than 17 million customers through a multi-channel access network which includes over 620 branches and extension counters, 2,200 ATMs, call centres and Internet banking.[2]

Figure 5.1
Structural Set-Up of ICICI Prudential Mutual Fund

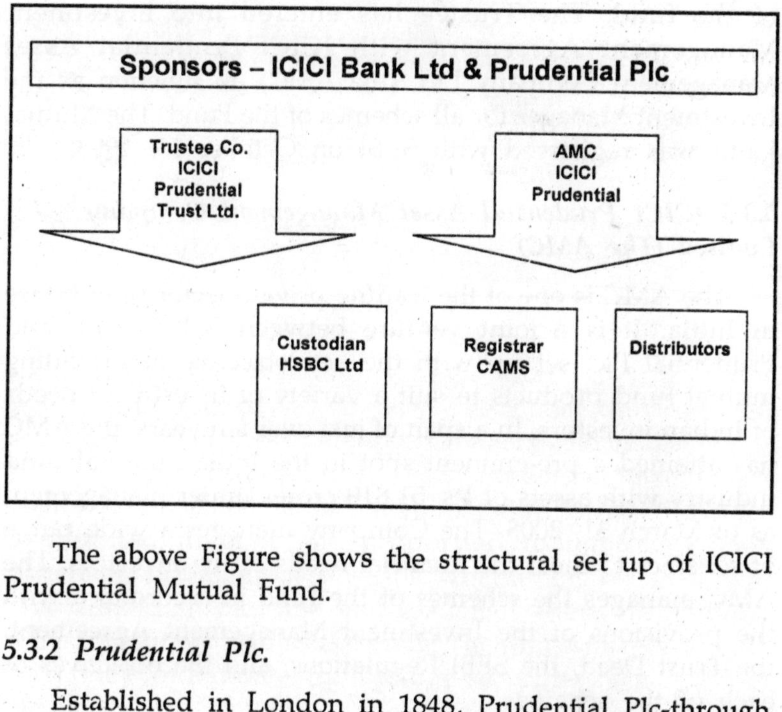

The above Figure shows the structural set up of ICICI Prudential Mutual Fund.

5.3.2 *Prudential Plc.*

Established in London in 1848, Prudential Plc-through its businesses in Europe, UK, USA, and Asia-provides retail financial services products and services to more than 16 million customers, policyholders and unit holders worldwide. Prudential has brought to the market an integrated range of financial services products that now includes life insurance, pensions, mutual funds, banking, investment management, and general insurance.

5.3.3 *Trust*

ICICI Prudential Mutual Fund was constituted as a Trust in accordance with the provisions of the Indian Trusts Act, 1882. The Trust Deed has been registered under the Indian Registration Act, 1908.

5.3.4 *Trustee Company*

ICICI Prudential Trust Ltd. (Trust Company) is the trustee of the fund. The Trustee has entered into investment Management Agreement with ICICI Prudential Asset Management Company Ltd. (the AMC), to function as the Investment Manager for all schemes of the Fund. The Mutual Fund was registered with SEBI on October 13, 1993.

5.3.5 *ICICI Prudential Asset Management Company Limited (The AMC)*

The AMC is one of the leading private sector fund house in India. It is a joint venture between ICICI Bank and Prudential Plc. set up with the key objective of providing mutual fund products to suit a variety of investment needs of Indian investors. In a span of just over ten years, the AMC has attained a pre-eminent spot in the Indian mutual fund industry with assets of Rs. 51,810 crores under management as of March 31, 2008. The Company manages a wide range of schemes to meet the financial needs of the investors. The AMC manages the schemes of the fund in accordance with the provisions of the Investment Management Agreement, the Trust Deed, the SEBI Regulations, and the objectives of each of the schemes.

5.3.6 *Custodian - The Hong Kong and Shanghai Banking Corporation Limited*

The Hong Kong and Shanghai Banking Corporation Limited, provides the custodial services to ICICI Prudential Mutual Fund which are as follows:

- Post-trading and custodial services to the Mutual Fund.
- Ensure that the benefits due on the holdings are received on time.
- Detailed management information as required by the AMC.
- Maintain confidentiality of the transactions.
- Be responsible for the loss or damage to the assets belonging to the scheme due to negligence.

5.3.7 Registrar - Computer Age Management Services (P) Limited (CAMS)

As registrar and transfer agent to the ICICI Premier, ICICI InfoTech handles all transfer related work, communications with investors, maintains investor data and processes all unit transactions.

5.3.8 Distributors

The distributors are the network through which the various schemes of ICICI Prudential mutual fund reach the investors. The distributors sell the schemes to the investors for which they are paid an incentive in the form of commission.

5.4 An Overview of the Organisation

ICICI has emerged as the most popular brands in the country. The Company puts in lots of efforts to build, strengthen and re-inforce the brand of ICICI Prudential among the investing public. ICICI Prudential Asset Management Company has forged a position of pre-eminence in the Indian mutual fund industry as one of the largest companies in the country with its consistent long term performance, innovative products, superior technology and a powerhouse of the best talent in the industry. ICICI Prudential mutual fund has been a consistent, focused and performance based company that has generated long term returns for its investors. The highlights of the company are given below in the following paragraphs.

5.4.1 *Total Assets Under Management*

The company which began in the year 1998, with an AUM of Rs 160 crores, managing only two funds at the time of its inception has since expanded its assets under management to Rs. 56772.58 crores as on December 31, 2007 spread over 40 funds thus making the company the largest asset management company in the private sector and the second largest in the mutual fund industry in India. Its impressive track record which bears testimony to this fact is shown below in table 5.1.

Table 5.1

ICICI Prudential's Total Assets Under Management

ICICI AUM	*Inception - May 1998*	*As on Dec 31, 2007*
Assets Under	Rs. 160 Crores Management	Rs. 56772.58 Crores

Source: www.icicipruamc.com

It can be observed from the table that the company has grown tremendously since its inception. The company attributes this aggressive growth to the increased awareness of mutual funds among the retail investors and to the dedicated distributors.

5.4.2 *Range of Products Offered*

The Company manages a wide range of products to meet the varying investment needs of its investors. The fund managers of this company are very talented and take great care in designing specialised products to suit the needs of every individual investor. In order to understand the range of products offered by the company let us first observe the following table.

Table 5.2
Products offered by ICICI Prudential AMC
(Figures as on 31st Dec.2007)

Total No. of Main Schemes	128
List of Options under Main Schemes	
Equity Schemes	40
Debt Schemes	274
Short term debt Schemes'	27
Equity and Debt Schemes	10
Money Market Schemes	0
Gilt Fund	7
Total No. of Schemes including Options	358

Source: Compiled from the Annual reports of ICICI Prudential Asset Management Company for the year 2006-2007

From the above table, it can be seen that the company has a wide range of schemes in order to meet the different investment objectives of the investors. The total number of schemes of the company as on December 31, 2007 stood at 358 including options. The AMC manages the schemes of the fund in accordance with the provisions of the Investment Management Agreement, the Trust Deed, the SEBI Regulations, and the objectives of each of the schemes. Table 5.2 clearly reflects the policies and beliefs of the company. The company has launched more number of debt schemes when compared to the equity schemes. This policy shows that company tries to play safe.

5.4.3 Distribution and Marketing Strategies

ICICI Prudential mutual fund has established a multi-channel approach to distribute its various products and has today an extensive network of customer service centres in 26 cities and over 12,000 customer contact points, comprising partner banks, financial distribution houses and financial advisers. The customer-centric approach of the company begins with educating and training its agents and distributors to understand customer requirements and counsel them accordingly. The company is allowed by SEBI to spend up to 6 percent of a scheme as marketing expense, and the company typically spends part of this allocation on distributors. The following figure shows the distribution structure of the company.

ICICI Prudential Mutual Fund has distributors who have a national presence. It. has also tied up with United Bank of India (UBI) for the distribution of its mutual fund schemes in order to popularize mutual funds as an investment avenue in hitherto under- tapped areas. Over the years, the company has provided innovative services like ICICIPru InstaCall (a 24-hour call centre enabling investors across India to update their account information, sell and switch between their investments in various schemes), ICICIPru InstaCheque (over-the-counter redemptions) and www.pruicici.com and http://www.pruicici.com (a transaction-enabled website with customized financial planning tools), designed to increase customer convenience and further empower the customer. ICICI Prudential undertakes customer education with the aim of reaching ever-larger sections of customers through mass media, mostly television

The company is also tapping new investor segments to boost business. As part of this strategy, marketing managers of this company are focusing their efforts on a hitherto untapped segment – namely daily wage earners and other unorganized sector workers – by offering them SIPs for very nominal amounts in their debt and liquid fund schemes.

5.5 Analysis of Sample Schemes of ICICI Prudential Mutual Fund

The performance of the sample schemes chosen for the purpose of the study have been examined in the following paragraphs. As seen earlier, table no 5.2 shows that the total number of schemes as on 31st Dec.2007 stands at 358 which includes the plans and options. As research has its own limitations and considering the time span and other factors of the study as discussed earlier, only the following schemes (four equity schemes, four debt schemes and one balanced scheme with growth options) have been selected for the purpose of analysis. The figure shown below displays the sample schemes chosen for the purpose of the study.

Figure 5.2
Sample Schemes of ICICI Prudential Asset Management Company Selected for the Purpose of the Study

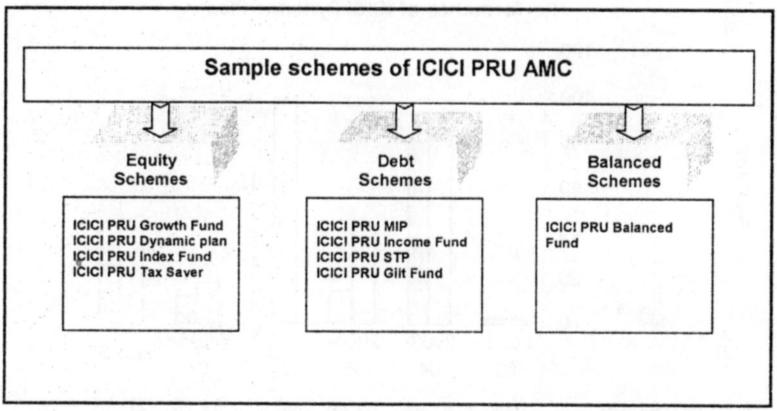

From the above figure, it can be seen that the analysis will be done only for the above schemes. The sample scheme's objectives, their sector allocation and their performance from their inception date have been discussed in detail in the following paragraphs.

5.5.1 *Analysis of Equity Schemes*

I. ICICI Prudential Dynamic Plan

ICICI Prudential Dynamic Plan was launched on October, 18, 2002 with an investment objective of generating capital appreciation. This scheme is a well diversified equity plan that follows the growth investment philosophy to invest in a portfolio of large, mid and small-cap stocks. The fund size stood at Rs. 2,453.08 crores as on 31-Dec-2007. The NAV of the fund as on 31-Dec-2007 stood at Rs. 92.63 for growth option, Rs. 26.24 for dividend option and Rs. 14.11 for institutional Option respectively. The performance of the scheme for the five year study period is shown below:

Graph 5.1
Performance of ICICI Prudential Dynamic Plan

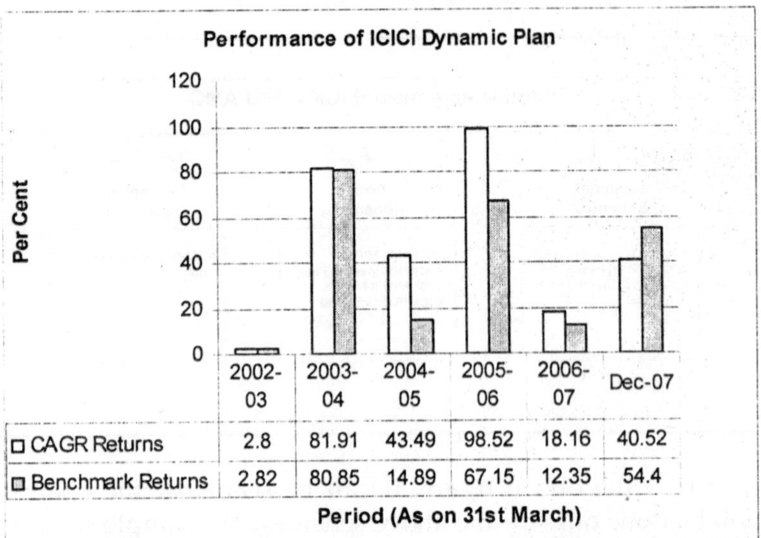

	2002-03	2003-04	2004-05	2005-06	2006-07	Dec-07
CAGR Returns	2.8	81.91	43.49	98.52	18.16	40.52
Benchmark Returns	2.82	80.85	14.89	67.15	12.35	54.4

Source: Compiled from Key Information Memorandum and Fund Fact Sheet Volumes of ICICI Prudential Mutual Fund

The scheme is benchmarked to S&P Nifty and the scheme's returns have consistently outperformed its benchmark returns during the study period. The last three years returns indicate clearly that the fund has performed consistently despite volatility. The major advantage of this fund is, it is aimed at capturing opportunities in the market across market capitalizations and it has the ability to move gradually into cash when the market gets over-valued. ICICI Prudential Dynamic Plan is more suited for conservative or risk-averse investors who have a long term investing horizon of more than five years. The scheme has exposure to large cap stocks, and the scheme has shown the flexibility to switch between different market capitalisation buckets, according to the sentiments of the markets. This has helped the scheme to outperform.

II. ICICI Prudential Growth Plan

ICICI Prudential Growth Plan was launched on 09-07-1998. The fund seeks to invest in large, profitable and well known companies, and aims to benefit from the best long term investments that the market has to offer in the large-cap space. Now, let us have a look at the following graph in order to understand the performance of this scheme. Graph 5.2 shows that the size of the fund stood at Rs.556.61 crores as on 31-Dec-2007 and the scheme has grown at a rate of 29.13 percent, whereas the scheme's benchmark index S&P Nifty has appreciated by 18.27 percent in the same period. The investments are spread across sectors like banks, software, industrial goods and rest in other safe sectors in order to ensure risk diversification. A close observation of the sectors reveals that stocks are selected through rigorous fundamental bottom up analysis.

When it comes to performance of the scheme, due to its large cap focus the scheme has managed to perform decently in spite of a volatile market. During the year 2003, 2004 and 2005, the scheme has continuously outperformed its benchmark (refer 5,2). But the next two years saw a dip in the performance. The reason can be attributed to high inflation and volatility. Even across the same category, peer average was also not very appealing during this period.

Graph 5.2
Performance of ICICI Prudential Growth Plan

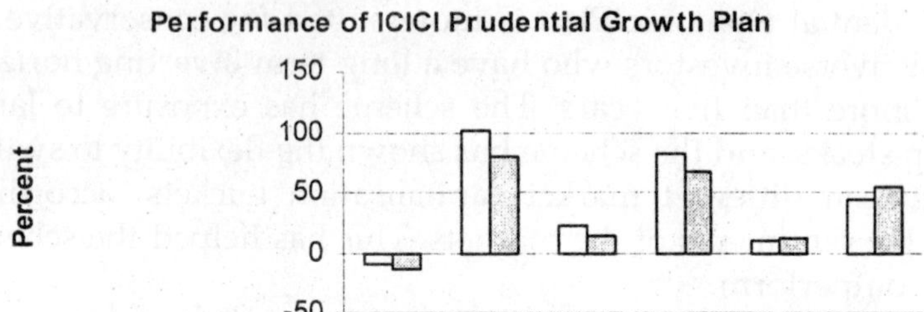

	2002-03	2003-04	2004-05	2005-06	2006-07	Dec-07
□ CAGR Returns	-9.81	100.01	22.6	82.83	10.21	44.11
□ Benchmark Returns (S&P CNX Nifty	-13.4	80.85	14.89	67.15	12.35	54.4

Period (As on 31st March)

□ CAGR Returns □ Benchmark Returns (S&P CNX Nifty

Source: Compiled from Key Information Memorandum and Fund Fact Sheet Volumes of ICICI Prudential Mutual Fund

III. ICICI Prudential Index Fund

This fund is an Open Ended Index Linked Growth Scheme and was launched on 26-02-2002 with a fund size of Rs. 29.03 crores as on 31-Dec-2007 and the NAV during the same period stood at Rs. 55.06. The objective of the plan is to invest in companies whose securities are included in nifty. Graph 5.3 shows that this fund has performed extremely well over the last 5 year period and has also emerged as the top performer in its category. This fund is a cost effective investment option. This fund has performed consistently and always has outperformed its benchmark except the year 2004-05.

The objective of the plan is to invest in companies whose securities are included in nifty and subject to tracking errors. This objective of the scheme has been achieved to a certain extent by investing in almost all the stocks comprising the

Graph 5.3
Performance of ICICI Prudential Index Fund

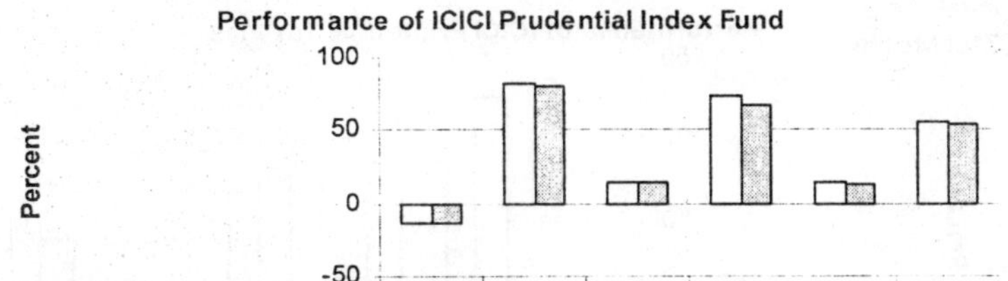

	2002-03	2003-04	2004-05	2005-06	2006-07	Dec-07
CAGR Returns	-13.5	82	13.53	73.56	13.83	56.08
Benchmark Returns(S&P CNX Nifty)	-13.4	80.85	14.89	67.15	12.35	54.4

Period (As on 31st March)

CAGR Returns Benchmark Returns(S&P CNX Nifty)

Source: Compiled from Key Information Memorandum and Fund Fact Sheet Volumes of ICICI Prudential Mutual Fund

S&P CNX Nifty. Hence it can be safely concluded that this index fund serves the investors by holding a portfolio comprised of well-managed diversified equity funds with proven track records across parameters and time frames.

IV. ICICI Prudential Tax Plan

ICICI Prudential Tax Plan is an open-ended equity linked saving scheme (ELSS) and was launched on August 1999. The fund size of the scheme stood at Rs. 1,035.26 crores as on 31-Dec-2007 and the NAV was Rs. 130.53 for the growth option and Rs. 28.43 for the dividend option respectively. This scheme has a lock-in period of 3 years, which ensures that the investors compulsorily remain invested over this period.

Graph 5.4
Performance of ICICI Prudential Tax Plan

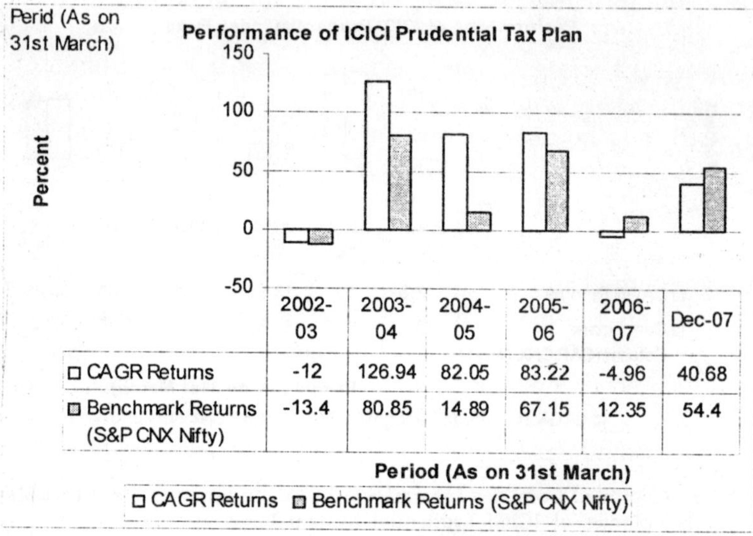

	2002-03	2003-04	2004-05	2005-06	2006-07	Dec-07
CAGR Returns	-12	126.94	82.05	83.22	-4.96	40.68
Benchmark Returns (S&P CNX Nifty)	-13.4	80.85	14.89	67.15	12.35	54.4

Source: Compiled from Key Information Memorandum and Fund Fact Sheet Volumes of ICICI Prudential Mutual Fund

ICICI Prudential Tax Plan is one of the more aggressive funds in the ELSS category and is very popular for exploiting market conditions. Even as a number of tax-savings funds have shed their mid-cap bias and shifted their focus on others, ICICI Prudential continues to hold to its strategy of relatively higher exposure to the mid and small-cap market cap segment.

In its so many years, the fund has under-performed its category only few times and during those times it has also recovered very quickly. During the year 2003 and 2005 it has produced tremendous results as against its benchmark of 80.85 percent and 67.15 percent respectively. But again subsequent two years were not too good and the scheme displayed very poor results.

5.5.2 Analysis of Debt Schemes

I. ICICI Prudential Monthly Income Plan

ICICI Prudential Monthly Income Plan was launched on 10-11-2000 and is a conservatively managed fund that invests predominantly in debt securities and a very limited equity exposure with the objective of stability of income, and has the track record of uninterrupted monthly dividends since inception. The total fund size stood at Rs. 563.39 crores as on 31-Dec-2007.

Graph 5.5
Performance of ICICI Prudential Monthly Income Plan

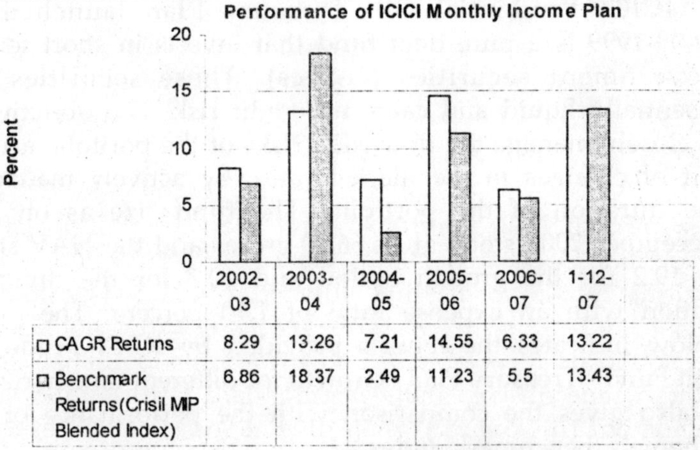

	2002-03	2003-04	2004-05	2005-06	2006-07	1-12-07
CAGR Returns	8.29	13.26	7.21	14.55	6.33	13.22
Benchmark Returns(Crisil MIP Blended Index)	6.86	18.37	2.49	11.23	5.5	13.43

Source: Compiled from Key Information Memorandum and Fund Fact Sheet Volumes of ICICI Prudential Mutual Fund

The scheme has been a consistent performer across various time frames and has grown at a CAGR of 10.52 percent since its inception. It's judicious asset allocation among debt &

money market instruments with a dash of equity exposure and correct timing has been instrumental in showing reasonably an average performance. If we observe the above graph it can be seen that the scheme has continuously outperformed its bench mark and has shown a satisfactory performance during the year 2004-05 and 2005-06 with returns of 7.21 percent and 14.55 percent as against its benchmark. The scheme has strictly adhered to its investment objective of generating regular income through investments in fixed income securities and long term capital appreciation by investing a portion in equity and equity related instruments and has never gone beyond its allocation.

II. ICICI Prudential Gilt Fund-Treasury plan

ICICI Prudential Gilt Treasury Plan launched on 19-08-1999 is a pure debt fund that invests in short tenure Government securities (G-Secs). These securities are essentially liquid and carry no credit risk. The objective is to closely manage the downside risks of the portfolio arising out of changes in the market rates, by actively managing the duration of the portfolio. The fund size as on 31st December 2007 stood at Rs.66.29 crores and the NAV stood at 19.2 for the growth option and 10.7 for the dividend option with an expense ratio of 1.10 percent. The graph below indicates the returns provided by ICICI Prudential Gilt Fund - Treasury Plan - Growth for different time horizons. It also gives the comparison with the performance of the scheme's benchmark index.

The fund size as on 31st December 2007 stood at Rs.66.29 crores. This fund has invested 53.07 percent in CPs, CDs and Term Deposits. The objective of this nature of allocation is to avoid credit risk. Major portion which comprises around 33.47 percent has been invested in Government Securities to play safe.

If we observe the performance as shown by the figures in the graph, it can be seen that in spite of sector allocation being done cautiously, the schemes CAGR has managed to

Graph 5.6
Performance of ICICI Prudential Gilt Fund

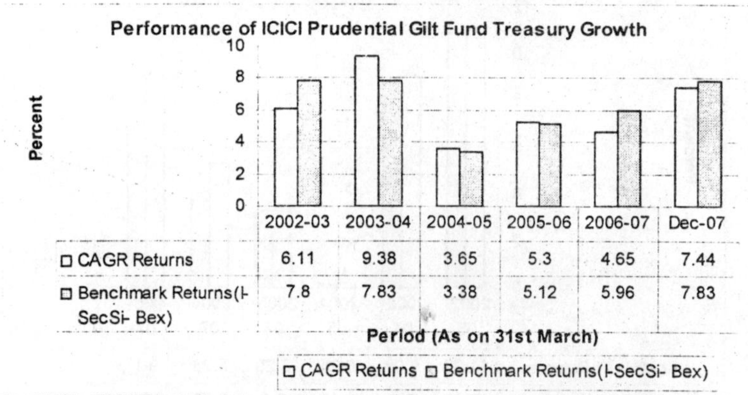

Source: Compiled from Key Information Memorandum and Fund Fact Sheet Volumes of ICICI Prudential Mutual Fund

outperform its benchmark on an average basis only. Infact, the scheme has underperformed during the year 2006-07 with a return of 4.65 percent as against benchmark return of 5.96 percent.

III. ICICI Prudential Income Plan

ICICI Prudential Income Plan is a debt fund that invests entirely in both short and long term debt securities of the Government and corporate sector. The inception date of this scheme was 09-07-1998. The Fund Size of this scheme was Rs. 339.31 crores as on 31-Dec-2007. The objective of the scheme is to earn a rate of interest that generates income for investors. This fund minimizes risks from liquidity, credit and interest rates in a balanced manner. A close observation of this plan shows that Income plan has the potential to earn total return from both interest and capital gains. A look at the returns figures shows that the returns have always outperformed the benchmark returns except for two quarters. The CAGR for December 2007 stood at 9.10 percent as against

Graph 5.7
Performance of ICICI Prudential Income Plan

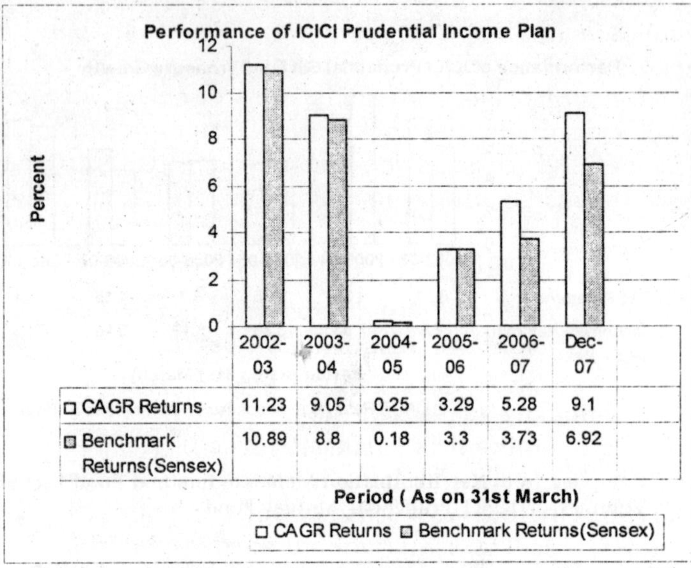

Source: Compiled from Key Information Memorandum and Fund Fact Sheet Volumes of ICICI Prudential Mutual Fund

its benchmark returns of 6.92 percent. The portfolio selection has been very carefully done by the fund manager with 37.26 percent invested in Government securities, 32.62 percent in PSU/PFI bonds and 24.11 percent invested in private corporate securities.

IV. ICICI Prudential Short Term Plan

ICICI Prudential Short Term Plan was launched on 25-10-2001 and the size of the fund as on December 31, 2007 stood at Rs. 627.51 Crores. This fund invests in a basket of debt securities, which have a shorter maturity term The scheme has invested around 61 percent in private Corporate Securities and around 26 percent in CDs and Term Deposits. The portfolio also comprises of short term instruments issued by the corporate sector and takes view-based limited G-Sec exposure. The scheme has shown remarkable performance ever since its inception and is benchmarked against Crisil Short Term Bond Fund Index. Prudential ICICI AMC was the third one to come up with Short Term Debt scheme. It has been ranked in the top quartile in its category across various time frames. The scheme has always outperformed its benchmark index and its category's average.

Graph 5.8

Performance of ICICI Prudential Short Term Plan

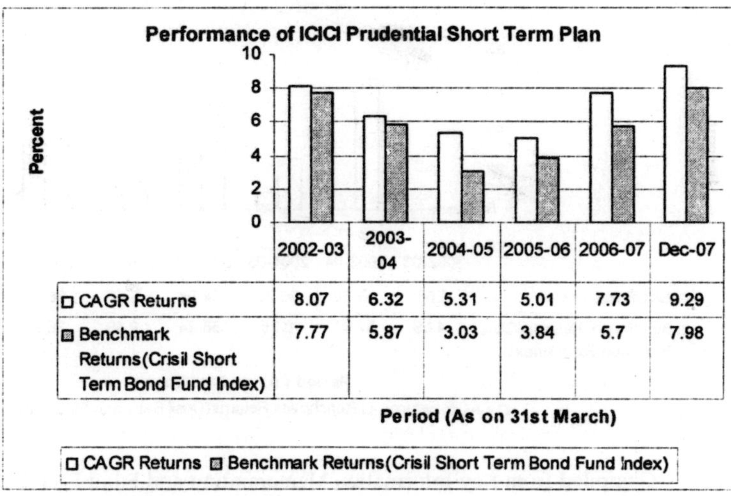

Source: Compiled from Key Information Memorandum and Fund Fact Sheet Volumes of ICICI Prudential Mutual Fund

5.5.3 *Analysis of Balanced Scheme*

I. ICICI Prudential Balanced Fund

ICICI Prudential Balanced Fund is an open-ended fund that allocates equally to both equity and debt. This dynamic allocation along with core debt portfolio reduces the volatility of return. Balanced fund brings the twin benefits of growth from equity markets and steady income from debt markets. The Inception date of this fund was 03-11-1999 and the fund size as on Dec 31, 2007 stood at Rs. 469.43 crores. The performance record of this fund is shown in the following graph.

Graph 5.9

Performance of ICICI Prudential Balanced Fund

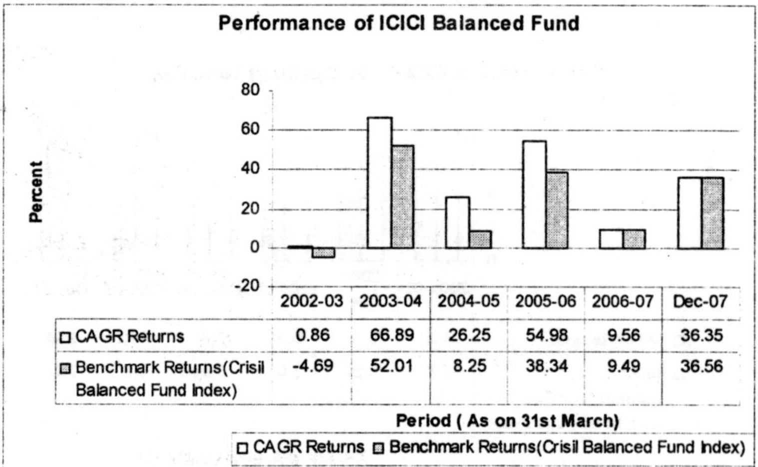

	2002-03	2003-04	2004-05	2005-06	2006-07	Dec-07
CAGR Returns	0.86	66.89	26.25	54.98	9.56	36.35
Benchmark Returns(Crisil Balanced Fund Index)	-4.69	52.01	8.25	38.34	9.49	36.56

Source: Compiled from Key Information Memorandum and Fund Fact Sheet Volumes of ICICI Prudential Mutual Fund

This fund has beaten the average category returns of 2004, 2005, 2006 and 2007 continuously. Like most funds, this fund was launched during a turbulent period where there was a tech bubble. During the tech bubble, the fund delivered a return of 68 percent in five months only to end with a 45 percent loss by the end of 2000. Since then, it began to spread its assets across various sectors and has managed to perform well since then. It has managed to invest in stocks that have the capacity to bring down the risks This is one reason why investors find this fund more attractive which is evident from the fact that last four years has consistently been delivering an above average return.

5.6 Conclusion

From the above, it is evident that ICICI Prudential AMC has a prominent position in the market and poses a very big threat to its competitors. Even though, in the initial stages, ICICI Prudential drew from the experience of Prudential's global network and the Indian parent's local knowledge, it developed its capability and eventually grew to become a matured company. Some of the major milestones that the company has crossed over the decade are:

- ICICI Prudential AMC is the first private sector mutual fund that challenged the leadership position of the public sector mutual funds.
- ICICI Prudential AMC is the first private MF player in the country – and the second overall in the MF industry – to cross the five figures mark (Rs. 10,000 crore) in terms of assets under management.
- This AMC has the largest investor base which is 1.9 million currently.
- The AUM which stood at Rs 160 Crores at the time of its inception has increased manifold to Rs. 56772.58 Crores till December 31, 2007.
- ICICI Prudential Asset Management received the prestigious Lipper Fund Awards for 'Best Overall Fund Group over three years' ending 2007. The Lipper Fund Awards highlight funds that have excelled in delivering consistent strong risk-adjusted performance. Lipper awards are given to funds in 21 countries across Asia, Europe and America.
- ICICI Prudential AMC is the first AMC to venture in to the Portfolio Management Service (PMS) space.
- This AMC has the largest branch network in India with 245 branches and still expanding.

Some of the reasons for its success can be attributed to the following:

- o Good brand image
- o Innovative techniques in product development
- o Positive approach by the Management
- o Capacity to identify emerging opportunities
- o Strong distribution channels
- o Capacity to meet the needs of the investors
- o Constant focus in developing a distinct position in the industry
- o Reaching out to rural markets
- o Excellent Marketing and advertising strategies

References

1. www.icicipruamc.com
2. www.icicibank.com

6

Profile of HDFC Asset Management Company Ltd

6.1 Introduction

This chapter begins with an examination of the profile of HDFC Mutual Fund governed by HDFC Asset Management Company Limited (AMC). This will be followed by an evaluation of the sample schemes in the framework of Five year -Average Rate of return using the average of CAGR returns in comparison with its respective benchmark returns for the study period 2002 to 2007. The methodology followed will be the same as in the case of ICICI Prudential mutual fund where the profile of this company, the services and the performances of sample schemes selected for the purpose of the study is critically examined. The period of study is from January 2002 to December 2007. The author has also given some valid and logical recommendations in the last two chapters based on the findings of the performance of the schemes.

6.2. Brief Background of Sponsors, Trust, Trustee Company and Asset Management Company

HDFC Mutual Fund was setup on June 30, 2000 with

two sponsors namely Housing Development Finance Corporation Limited and Standard Life Investments Limited. Despite being a late entrant in the mutual fund industry, HDFC Mutual Fund is one of the largest mutual funds. A brief background of the sponsors is given below in the following paragraphs.

6.2.1 *Housing Development Finance Corporation Limited*

HDFC was incorporated in 1977, as the first specialised housing finance institution in India. HDFC provides financial assistance to individuals, corporates and developers for the purchase or construction of residential housing. It also provides property related services, training and consultancy. Of these activities, housing finance remains the dominant activity. HDFC has a client base of over 8,00,000 borrowers, 12,00,000 depositors, 92,000 shareholders and 50,000 deposit agents. HDFC has received the highest rating for its bonds and deposits program for the ninth year in succession.[1]

6.2.2 *The Standard Life Investments Limited*

Standard Life Investments Limited is one of the world's major investment companies and is responsible for investing money on behalf of five million retail and institutional clients worldwide. In order to meet the different needs and risk profiles of its clients, Standard Life Investments Limited manages a diverse portfolio, covering all of the major markets world-wide, which includes a range of private and public equities, government and company bonds, property investments and various derivative instruments.

6.2.3 *The Trust*

HDFC Mutual Fund (the "Fund") has been constituted as a trust in accordance with the provisions of the Indian Trusts Act, 1882. The Trust Deed has been registered under the Indian Registration Act, 1908. The Trustee has entered into an Investment Management Agreement with HDFC Asset Management Company Ltd. to function as the Investment Manager for all the Schemes of HDFC Mutual Fund.

6.2.4 *The Trustee Company*

HDFC Trustee Company Limited (the "Trustee") is the exclusive owner of the Trust Fund and holds the same in trust for the benefit of the Unit holders. The Trustee Company seeks to ensure that the Fund and the Schemes floated are managed by HDFC AMC in accordance with the Trust Deed, the regulations, directions and guidelines issued by the SEBI, the stock exchanges, the Association of Mutual Funds in India and other regulatory agencies.

Figure 6.1
Structure of HDFC Asset Management Company

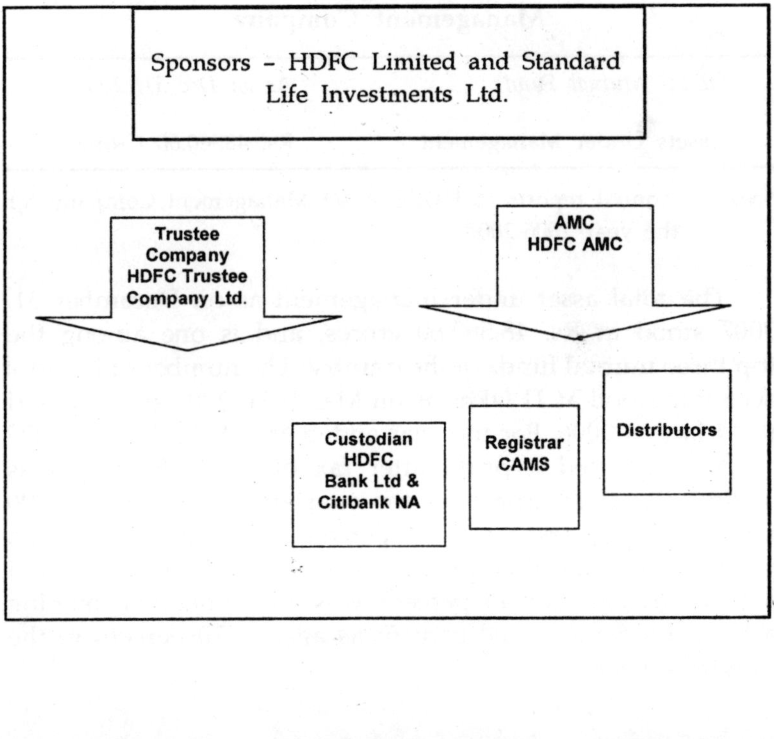

6.3 An overview of HDFC Asset management Company

HDFC Asset management Company was incorporated under the Companies Act, 1956, on December 10, 1999, and was approved to act as an Asset Management Company for the Mutual Fund by SEBI in the year 2000. HDFC AMC is a joint venture between housing finance giant HDFC and British investment firm Standard Life Investments Limited. In 2003, following a decision by the Zurich Insurance Company (ZIC), the Sponsor of Zurich India Mutual Fund, decided to divest its asset management business in India. Eventually an agreement was entered with ZIC by the AMC to acquire the asset management business whereby all the schemes of Zurich Mutual Fund in India had been transferred to HDFC Mutual Fund and renamed as HDFC schemes. The following table shows the assets under management of the company as on December 31, 2007.

Table 6.1
Total Assets Under Management of HDFC Asset Management Company

HDFC Mutual Fund	*As on Dec 31, 2007*
Assets Under Management	Rs. 48560.60 Crores

Source: Annual reports of HDFC Asset Management Company for the year 2006-2007

The total asset under management as on December 31, 2007 stood at Rs. 48,560.60 crores, and is one among the top three mutual funds of the country. The number of investor accounts stood at 21 lakhs as on March 31, 2007 as compared to 14 lacs in 2006. For the year ended March 31, 2007, HDFC - AMC reported a profit after tax of Rs. 67.54 crores as against Rs. 45.48 crores for the year ended March 31, 2006 representing a growth of 49 percent[2]. During the year, an interim dividend of 60 percent was paid in March 2007 and a final dividend of 40 percent was recommended, making a total dividend of 100 percent as against 70 percent in the previous year.[3]

6.3.1 Products of HDFC Mutual Fund

HDFC Mutual Fund, equipped with an insight into the mindset and needs of the Indian investor, offers a basket of around 23 schemes comprising equity funds, hybrid funds and debt funds. This vast choice, managed by professional and highly experienced fund managers, enables a customer to choose an investment option that best fits their needs.

From the table 6.2 shown below, it can be seen that the company has a wide range of schemes in order to meet the different investment objectives of the investors.

The products of HDFC Mutual Fund are as follows:

- Equity Funds
- Balance Funds
- Debt Funds

Apart from this it also provides the following value added services:

- SIP (Systematic Investment Plan)
- STP (Systematic Transfer Plan)
- SWAP (Systematic Withdrawal Advantage Plan)

Table 6.2

Scheme Details of HDFC AMC as on December, 31, 2007

Details	*No.*
Total Number of Main Schemes	76
List of Options under Main Schemes	
Equity Schemes	30
Debt Schemes	232
Short term debt Schemes'	15
Equity and Debt Schemes	6
Money Market Schemes	0
Gilt Fund	4
Total Number of Schemes including Options	**287**

Source: Compiled from the Annual reports of HDFC Asset Management Company for the year 2006-2007

HDFC Mutual Fund is one of the dominant players recognized for its high level of ethical and professional conduct and its commitment towards enhancing investor's interest. As a fund house, HDFC Mutual Fund is known for its process-driven investment approach. The fund has a portfolio of strong performing schemes like HDFC Equity, HDFC Top 200 and HDFC Prudence, to name a few. These funds have proven track records across time frames and market phases. It also includes those launched by the fund itself along with those acquired on the merger of Zurich Mutual Fund with itself some time ago. Since its incorporation, the AMC has attained a pre-eminent spot in the Indian mutual fund industry with assets of Rs. 48560.6023 Crores under management as of December 31, 2007.

6.3.3 *Brand Building*

Customer orientation in designing the products has helped them find a secure place in the market and this is one reason why this fund is still a premium brand. The company has worked very hard to gain recognition among the investing public and in order to retain the brand image, it is still continuing to strengthen the image.

6.3.4 *Operations and Consumer Service*

The company always puts the customers first. Operations and Customer Service are its key focus area and play an instrumental role in their success. The company is dedicated towards customer satisfaction and works hard to cater to their unique requirements. This company is the first and only AMC to be assigned "Fund House Level 1 Rating" by Crisil. The rating reflects highest fund governance levels and fund management practices at HDFC AMC.

6.3.5 *Personnel*

The company believes that the employees are important stakeholders in the growth and development of the organization. The company believes that the desire to know more, skills to consistently perform at higher levels and a winning attitude, as the qualities of a good employee. The employees of this company are passionate about their chosen field of work, want to grow and are driven to make a difference. The spirit of teamwork and companionship is visible in all employees, regardless of their stature or position.

6.3.6 Portfolio Management Services (PMS)

The Company also commenced portfolio management activities. Under the Portfolio Management Services, HDFC PMS offers discretionary Services. These services are offered to each client under a specific agreement entered into between the Portfolio Manager and the client on an exclusive basis.

6.3.7 Distribution and Marketing Strategies

HDFC Mutual Fund is one of the largest mutual funds in India with an investor base of over 25 lakh. The investors are serviced primarily by their wide network of distributors. HDFC mutual fund recognizes their distributors as the most important link between the investors and the company. To help distributors to advice and service their clients better, the company, together with their registrar (CAMS) offer a range of facilities to them. It has also launched country's first-ever mutual fund service to enable investors to buy and sell mutual fund units through automatic teller machines (ATMs). The company has also tied up with Union Bank of India to distribute its products across India.

As per SEBI rule, the company is allowed to spend up to 6 percent of a scheme as marketing expense, and the company typically spends part of this allocation on distributors. HDFC Bank has launched neighbourhood marketing initiatives in tier-two cities and towns to create awareness about its various products and services. It has also launched a customer analysis system to understand the preferences of the investor.

6.4 Analysis of sample schemes of HDFC Mutual Fund

The authors after having examined the profile of the

company next examines the performance of the sample schemes. The methodology followed in examining the sample schemes will be the same as in the case of the previous chapter. Another common factor in the choice of selection of schemes of this company to facilitate comparison with the other two companies is the similar investment objectives that falls under the same category. The schemes that have been selected for the purpose of analysis and their objectives, their sector allocation and their performance from their inception date have been discussed in detail in the following paragraphs.

Figure 6.2
Sample Schemes of HDFC Asset Management Company Selected for the Purpose of Study

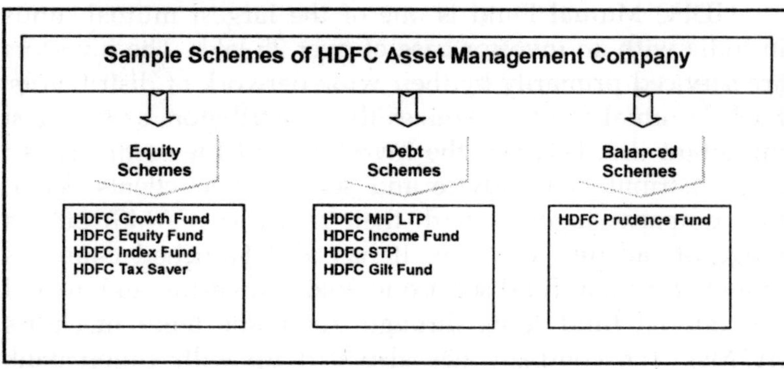

As mentioned earlier in the study, four equity schemes, four debt schemes and one balanced scheme have been selected as shown below in the following paragraphs:

6.4.1 Analysis of Equity schemes of HDFC Mutual Fund

I. HDFC Growth Fund

HDFC Growth Fund is an open-ended equity diversified scheme, which aims to generate long term capital appreciation from a portfolio that is invested predominantly in equity and equity related instruments. The scheme was launched in August 10, 2000. The Net Asset Value of this fund stood at Rs. 394.48 crore as at March 31, 2007. The performance of the fund for the five year study period is shown below.

Graph 6.1
Performance of HDFC Growth Fund

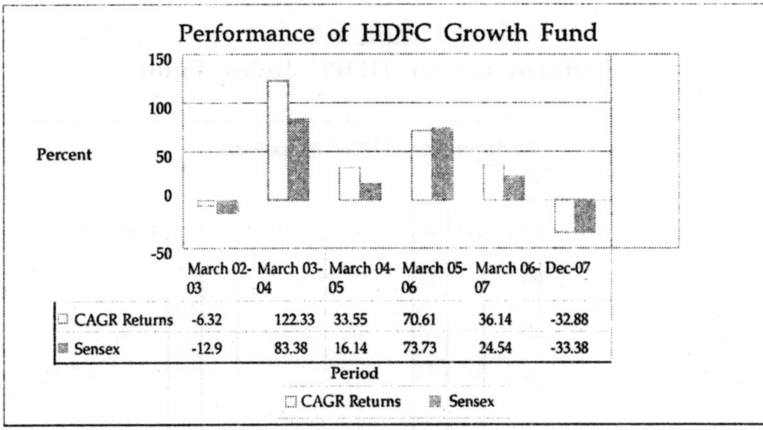

Source: Compiled from the Annual reports of HDFC Asset Management Company for the year 2006-2007

The performance of the scheme has been very good during 2004 and 2005. The returns during this period outperformed its benchmark. But the next consecutive two years saw a down turn. HDFC Growth fund is a well diversified. HDFC Growth fund, despite a decent corpus size, active fund management style and a good brand name failed to match the expectations of the investing people. Although the long-term performance is decent, and has generated stable returns since its inception, there is a lack of a mix of small cap and midcap stocks in the portfolio.

II. HDFC Index Fund

Index funds are a cost-effective investment option that invests 80 to 90 percent of the net assets of the Plan in companies whose securities are included in Sensex and between 10 percent and 20 percent of the net assets in companies whose securities are not included in the Sensex and was launched in July 17, 2002. This fund actually offers three plans to investors – Sensex Plan, Nifty Plan and Sensex plus Plan. The performance of this fund is shown in the following graph.

Graph 6.2
Performance of HDFC Index Fund

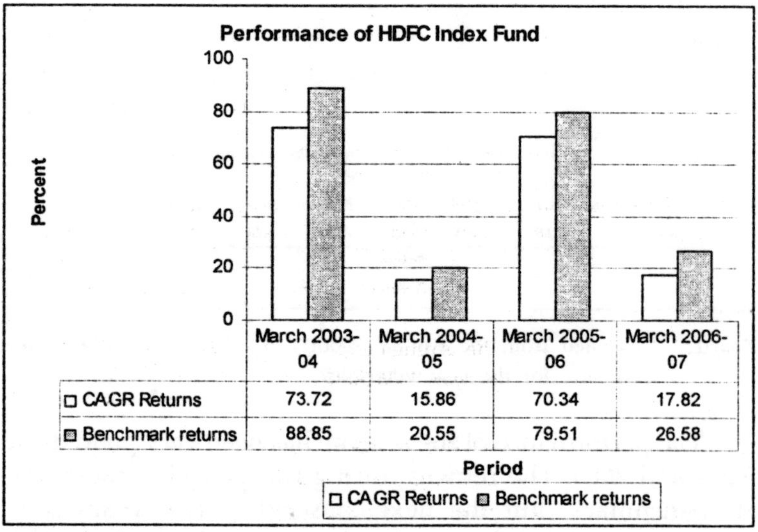

Source: Compiled from the Annual reports of HDFC Asset Management Company for the year 2006-2007

Index funds have continuously underperformed its benchmark returns. Even the peer average has been very unsatisfactory. During the study period, the five year return has continuously shown underperformance which reflects the market scenario. The sector allocation has been a well diversified one with 14.76 percent invested in petroleum products. The HDFC Sensex plus plan too has kept up with this trend. In keeping with its initial objectives, the fund has delivered higher returns than passive Sensex funds by investing a small portion of its assets outside the index stocks.

III. HDFC Equity Fund-Growth plan

HDFC Equity Fund was launched in January 1995. HDFC Equity Fund (HEF) is an open-ended diversified equity fund. HEF is a high risk-return investment proposition and has a good track record to show for. The fund has managed to pitch in a reasonable performance which is shown in the following graph.

Graph 6.3
Performance of HDFC Equity Fund

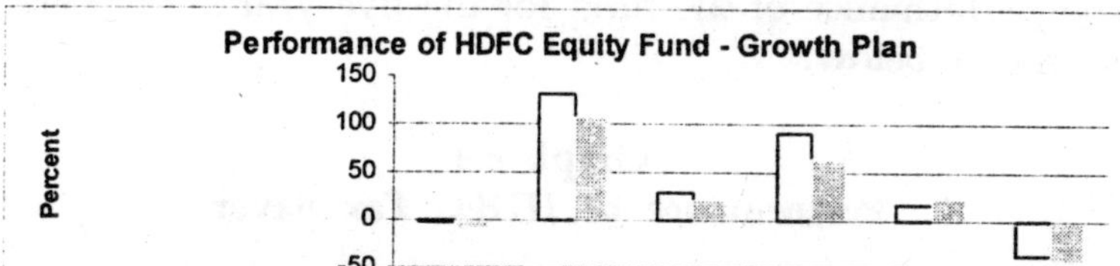

	March 02-	March 03-	March 04-	March 05-	March 06-	Dec-07
CAGR Returns	-1.46	131.8	29.54	90.24	17.83	-34.88
Benchmark Returns (S&P CNX 500)	-10.21	107.81	21.64	64.16	24.87	-39.38

Period

CAGR Returns Benchmark Returns (S&P CNX 500)

Source: Compiled from the Annual reports of HDFC Asset Management Company for the year 2006-2007

HDFC Equity, with its impressive track record, is a good investment option. For more than a decade, the fund has weathered different phases in the market and delivered attractive value to long-term investors. The consistency in performance across quarters during study period shows its ability to sail though any sluggish market phase.

HDFC Equity has not only outpaced the indices, but also a host of peer funds. This remains one of the best performing funds in its category. The portfolio is characterized by concentrated stock and sectoral holdings. Also the fund invests in stocks of both the large and mid cap varieties. The fund is appropriate for investors looking for a long-term option.

IV. HDFC Tax Saver

HDFC Tax saver Fund was launched in 31st March 1996. This scheme was taken over by HDFC Mutual Fund from erstwhile Zurich India Mutual Fund. The investment objective of the Scheme is to achieve long-term growth of capital. Being an ELSS, the scheme has allocated a minimum of 80 percent in equity and equity related instruments and the balance of the 20 percent in debt and liquid instruments. The ELSS has advantage over other schemes as it has a lock in period of three years and so the fund manager can effectively mobilize the resources to get the best of returns. The performance of the fund for the five year study period is shown below.

Graph 6.4
Performance of HDFC Tax Saver

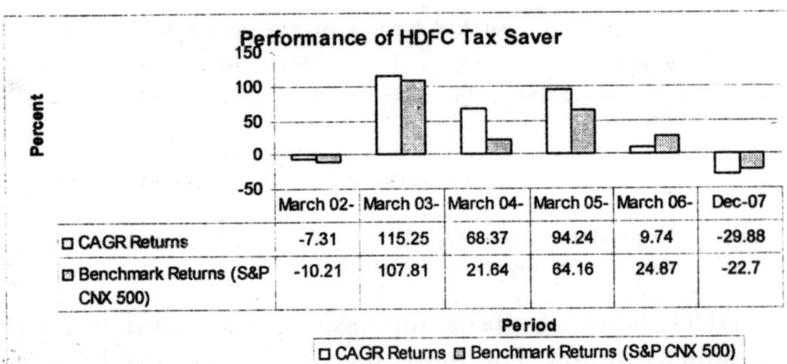

Source: Compiled from the Annual reports of HDFC Asset Management Company for the year 2006-2007

The scheme is one of the best performing funds in the ELSS category. It has generated 45.49 percent return since inception on an annualized basis. It has managed to outperform its benchmark and peer's average in various time periods. The scheme has generated 115.25 percent, 68.37 percent, and 94.24 percent returns during 2004, 2005 and 2006 respectively. In the last 5 years the scheme has always been among the top 3 schemes in its category on the returns criteria. The scheme has also performed well in the risk adjusted return criteria. The scheme had 94.35 percent holdings in equity and equity related holdings during December 2007.

6.4.2 Analysis of Debt schemes of HDFC Mutual Fund

I. HDFC MIP Long Term Plan

HDFC MIP Long Term Plan was launched by HDFC Mutual Fund in December 2003, when hybrid products were the flavor of the season. The objective of the Scheme is to generate regular returns by investing primarily in Debt & Money Market Instruments. The fund managed assets worth Rs. 140,145.97 crores as on December2007, which was a 44 percent increase, when compared to the last year. The scheme is aimed at the aggressive investors and the performance of the scheme is shown below:

Graph 6.5
Performance of HDFC MIP Long Term Plan

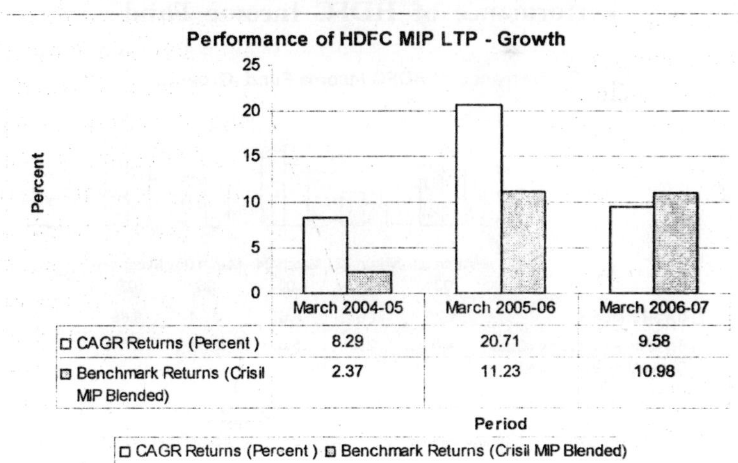

Source: Compiled from the Annual reports of HDFC Asset Management Company for the year 2006-2007

HDFC MIP has always been amongst the top performers in its category. The scheme has outperformed its benchmark - Crisil MIP Blended Index as well as its average peer group across all time frames and that too with a handsome margin. In the equity segment, the fund has allocated 25.87 percent as on December 2007 and 66.54 percent in debt segment.

In the one year period 2005-2006 it generated 20.71 percent as against its benchmark returns of 11.23 percent displaying very good performance. The scheme has always stood on the top across all selected time frames.

II. HDFC Income Fund

HDFC Income Fund was launched in August 10, 2000 and the objective of the scheme is to maintain a balance of safety, yield and liquidity and at the same time optimize returns. The scheme is mandated to invest 80 percent -100 percent of its assets in Debt securities and 0-20 percent in Money Market instruments. The performance of the scheme is displayed in the following graph.

Graph 6.6
Performance of HDFC Income Fund

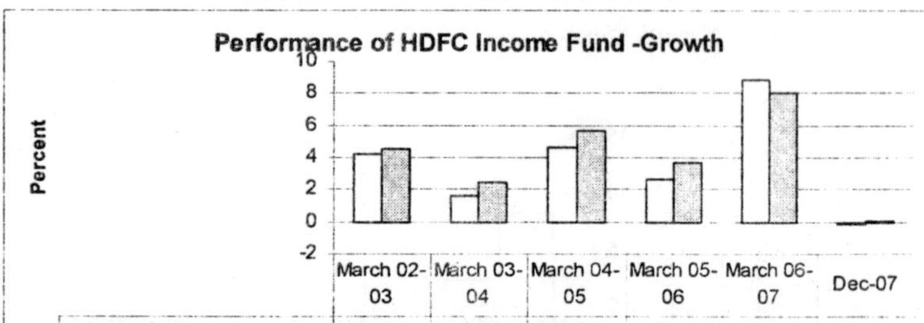

	March 02-03	March 03-04	March 04-05	March 05-06	March 06-07	Dec-07
CAGR Returns	4.25	1.67	4.65	2.64	8.85	-0.15
Benchmark Returns (Crisil Composite Bond Fund Index)	4.5	2.4	5.62	3.69	8.04	0.08

Source: Compiled from the Annual reports of HDFC Asset Management Company for the year 2006-2007

An observation of the above graph shows that the fund has displayed its strength in both good and bad times and thus makes it attractive. Over last one year the scheme's asset allocation indicates that the fund manager intended to derive the best out of volatile debt markets by investing 62.4 percent in debentures. It has consistently beaten its benchmark over the last five years during the study period. It has reduced risk by spreading its portfolio across 40-50 securities. This strategy has helped the fund to overcome volatility. Thus, the fund has managed to achieve one of the best risk-reward profiles in the group.

III. HDFC Short Term Plan

HDFC Short Term Plan was launched in February 28, 2002. This plan is an additional plan under the existing ICICI Prudential Income Plan with characteristics similar to ICICI Prudential Income Plan. The objective of the plan is to seek to generate regular returns through investments in a basket of debt and money market securities. Short-term plan may be ideal for investors with short-term funds on their hands. The performance of the fund for the five year study period is shown below.

Graph 6.7
Performance of HDFC Short Term Plan

Performance of HDFC Short Term Plan - Growth

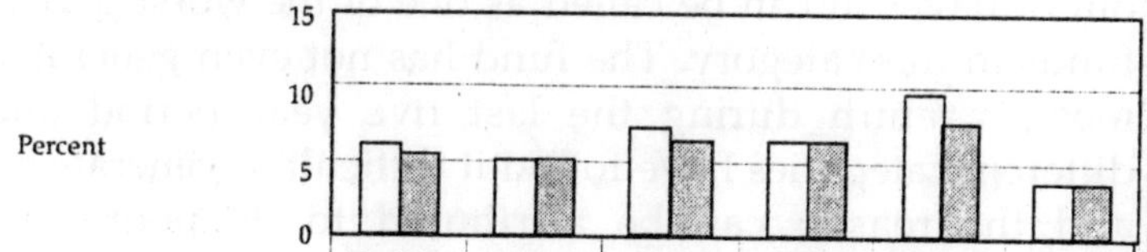

	March 02-03	March 03-04	March 04-05	March 05-06	March 06-07	Dec-07
□ CAGR Returns	6.13	5.08	7.16	6.45	9.64	3.72
▩ Benchmark Returns (Crisil Liquid Fund Index)	5.49	5.13	6.37	6.41	7.63	3.6

Period

□ CAGR Returns ▩ Benchmark Returns (Crisil Liquid Fund Index)

Source: Compiled from the Annual reports of HDFC Asset Management Company for the year 2006-2007

As can be seen from the above graph, the scheme has outperformed its benchmark for three consecutive years during the study period. The scheme has delivered 6.49 percent per annum returns since inception. In the tight liquidity and rising interest rate environment, the scheme was running a lower maturity compared to the benchmark index, which helped the scheme performance. The short-term plan is a significantly large fund with assets under management of around Rs 2,600 crore. The fund has 75.4 percent of net assets in Debentures and 22.63 percent in money market instruments. The fund has only a limited exposure to government securities. This enhances the credit risk of the portfolio.

IV. HDFC Gilt Fund

The objective of HDFC Gilt fund which was launched in August 19, 1999 is to generate steady and consistent returns from a basket of government securities across various maturities through proactive fund management aimed at controlling interest rate risk. Among all the different categories of mutual fund schemes in India, Gilt funds as a category have been the worst performing in the last one year.

During the study period, HDFC Gilt Fund has continuously underperformed its benchmark and has fallen out of flavor. It can be called as one of the worst performing funds in this category. The fund has not even generated any meager return during the last five year period and the different categories have found it difficult to generate returns and the reason can be attributed to its poor portfolio allocation. The company has invested 93.55 percent in Government securities which due to inflation and falling interest rates has generated poor yield. An unfavorable market has also prevented the scheme from generating decent returns. Investments in gilt funds are vulnerable to interest rate risks. When interest rates rise, prices of government securities fall; this in turn has an adverse impact on the performance of gilt funds.

Graph 6.8
Performance of HDFC GILT FUND-Short Term Plan

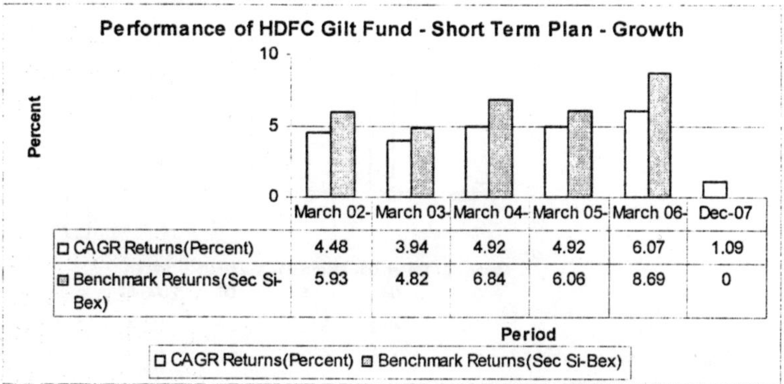

Source: Compiled from the Annual reports of HDFC Asset Management Company for the year 2006-2007

6.4.3 Analysis of Balanced scheme of HDFC Mutual Fund

I. HDFC Prudence Fund

HDFC Prudence Fund is one of the best performing schemes in the balanced category. The scheme was launched in February 1, 1994 with the objective to provide periodic returns and capital appreciation over a long period of time, from a judicious mix of equity and debt investments, with the aim to prevent/ minimize any capital erosion. The fund was launched in December 1993 by the erstwhile Zurich Mutual Fund. When HDFC Asset Management Company bought over the funds of Zurich, the scheme was renamed as HDFC Prudence Fund.

The following graph shows the performance of this scheme.

Graph 6.9
Performance of HDFC Prudence Fund

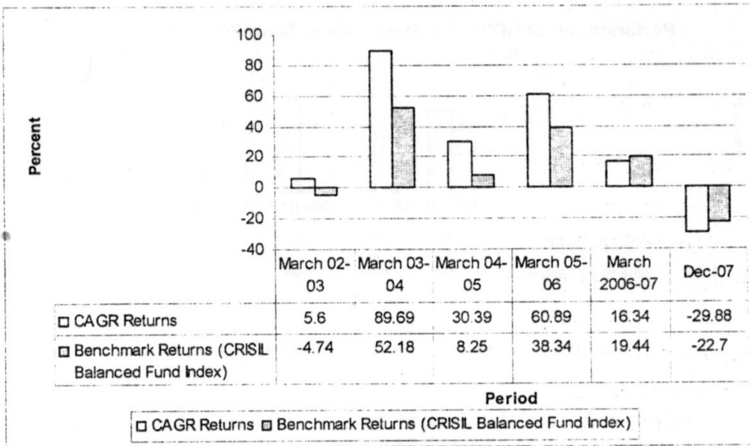

Source: Compiled from the Annual reports of HDFC Asset Management Company for the year 2006-2007

The performance of the scheme has been outstanding since its inception and it has been able to outperform its benchmark and peers by a wide margin. During the study period, the scheme has continuously outperformed its benchmark. The scheme has generated returns of 89.69, 30.39 and 60.89 percent respectively as against 52.18, 8.25 and 38.34 benchmark returns respectively for the year as on March 2004, 2005 and 2006 respectively. The total equity & equity related holdings stands at 75.29 and the debt / money market instrument stood at 15.22 percent as on December 31, 2007. The scheme has also been ranked as the best performing scheme in the balanced scheme category for the three-year period in the ICRA Online quarterly rankings as on June 2005.

6.5 Conclusion

HDFC Mutual Fund is one of the well-established fund houses in the country with a very consistent performance since its inception in 2000. HDFC Mutual Fund has a reasonable track record and has competitive advantages, which gives sustainability to the businesses. HDFC's success can be attributed to the company's commitment and dedication to give the investors long-term benefits by constantly reviewing the markets for new trends and by identifying new growth sectors and by offering innovative products.

HDFC Mutual Fund has solid infrastructure with which a sound financial analysis is successfully conducted. The company also does the required research and analysis, based on which the investors are also told about the new growth sectors and the sectors in which investing will pay huge benefits after a certain period of time. The success mantra of the HDFC Mutual Fund lies in the fact that it works for the benefit of the investor and at the same time keeps in mind the new market trends. This mutual fund also pays an emphasis on controlling and managing the risk of the latest market trends.

The success story of HDFC Mutual Fund is also evident from the fact that it has been assigned the "CRISIL Fund House Level-1" rating. This rating proves the fact that HDFC Mutual Fund has expertise in fund management. It also has the highest level of governance in the field of investing. It is the only fund house to have been assigned this rating for two years in succession.

References

1. Annual Report of HDFC Asset management company, 2006-2007
2. Source: Annual reports of HDFC Asset Management Company for the year 2006-2007.
3. Financial report of HDFC Asset Management Company for the year 2006-2007.

7

Profile of Franklin Templeton Asset Management (India) Pvt. Ltd.

7.1 Introduction

This chapter examines the profile of Franklin Templeton Investments. The performance of the sample schemes will be examined in the framework of Five year -Average Rate of return using the average of CAGR returns in comparison with its respective benchmark returns for the study period 2002 to 2007 as in the case of previous chapters. The methodology is the same as in the case of other two companies. This chapter further examines the products of this company, the services and the performances of sample schemes selected for the purpose of the study. Since it is difficult to examine all the schemes of this company including funds and options, only the sample schemes and their performance is critically examined. The period of study is from January 2002 to December 2007. The authors have also given some valid and logical recommendations in the last two chapters based on the findings of the performance of the schemes.

7.2 Brief Background of Sponsors, Trust, Trustee Company and Asset Management Company

Franklin Templeton Asset Management Company, a company incorporated under the Companies Act, 1956, is a part of the Franklin Templeton Group. The sponsor of the Fund, Templeton International Inc., is a wholly owned subsidiary of Templeton Worldwide Inc., which in turn is a wholly owned subsidiary of Franklin Resources Inc. As a part of the group's major thrust on investing in markets around the world, the India office was set up in 1996 as Templeton Asset Management India Pvt. Limited. It started the mutual fund business with the launch of Templeton India Growth Fund in September 1996, and since then the business has grown at a steady pace. Templeton took over Pioneer ITI Mutual Fund in July 2002. The acquisition led to the assets under its management increasing to US$ 1,695 million from US$ 872 million in July 2002[1].

The fund house has established its position in the Indian mutual fund industry and it has been in the market for quite some time now. Now the background and details of the sponsors and the other important parties associated with the company is briefly presented in the following paragraphs.

7.2.1 Sponsor - Templeton International Inc.

Franklin Templeton Mutual Fund is sponsored by Templeton International, Inc. Templeton International Inc., is a wholly owned subsidiary of Templeton worldwide Inc., which in turn is a wholly owned subsidiary of Franklin Resources Inc. Templeton International, Inc. Franklin Templeton has offices in over 29 countries. The sponsor was responsible for setting up and establishing the Franklin Templeton Mutual Fund. The Sponsor is represented by directors on the board of the trustee company and the Asset Management Company in accordance with the SEBI Regulations.[2]

Figure 7.1
Structural Set-Up of Franklin Templeton Mutual Fund

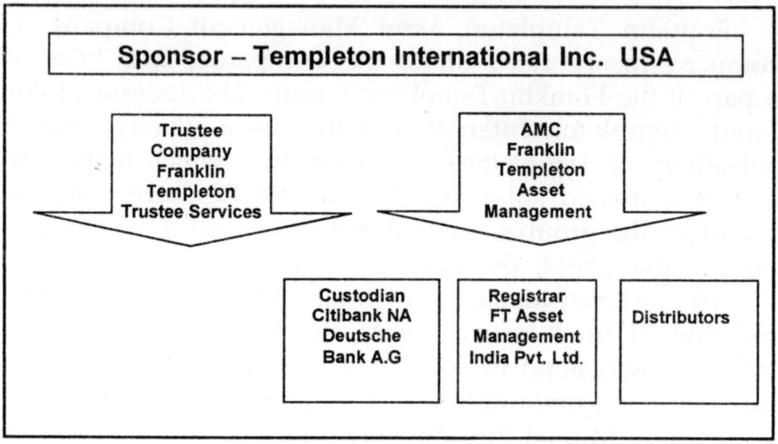

7.2.2 Trust - Franklin Templeton Mutual Fund

Franklin Templeton Mutual Fund (FTMF) was constituted as a Trust. It was sponsored by Templeton International, Inc. with Franklin Templeton Trustee Services Pvt. Ltd. (the "Trustee") as the Trustee. The Trustee has entered into an Investment Management Agreement dated January 5, 1996 with Franklin Templeton Asset Management (India) Pvt. Ltd. (the "AMC") appointing the AMC as the Investment Manager for all the schemes of FTMF. FTMF is registered with SEBI.[3]

7.2.3 Trustee - Franklin Templeton Trustee Services Pvt. Ltd.

Franklin Templeton Trustee Services Pvt. Ltd., a company incorporated under the Companies Act, 1956 is the Trustee to Franklin Templeton Mutual Fund. The Trustees ensure that FT Mutual fund and the schemes floated there under are managed by the AMC in accordance with the Trust Deed, the regulations, directions and guidelines issued by SEBI, the Stock Exchange and other regulatory agencies.

7.2.4 *Asset Management Company - Franklin Templeton Asset Management (India) Pvt. Ltd.*

Franklin Templeton Asset Management (India) Pvt. Ltd., a company incorporated under the Companies Act, 1956 is the Investment Manager of Franklin Templeton Mutual Fund. Franklin Templeton Holding Ltd. is a wholly owned subsidiary of Templeton Asset Management Ltd. The Investment Manager has been approved by SEBI to act as the Asset Management Company of Franklin Templeton Mutual fund.

7.2.5 *Custodian*

Citibank N.A. and Deutsche Bank A.G. are the custodians of the company, The duty of the Custodian is to keep in safe custody all the securities and other such instruments belonging to the Fund, ensure smooth inflow-outflow of securities and such other instruments as and when necessary, in the best interest of the investors, and ensure that the benefits due are recovered.

7.3 An Overview of the Organisation

Franklin Templeton had an early presence in India's investment market and was one of the first international firms to set up a local asset management business in 1995. Franklin Templeton Investmentsstarted their India operations in 1996 as Templeton Asset Management India Pvt. Limited. It flagged off the mutual fund business with the launch of Templeton India Growth Fund in September 1996.The Company, later acquired onetime Pioneer-ITI, to expand its operations. The fund has been launching new schemes and it is also one of the biggest players on the equity side in the Indian mutual fund industry. Pioneer ITI brought a strong equity team to Franklin Templeton and helped boost the asset manager's retail distribution activity and rapidly develop the mutual funds business.

The consistent and focused approach of the company has

generated long term returns for its investors. The Performance of the company, its assets under management and range of products offered are given below in the following paragraphs.

Table 7.1
Total Assets Under Management of Franklin Templeton Asset Management (India) Pvt. Ltd.

Franklin Templeton	As on Dec 31, 2007
Assets Under Management	Rs.31175.54 Crores

Source: Annual reports of Franklin Templeton Investments for the year 2006-2007

The total assets under management stood at Rs. 31175.546 Crores as on December 2007 and over the years, Franklin Templeton has emerged as one of the largest and renowned mutual funds in the country. Some of the considerations that Franklin Templeton had while entering India were high savings rate, high disposable income, young population, and changing regulatory climate. The investment philosophy of the company encompasses rigorous risk management processes, which include a dedicated risk manager who works closely with the investment teams in monitoring and evaluating the performance of the schemes.

7.3.1 Products Offered

The Company manages a wide range of products to meet the varying investment needs of its investors. In order to understand the products of the company we will first look at the following table.

Franklin Templeton AMC has a wide range of schemes in order to meet the different investment objectives of the investors. The total number of schemes of the company as on December 31, 2007 stood at 201 including options. Templeton AMC started off by launching its Templeton India Growth fund, a diversified equity fund. In the next few years it added to its product line by launching an income fund

Table 7.2
Products Offered by Franklin Templeton Mutual Fund as on December 31, 2007

Details	*No.*
Total Number of Schemes	74
List of Options under Main Schemes	
Equity Schemes	37
Debt Schemes	125
Short term debt Schemes'	15
Equity and Debt Schemes	14
Money Market Schemes	0
Gilt Fund	10
Total Number of Schemes including Options	201

Source: Compiled from the Annual reports of Franklin Templeton Investments for the year 2006-2007

(Templeton India Income), a liquid fund (Templeton India Liquid) and a government securities fund (Templeton India Government Securities Fund).

The early years were not too good. But gradually Templeton AMC had virtually every possible type of mutual fund product. In fact in many categories there was overlapping of products. Some of the recent launches have received a very good response from the investors. This includes Franklin India Flexi Cap fund and Franklin India Special Situations fund but at the same time two of its oldest schemes Franklin India Bluechip Fund and Franklin India Prima Fund are also huge in terms of their assets under management. Prima Fund even had to close its offering for new investors for several months when the market was red hot and investors were pouring money into mutual funds in large amounts. It also added to its product line by launching an income fund (Templeton India Income), a liquid fund (Templeton India Liquid) and a government securities fund (Templeton India Government Securities Fund). Not only that, along with the Pioneer products and assets came a vast pool of retail investors. The Rs. 4,022 crore of assets took Templeton AMC's total AUM to nearly Rs. 8,000 crore, making it the largest AMC at the time. More important was the manner in which the merger was handled. Not a single equity fund manager of erstwhile Pioneer ITI left the new organization. Undoubtedly this gave Pioneer ITI investors much comfort and even now the schemes continue to flourish with equity managers who have one of the longest track records in the industry. The fund house also initiated a product rationalization exercise in 2004 with the objective to eliminate duplication of schemes that had occurred due to the acquisition in 2002, and also to reposition/merge schemes that did not have a long-term sustainable proposition from the investors' perspective.

Today, Franklin Templeton has evolved to a stage where it has many innovative products in its stable. These include India's first InfoTech fund, only private sector pension scheme and the Templeton Floating Rate Income Fund, the first floating rate income fund to be launched in India. The AMC also manages Franklin India International Fund, which invests in US government securities.

Templeton has also been the first AMC to launch institutional plans on the debt side. These schemes are meant for big-ticket investors and pass on the lower cost of mobilizing funds in the form of lower expenses. After this, launching institutional plans became a craze in the mutual fund world. Templeton however, took a measured approach and did not launch an institutional plan in its short-term and cash fund. The rationale was that expenses were already low in these funds. This has allowed Templeton to maintain higher profitability in these schemes.

7.3.3 Distribution Strategies

Like other companies, Franklin Templeton mutual fund has also established a multi-channel approach to the distribution of its various products and has today an extensive network of customer service centers. In addition to the large office network of around 33 branches, FT India has been regularly tying-up with banks for the distribution of its mutual fund products. This has given the company products accessibility across the country. For example, it has tied up with State Bank of Indore for the distribution of its schemes. The alliance initially started with plans to cover 33 cities and is planned to roll out to at least 100 locations in a phased manner. Not only that, it now has access to Pioneer ITI's strong retail base and distribution network. Most of Templeton's distribution had been initially been through banks and broker distributors, whereas a large part of Pioneer ITI's sales were through independent distributors. Franklin Templeton also plans to expand its distribution reach to suburban and rural areas where most small investors live. As a part of this plan, the company also plans to train financial advisors who would be able to take Templeton products to all regions of the country.

7.3.4 *Portfolio Management Services*

In a market which is very unpredictable, and to follow a regular investing approach rather than investing a lump sum, Franklin Templeton's portfolio management services which was named as "PROWESS" was started by the company. PROWESS focuses on providing with the investors options which would aim at wealth creation and risk minimisation. The focus of PROWESS was to identify attractive investment opportunities taking advantage of the disciplined approach to investing, which has been the hallmark of Franklin Templeton over the years.

7.4 Analysis of sample schemes of Franklin Templeton Mutual Fund

The authors after having examined the profile of the company will now focus on scheme analysis of the sample schemes. The methodology followed in examining the sample schemes will be the same as in the case of the previous chapter. In order to facilitate comparison with the other two companies, the sample schemes have been chosen very carefully with similar investment objectives. The schemes that have been selected for the purpose of analysis and their objectives, their sector allocation and their performance from their inception date have been discussed in detail in the following paragraphs.

Figure 7.2
Sample Schemes of Franklin Templeton Mutual Fund Selected for the Purpose of the Study

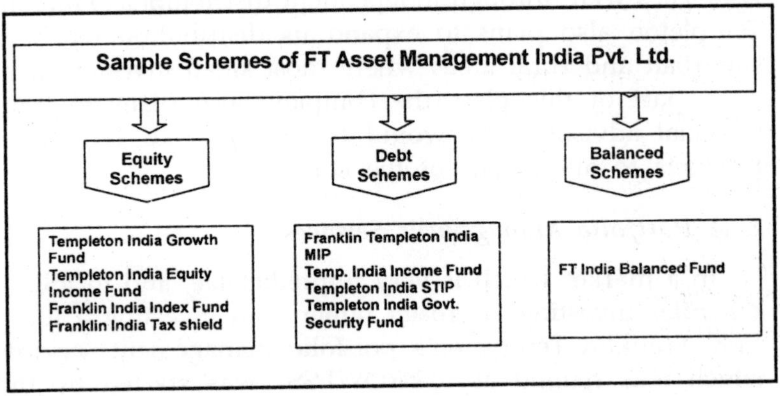

7.4.1 *Analysis of Equity schemes of Franklin Templeton Mutual Fund*

I. Templeton India Growth Fund

Templeton India Growth Fund is an open ended growth scheme and the scheme was launched on September 10, 1996. The objective of this scheme is to provide long-term capital growth to its unit holders. The fund size as on December 31, 2007 stood at Rs. 408.19 crores. The performance of this scheme for the five year study period is shown in the following graph:

Graph 7.1
Performance of Templeton India Growth Fund

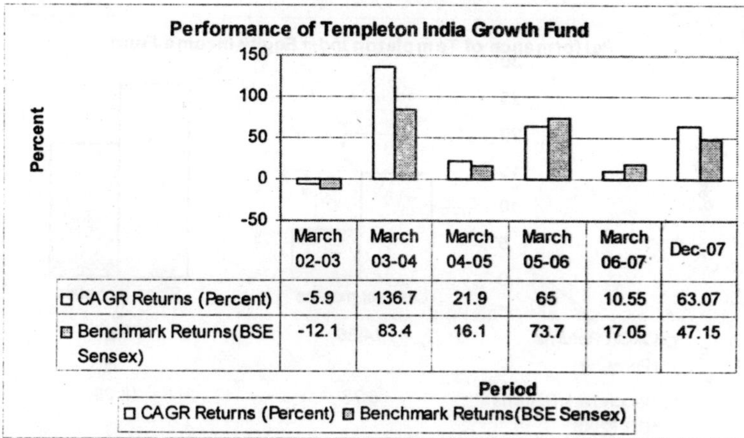

	March 02-03	March 03-04	March 04-05	March 05-06	March 06-07	Dec-07
CAGR Returns (Percent)	-5.9	136.7	21.9	65	10.55	63.07
Benchmark Returns(BSE Sensex)	-12.1	83.4	16.1	73.7	17.05	47.15

Source: Compiled from Key Information Memorandum and Fund Fact Sheet volumes, Franklin Templeton Investments.

The above graph shows that this scheme has outperformed its benchmark for two years during 2004 and 2005. But 2006 and 2007 has not been a satisfactory year because of the sudden fall in returns. The total equity allocation stood at 99.39 percent as on December 2007 and 0.69 percent in other current assets. Templeton Equity managers adopt a long term disciplined approach to investing and use the widely known philosophy of 'value investing'.

II. Templeton India Equity Income Fund

Templeton India equity income fund was launched in May, 2006 which seeks to provide a combination of regular income and long-term capital appreciation by investing primarily in stocks that have a current or potentially attractive dividend yield. Templeton India Equity Income Fund (TEIF) is a good option for investors looking to diversify their equity portfolio. Templeton Equity Portfolio Managers follow the long term disciplined approach of investing.

Graph 7.2
Performance of Templeton India Equity Income Fund

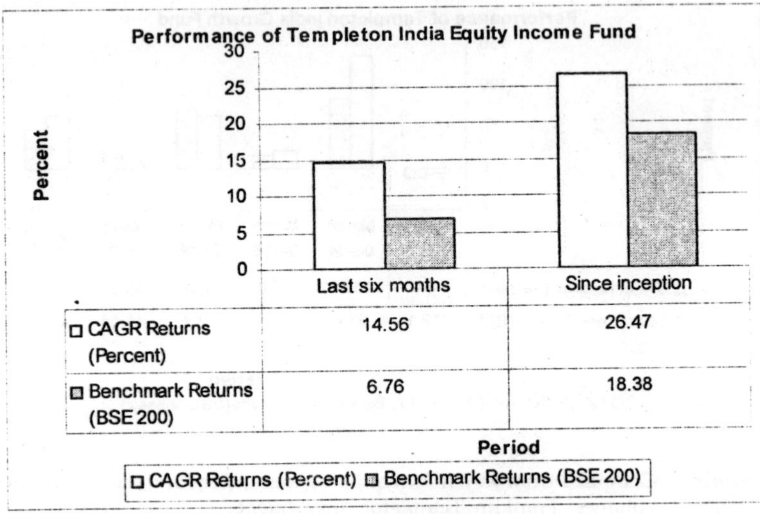

Source: Compiled from Key Information Memorandum and Fund Fact Sheet volumes, Franklin Templeton Investments.

Their main focus is on stocks with attractive dividend yields and they use the value style of investing. The fund size is Rs. 1737.41 crores as on December 2007. The performance of the scheme since inception is given above in graph 7.2. Global investment and value investing strategy are two key features of this fund that provides some cushion to any decline in the market. The performance since its inception fares well against the benchmark. With a return of 26.47 percent, TEIF has outperformed its benchmark BSE 200's return of 18.38 percent. But with just the last one year performance it cannot be said that fund is a good bet. TEIF follows the strategy of investing in stocks that trade at a discount. The portfolio of this fund is well diversified with 97.50 percent in total equity holdings and it tries to provide stability even during volatile market phases. But since the fund was launched only recently, it is difficult to assess the performance of this fund.

III. Franklin Ind.a Index Fund

The objective of Franklin India index fund is to provide returns before expenses that correspond to the benchmark returns. The fund size of this plan stood at Rs. 86.88 crores. The scheme that was launched in August, 2000 follows a passive style of equity investing investment objective and the expense ratio of this scheme is 1 percent. The performance of this scheme for the five year study period is given below in the following graph.

Graph 7.3
Performance of Franklin India Index Fund

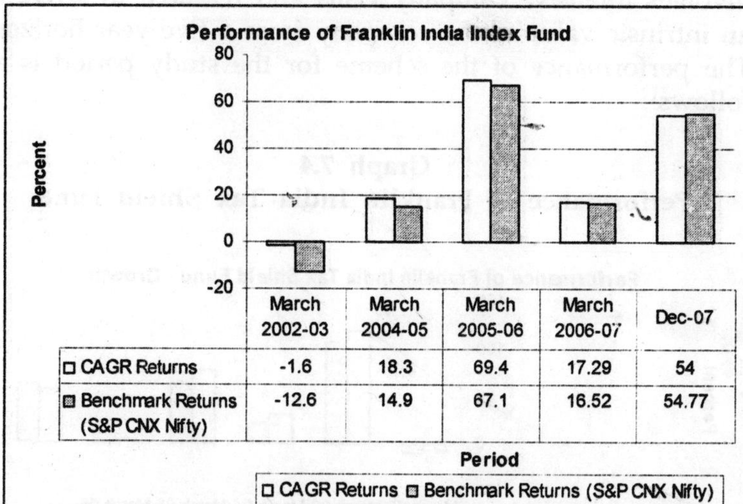

Source: Compiled from Key Information Memorandum and Fund Fact Sheet volumes, Franklin Templeton Investments.

During 2003 and 2004 the scheme underperformed its benchmark returns but successfully managed to overcome volatility and outperformed its benchmark returns (18.3 percent, 69.4 percent and 17.29 percent as against 14.9, 67.1and 16.52 of the year 2005, 2006 and 2007 respectively). (See graph 7.3). The total equity holdings of this fund stood at

99.63 percent and other current assets at 0.37 percent. The top five holdings are Reliance Industries, ONGC, NTPC, Bharti Airtel and Reliance Communication.

IV Franklin India Tax Shield Fund

Franklin India Tax shield is an open-end Equity Linked Savings Scheme (ELSS) which aims to provide medium to long term growth of capital along with income tax rebate. Fund Size of the scheme as on Dec 31, 2007 stood at Rs. 628.45 crores. The fund adopts a flexible strategy of generating above-average returns in the long-term. The fund managers follow bottom- up approach to identify bargain stocks. This involves intensive company visits and research to arrive at an intrinsic value of the company from a five year horizon. The performance of the scheme for the study period is as follows:

Graph 7.4
Performance of Franklin India Tax Shield Fund

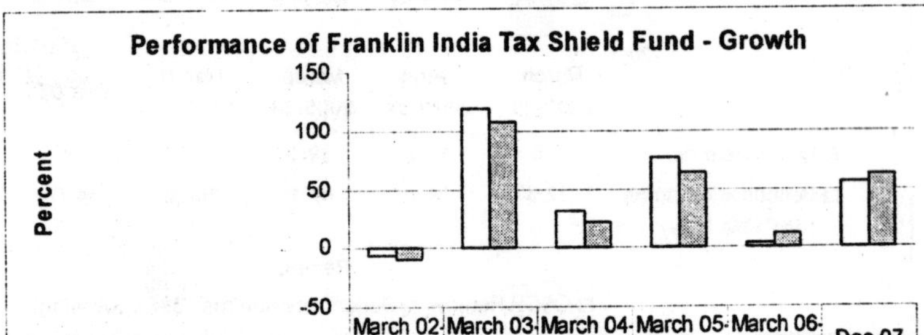

	March 02-03	March 03-04	March 04-05	March 05-06	March 06-07	Dec-07
□ CAGR Returns	-5.4	118.6	31.6	76.9	3.29	56.02
▨ Benchmark Returns (S&P CNX 500)	-9.6	107.8	21.6	64.2	12.11	62.51

Source: Compiled from Key Information Memorandum and Fund Fact Sheet volumes, Franklin Templeton Investments.

Franklin India Tax shield has consistently managed to outperform its benchmark. The scheme has yielded 38.5 percent annualized returns since inception in April 1999. The fund has generated healthy returns for the investors by way of capital appreciation and income distribution. It managed to out perform the benchmark returns during 2004, 2005 and 2006 but 2007 saw a reverse and the scheme suddenly underperformed its benchmark returns by yielding only 3.29 percent as against 12.11 percent. Its portfolio is well diversified across 42 stocks. Thus we can see that the fund manager follows an active investment strategy and takes defensive/ aggressive postures depending on prevailing market conditions.

7.4.2 Analysis of Debt schemes of Franklin Templeton Mutual Fund

I. Franklin Templeton Monthly Income Plan

FT India MIP is one of the first few MIPs launched in the country. The scheme was launched with an objective to provide regular income through a portfolio of predominantly high quality fixed income securities with a maximum exposure of 20percent to equities. The scheme is managed with a fund size of Rs. 118.48 crores as on December 2007. The performance of the scheme for the study period is given below:

The scheme's performance has been outstanding since its inception and it has managed to beat its peers as well as its benchmark, Crisil MIP Blended Index across all time frames. The performance of the scheme during the study period has also been very good and it has managed to outperform its benchmark returns by a handsome margin. The fund had an exposure in equities to the tune of 21.05 percent and its exposure to debt instruments was 45.53 percent. While they offer the opportunity to earn higher returns than possible from pure debt funds, their returns may be lower, if the equity component performs poorly.

Graph 7.5
Performance of FT India Monthly Income Plan

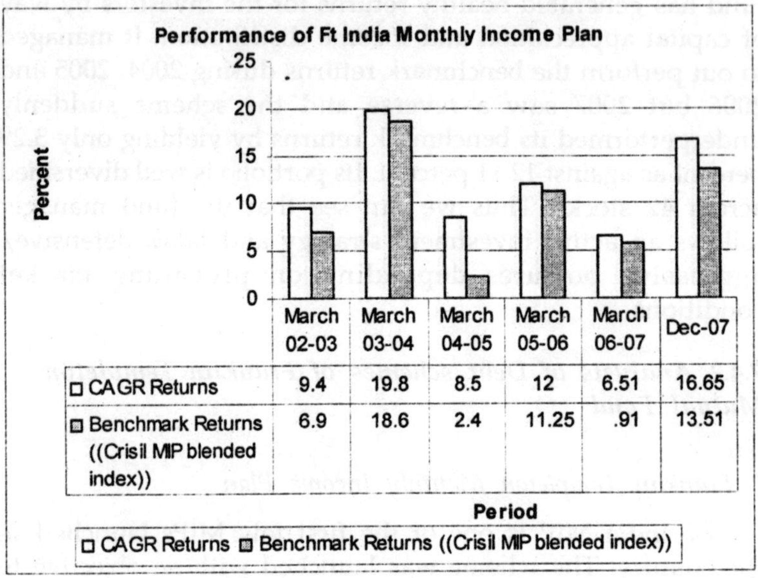

Source: Compiled from Key Information Memorandum and Fund Fact Sheet volumes, Franklin Templeton Investments.

II Templeton India Income Fund

The objective of Templeton India Income Fund is to generate a steady stream of Income through investment in fixed income securities. The scheme was launched in March 5, 1997. The Fund Manager's strategy is to earn steady returns in the fixed income market by actively managing the funds portfolio on interest rate movements and credit risks. The fund size as on December 31, 2007 stood at Rs. 197.03 crores. The performance of the scheme for the study period is shown below;

Graph 7.6
Performance of Templeton India Income Fund

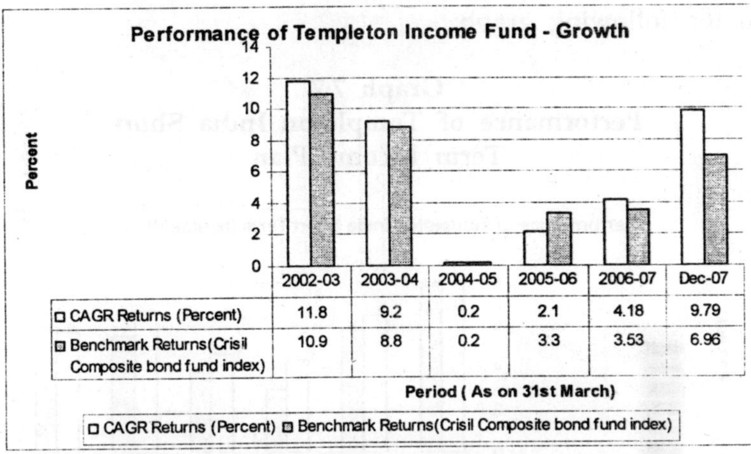

Source: Compiled from Key Information Memorandum and Fund Fact Sheet volumes, Franklin Templeton Investments.

As can be seen from the above graph, the year 2003 and 2004 has been good for the scheme. It managed to out perform the benchmark returns. But during 2005, the performance stood at par with the benchmark returns and dipped below the benchmark in the year 2006. But again in 2007, the fund manager re-allocated the portfolio and once again managed to out perform the benchmark returns.

The scheme had an exposure to gilts to the tune of 59.43 percent and 29.08 percent in PSU/PFI bonds. Even though the scheme is an average performer the allocation is very interesting and has been given careful consideration by the fund manager.

III. Templeton India Short Term Income Plan

The objective of Templeton India Short term income plan is to provide stable returns by investing in shorter term fixed income securities. The fund was incepted in January 2002 and the size of the fund stood at Rs. 1951.31 crores as on

December 2007. The fund manager adopts the strategy of providing a steady stream of income while avoiding interest rate volatility. The performance of the scheme is shown below in the following graph:

Graph 7.7
Performance of Templeton India Short Term Income Plan

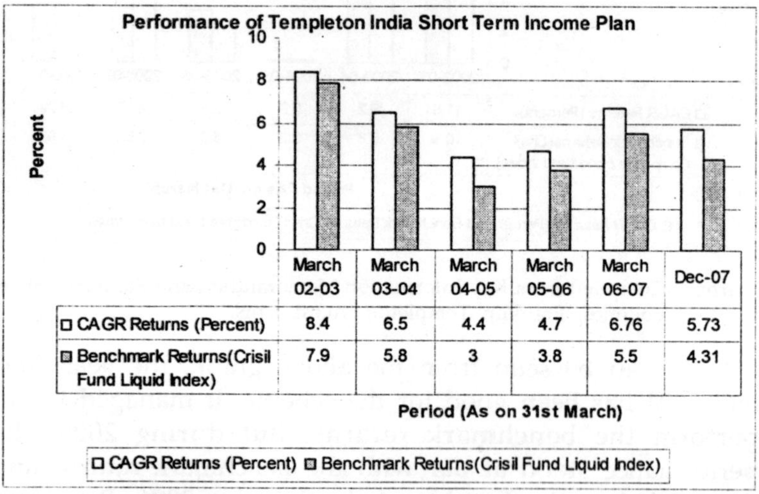

	March 02-03	March 03-04	March 04-05	March 05-06	March 06-07	Dec-07
CAGR Returns (Percent)	8.4	6.5	4.4	4.7	6.76	5.73
Benchmark Returns(Crisil Fund Liquid Index)	7.9	5.8	3	3.8	5.5	4.31

Source: Compiled from Key Information Memorandum and Fund Fact Sheet volumes, Franklin Templeton Investments.

This fund has managed to out perform the benchmark returns consistently during the study period. Even across the peer category, the scheme has managed to beat the peer average and so it can be called as a safe bet. The portfolio holdings of this scheme as on December 2007 shows that 70.35 percent of the funds have been invested in corporate debt and 10.77 percent in PSU/PFI bonds. It can be concluded that Templeton India Short-Term Income Plan is an effective investment avenue for intermediate term funds.

IV Templeton India Government Securities Fund

Templeton India Government Securities Fund is an open

end dedicated Gilts scheme with the objective to generate credit risk-free return through investments in sovereign securities issued by the Central Government and/or State Government and/or any security unconditionally guaranteed by the Central Government and/or State Government for repayment of Principal and Interest. The inception date of this scheme is February, 2002. The expense ratio of the scheme is 0.90 percent and the size of the fund as on December 2007 stood at Rs. 14.6230 crores for the growth option.

Graph 7.8

Performance of Templeton India Government Securities Fund – Treasury Plan

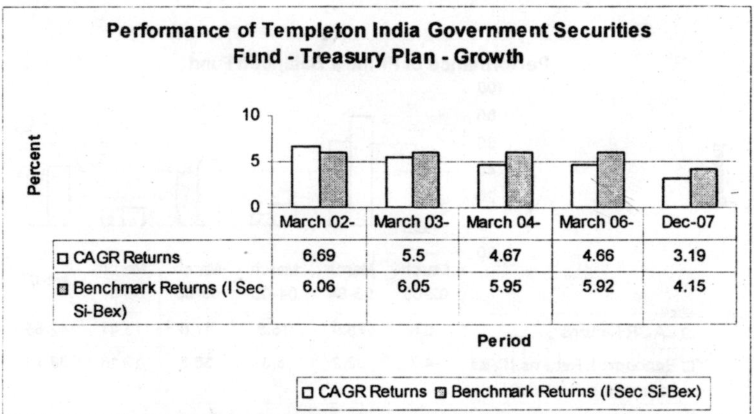

Source: Compiled from Key Information Memorandum and Fund Fact Sheet volumes, Franklin Templeton Investments.

Graph 7.8 shows that this scheme has outperformed its benchmark returns only in 2003. From 2004 the scheme has under performed the benchmark and has not matched the expectations of the investor. The poor performance of the scheme is reflected even in the peer average across the category. The scheme's portfolio comprises of gilts to the tune of 94.02 percent. The reason can be attributed to interest rate risk. These funds are prone to volatility and price sensitivity.

7.4.3 *Analysis of Balanced Scheme of Franklin Templeton Mutual Fund*

I. Franklin Templeton India Balanced Fund

Being an equity-oriented balanced fund with an objective to provide long term growth of capital and current income, this fund offers an opportunity to invest partly in debt, which has return potential. The Fund Size as on Dec 31, 2007 stood at Rs. 355.90 crores. The performance of the scheme during the study period is as follows.

Graph 7.9
Performance of FT India Balanced Fund

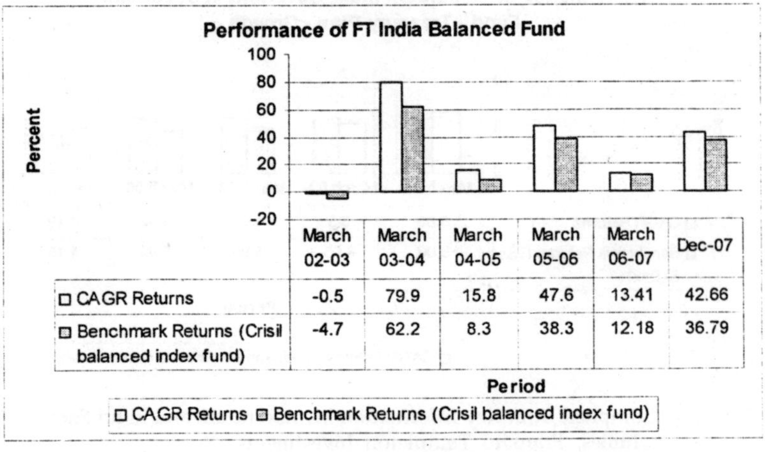

Source: Compiled from Key Information Memorandum and Fund Fact Sheet volumes, Franklin Templeton Investments.

The large-cap exposure has aided the performance of this scheme and the scheme has delivered consistent returns from the year 2004 and has outperformed its benchmark with a decent margin. The fund manager has succeeded in striking an optimum balance between growth and stability, by maintaining a diversified portfolio of equities and managing interest rate movements and credit risk on the fixed income component.

7.5 Conclusion

Franklin Templeton has emerged as a successful player in the asset management sector of India since its launch of operations in 1996. The takeover of Pioneer ITI Mutual fund also provided FTMF a vast market to reach the investors with localized, innovative and value-added products. Franklin Templeton has played a pioneering role in the mutual fund industry with regard to its focus on investor education and awareness programmes. Another major reason for its success is it continues to be focused on educating investors and financial advisors and conducts extensive training programmes for financial advisors all over the country. The company has also launched focused promotional media campaigns in order to shift the investment preference of customers from traditional saving instruments like fixed deposits to mutual funds. One of the major reasons for its success has been its strategy to "Think Global. Act Local". As part of this strategy, it focused on launching products, tailor-made for Indian investors. It has adapted its international products, processes and practices to suit Indian investors. The most important reason for the success of the company can be attributed to the talented local management across all functions of the organization in India. So it can be concluded that Investing in investor education, launching localized value-added products, strategic acquisition, local talent, excellent track record of funds and strong distribution network are the important factors for the success of this fund.

References

1. Annual reports of Franklin Templeton Investments.
2. Franklin Templeton mutual fund, Statement of additional information.
3. Abridged Annual Report, Templeton Investments Ltd, 2006-2007.

8

Performance Evaluation of Selected Sample Schemes

8.1 Introduction

The main objective of this book is to evaluate the performance of the sample schemes. A significant number of studies have been trying to explain mutual fund performance across the world. In India too, many researchers have tried to explain the performance techniques based on the popular measures used in developed countries. Some of the magazines like Money Today, Business India, Dalal Street, Capital Market, Mutual Fund Insight-an exclusive magazine dedicated for mutual funds and others have been evaluating the mutual funds and have been competing with each other on how best to measure and compare funds. Higher returns or a rapidly appreciating NAV do not necessarily mean that the fund manager is doing the right thing. A well-managed fund should be a consistent performer and it should have the ability to outperform the peers and the benchmarks over different periods of time.

From the investor's point of view, the aim of investing for any individual investor is to generate returns in excess of the risk free return. In order to generate higher returns, an investor is willing to take risks. In a generic sense, risk means the possibility of a financial loss. This possibility of loss should always be considered. Generally high returns are associated with high degree of volatility. There are different factors such as market risk, sector risk, market cycles, market timing and other macro-economic factors which affect the performance of a fund. A good performance evaluation technique for mutual funds should always consider the risk-adjusted returns and not the returns alone. Keeping in mind all these factors sophisticated performance evaluation techniques have been developed by researchers, many of which originate in modern portfolio theory.

There are several ways to calculate risk-adjusted return to measure the performance of managed portfolios. Some of the popular performance measures are Jensen (1968), Sharpe (1966), and Treynor (1965). These measures offer good results but at the same time make the selection of a method difficult. Each has its strengths and shortcomings. All require particular data, such as an investment's rate of return, the risk-free return rate for a given period, and a market's performance and its standard deviation. Their common feature is that they all measure funds' returns relative to risk. However, they differ in how they define and measure risk and, consequently, in how they define risk-adjusted performance.

Since risk and performance measurement is an active area for academic research, the authors after reviewing major research studies on this topic have very sincerely made an attempt to evaluate the performance of sample funds in this chapter using *Sharpe Ratio,* a very popular performance measurement technique.

This chapter begins with a brief note on the evaluation parameters used in this study. Then the sample scheme's performance is evaluated using Sharpe's technique and the results will be examined. Next, hypothesis of the study will be tested after comparing Sharpe's ratio of the schemes with that of Sharpe's ratio of the schemes respective benchmark returns.

Lastly, the findings of the survey conducted to assess the perceptions of individual investors and distributors with regard to the sample companies will be presented. Using these observations, the second hypothesis of the study will be tested.

8.2 Sharpe's Ratio

As discussed earlier, the performance evaluation of the sample schemes is carried out using the Sharpe Ratio in this study. Among the different measures that are available, Sharpe's Ratio is the simplest and the most popular performance measure. Sharpe's Ratio is a ratio developed by "Nobel Laureate William F. Sharpe (1966)" to measure risk-adjusted performance and is considered to be one of the best tools for determining a fund's performance. This reward to variability ratio measures the excess return per unit of total risk (Standard Deviation).[1] The higher the Sharpe Ratio, the better a fund's historic risk-adjusted performance.

The Sharpe Ratio formula is given below:

Sharpe Ratio of the Mutual Fund Scheme = (Rp-Rf)/SDp

The Benchmark Comparison is = (Rm-Rf)/SDm

- o Where Rp is the average return of the mutual fund scheme portfolio
- o Where Rm is the average return of the benchmark portfolio
- o Rf is the average risk free rate
- o SDp, SDm is the standard deviation of the portfolio

The Sharpe Ratio is quite simple. It's broken down into just three components: asset return, risk-free return and standard deviation of return. Mathematically, it takes a fund's returns in excess of a guaranteed investment (T-bill) and divides by the standard deviation of those returns. The idea of the ratio is to see how much additional return is received for the additional volatility of holding the risky asset over a risk-free asset. This ratio has an advantage because it uses standard deviation as the volatility variable. The bigger the Sharpe Ratio, the better a fund has performed considering its riskiness. It is thus one single number, which represents the trade-off between risks and returns.

The main advantage of the Sharpe Ratio is that it brings different schemes on an even level, and it helps the investors to find out whether the excess returns earned are due to smart investment decisions, or due to excess risk undertaken by the fund manager. If investors only look at the return and volatility figures given by the standard deviation of the scheme, the decision-making process becomes tough, as it's difficult to interpret how the various schemes stand with respect to each other.

The Sharpe Ratio can also be considered for schemes across a range of categories to check whether any scheme is revealing any abnormal behaviour. In many cases, the Sharpe Ratio is calculated for a portfolio and not for a particular scheme. Researchers also believe that the Sharpe Ratio is most effective when it is used in conjunction with several other parameters. This also helps in clearing any inconsistencies that may be witnessed over a short period of time.

Some of the important points to be kept in mind while interpreting Sharpe Ratios are:

- This ratio facilitates comparison of one portfolio with that of the other by making an adjustment for risk.
- The Sharpe measure is a pure number. In isolation it has no meaning. It can only be used as a comparative tool.
- Sharpe Ratio should be used to compare the performance of a number of funds.
- Sharpe Ratio of a fund can alternatively be compared with that of its benchmark index.
- The higher a fund's Sharpe Ratio, the better a fund's returns
- The Sharpe Ratio uses standard deviation as its risk component; a low standard deviation can affect the results.
- The Sharpe Ratio do not account for any risks inherent in a fund's portfolio.

8.3 Risk Adjusted Performance Evaluation of the Sample Schemes

Chapter 5, 6 and 7 discussed in detail the profile of the sample companies and the performance of the sample schemes in the framework of Five year -Average Rate of return using the average of CAGR returns in comparison with its respective benchmark returns for the study period 2002 to 2007. It is always appropriate to assess performance over longer periods to smooth out very short term fluctuations in performance and the influence of the business cycle. Even though the performance of the schemes in comparison with its bench mark index for the said period has been already carried out, performance measurement should not be reduced to the evaluation of fund returns alone. It must also integrate other fund elements that would be of interest to investors, such as the measure of risk taken. Hence critical evaluation of the performance of selected mutual fund schemes in the framework of risk and return using the technique of Sharpe Ratio which is also popularly referred as Sharpe Ratio's a risk adjusted performance measure is attempted in this chapter.

8.4 Computation of Sharpe Ratio

This section aims at critical evaluation of sample schemes where the results are derived using the method of Sharpe Ratio. Before proceeding, it would be worthwhile to recall that the study utilised a sample of three major mutual fund companies selected on the basis of judgement sampling. They are ICICI Prudential Mutual Fund, HDFC Mutual Fund and Franklin Templeton Mutual Fund.

8.4.1 Classification of Schemes

The method used by the authors for selecting the sample schemes has been explained already in the first chapter. Briefly, based on their investment objectives, the schemes were classified first and grouped in terms of common investment objective. Next, four debt schemes, four equity schemes and one balanced scheme from each company was selected and this objective-wise classification was made to facilitate peer group comparison. Overall the study utilised a sample of 27 schemes and the authors have considered only the growth options of the schemes.

8.4.2 Computation of Average Rate of Return of the Schemes and Average Benchmark Returns[2]

In order to evaluate the performance of a managed portfolio, a measure of return is required. The CAGR returns and the benchmark returns of the sample schemes for the period April 2002 - March 31, 2007 is already presented in the scheme analysis section of chapters five, six and seven respectively. Data was sourced from the Annual reports, half-yearly reports and the monthly updates of the respective companies. To compute the scheme's average rate of return and its benchmark return for five year period, the CAGR returns and the benchmark returns of 2002, 2003, 2004, 2005 and 2006 were summed up and the average was found. The result will give us the Average rate of return of the scheme and the average bench mark return for the study period. Now, the list of sample schemes and the Average fund return computed from the CAGR returns for five year study period for the sample equity, debt and balanced schemes are given below.

Table 8.1
Average Rate of Return of the Equity Schemes for the period March 2002-2007

Sr. No.	*Name of the Schemes*	*Average Fund return of the MF schemes(percent)*	*Average Benchmark returns (percent)*
1	2	3	4
1.	ICICI Prud.Gr. Fund	41.00	32.36
2.	ICICI Pru Dy.Plan	49.00	36.00
3.	ICICI Prud. Index Fund	34.00	33.00

1	2	3	4
4.	ICICI Prud.l Tax Saver	55.00	33.00
5.	HDFC Growth Fund	51.26	37.00
6.	HDFC Equity Fund	53.60	41.65
7.	HDFC Index Fund	44.40	53.8
8.	HDFC Tax Saver	56.00	41.65
9.	Temp. India Gr. Fund	45.6	35.63
10.	Temp.India Eq. Inc.Fd	13.23	9.19
11.	Franklin Ind.Index Fund	36.7	33.40
12.	Franklin Ind. Tax Shield	45.0	39.22

Source: Computed from secondary data

Table 8.2
Average Rate of Return of the Debt Schemes for the period March 2002-2007

Sr. No.	*Name of the Schemes*	*Average Fund return of the MF schemes(percent)*	*Average Benchmark returns (percent)*
1.	ICICI Prudential Monthly Income Plan	10.0	8.89
2.	ICICI Prudential Income Plan	5.82	5.38
3.	ICICI Prudential Short Term Plan	6.50	5.24
4.	ICICI Prudential Gilt Fund	5.80	6.00
5.	HDFC MIP Long Term Plan	13.00	8.19
6.	HDFC Income Fund	4.40	4.85
7.	HDFC Short Term Plan	6.89	6.21
8.	HDFC Gilt Fund	4.87	6.50
9.	FT India Monthly Income Plan	11.24	9.00
10.	Templeton India Income Fund-Growth	5.50	5.35
11.	Temp. India Short Term Income Plan	6.15	5.20
12.	Templeton India Government Securities Fund - Treasury Plan - Growth	5.38	5.97

Source: Computed from secondary data

Table 8.3
Average Rate of Return of the Balanced Schemes for the period March 2002-2007

Sr. No.	*Name of the Schemes*	*Average Fund Return of the MF schemes (Percent)*	*Average Benchmark return (Percent)*
1.	ICICI Prud. Balanced Fund	31.7	20.68
2.	HDFC Prudence Fund	40.6	22.7
3.	FT India Balanced Fund	31.24	23.26

Source: Computed from secondary data

Table 8.4
Performance of Sample Schemes based on Average Rate of Return measure

Sr. No.	*Name of the Schemes*	*Ranks of Average Rate of Return of the schemes and their benchmarks Y*
1.	2.	3.
1.	ICICI Prudential Growth Fund	9
2.	ICICI Prudential Dynamic Plan	5
3.	ICICI Prudential Index Fund	18
4.	ICICI Prudential Tax Saver	1
5.	HDFC Growth Fund	4
6.	HDFC Equity Fund	16
7.	HDFC Index Fund	27
8.	HDFC Tax Saver	3
9.	Templeton India Growth Fund	8
10.	Templeton India Equity Income Fund	13

1.	2.	3.
11.	Franklin India Index Fund	14
12.	Franklin India Tax Shield Fund	11
13.	ICICI Prudential Monthly Income Plan	17
14.	ICICI Prudential Income Plan	21
15.	ICICI Prudential Short Term Plan	6
16.	ICICI Prudential Gilt Fund	23
17.	HDFC MIP Long Term Plan	12
18.	HDFC Income Fund	24
19.	HDFC Short Term Plan	20
20.	HDFC Gilt Fund	26
21.	FT India Monthly Income Plan	15
22.	Templeton India Income Fund-Growth	22
23.	Templeton India Short Term Income Plan	19
24.	Temp. India Govt. Sec. Fund - Tr. Plan - G	25
25.	ICICI Prudential Balanced Fund	7
26.	HDFC Prudence Fund	2
27.	FT India Balanced Fund	10

Source: Computed from secondary data

The tables 8.1, 8.2 and 8.3 shows the average rate of return of all the sample mutual fund schemes and their benchmark returns computed in the respective chapters based on the Rate of return measure. Table 8.1 shows the returns for all the equity schemes. In total 12 equity schemes were selected. Out of these 12 equity schemes four were from ICICI Prudential mutual fund, four schemes were from Franklin Templeton mutual fund and four schemes were from HDFC mutual fund. Out of the 12 equity schemes, 11 schemes have out performed their benchmark indices. The only scheme that has under performed is HDFC Index fund. A closer look at the other funds shows that the top five equity schemes on the basis of simple comparison with their benchmark returns are ICICI Prudential Tax Saver, HDFC Tax Saver, HDFC Growth Fund, ICICI Prudential Dynamic Plan and Templeton India Growth Fund . The other equity schemes have performed moderately.

Table 8.2 shows the average rate of return and the benchmark returns for all the debt schemes. Out of the twelve debt schemes, eleven schemes have out performed their benchmark indices. But unlike equity schemes, the difference is very marginal. From these schemes according to this method of comparison of scheme's return with their benchmark returns, ICICI Prudential Short Term Plan has performed extremely well in this category. The top performing schemes are: ICICI Prudential Short Term Plan, HDFC MIP Long Term Plan, FT India Monthly Income Plan .and ICICI Prudential Monthly Income Plan. ICICI Prudential Gilt Fund has under performed its benchmark index and has performed below satisfaction. In the case of balanced fund category all the three schemes shown in table 8.3 have performed satisfactorily.

Table 8.4 shows the performance of the schemes based on ranks. As we can observe from this table the top five companies on the basis of ranks are shown below:

1. ICICI Prudential Tax Saver
2. HDFC Prudence Fund
3. HDFC Tax Saver
4. HDFC Growth Fund
5. ICICI Prudential Dynamic Plan

Most of the fund managers in our country use this method to measure performance of schemes but researchers all over the world believe that the results shown according to this method is not correct as the risk element is not considered in this method. So, the average rate of returns and the average bench mark returns of the sample schemes shown above in the tables above will be used as the parameters to compute Sharpe Ratios to measure the risk adjusted measure of performance of the schemes.

8.4.3 Computation of Risk-Free Rate of Return

The annualized rate of return on a risk-less investment is called as the Risk-Free Rate of Return. This is the rate against which other returns are generally measured. The risk-free rate of return is used to see whether the investor is compensated for the additional risk taken with the risky asset. Traditionally, the risk-free rate of return is the shortest dated government T-bill as this type of security will have the least volatility. In order to compute risk adjusted return, the risk free rate has to be computed as:

$$\text{Average risk free rate} = \frac{\text{Annualized yield on 91 day t-bill}}{5}$$

This study uses the average 91 day t-bill for five years and the average 91 day t- bill has been computed as given below based on the five year annualized yield.

Table 8.5
Yield On 91 Day Treasury Bill Rates for the period 2002 To 2007

Sr. No.	*Period*	*91 day t-bill rate-Annualised*
1	2002-03	5.72
2	2003-04	4.51
3	2003-04	4.79
4	2004-05	5.65
5	2006-07	6.54

Source: RBI's Hand book of Statistics on Indian Economy for 2006-2007

Based on the formulae given above, Average risk free rate has been computed and the value = 5.4

Now from the table, we can see that starting from the year 2002 to 2007, the yield on t-bill on monthly basis has been calculated first and then annualised respectively. The average on the five year annualised yield will give us the average risk free rate which is **5.4** in this study.

8.4.4 Computation of Standard Deviation

Investors are interested not only in funds' returns but also in risks taken to achieve those returns. Risk can be interpreted as the uncertainty of the expected return, and uncertainty is generally equated with variability. Investors demand and receive higher returns with increased variability, suggesting that variability and risk are related. The basic measure of variability is the standard deviation, also known as the volatility. Standard Deviation, the statistical concept is the best measure of risk. Even though it is based on past returns it measures total risk and it is capable of measuring both specialised and diversified funds it can also be applied to equity and debt funds. It's significance lies in the fact that the sample is free from defects of sampling. It measures the absolute dispersion. The greater the standard deviation, the greater will be magnitude of the deviation of the values from their mean. The following table shows the standard deviation calculated for the mutual fund portfolio and for the benchmark of the portfolio.

The computation for the above table is very simple. The annual returns are calculated first and then the average fund returns for the study period are computed. The fluctuation of fund returns around the mean level is then calculated. Next step is to calculate the variance and the figures are then squared up and then the standard deviation is computed.

An important aspect to remember about standard deviation is, that it is a measure of the total risk of an asset or a portfolio, including both systematic and unsystematic risk. A higher standard deviation means that the returns of the fund have been more volatile than a fund having low standard deviation. In other words, high standard deviation means high risk.

Table 8.6
Standard Deviation of the Mutual Fund Portfolio Schemes and the Benchmark Portfolios

Sr. No.	*Name of the Schemes*	*Standard Deviation of the Mutual Fund Schemes*	*Standard Deviation of the Benchmark Portfolios*
1.	ICICI Prud. Growth Fund	42.65	35.66
2.	ICICI Prud. Dynamic plan	36.39	31.89
3.	ICICI Prudential Index Fund	37.25	39.47
4.	ICICI Prudential Tax Saver	42.19	35.66
5.	HDFC Growth Fund	43.08	36.28
6.	HDFC Equity Fund	49.7	40.63
7.	HDFC Index Fund	27.62	30.58
8.	HDFC Tax Saver	47.5	36.1
9.	Templ. India Growth Fund	60.28	36.70
10.	Temp. India equity inc. fund	12.70	8.67
11.	Franklin India index fund	32.00	35
12.	Frank. India Tax Shield Fund	46.6	41.8
13.	ICICI Prud. MIP	3.33	5.51
14.	ICICI Prud. Inc. Fund pl an	3.89	3.90
15.	ICICI Prudential STP	1.19	1.66
16.	ICICI Prudential Gilt fund	1.95	1.68
17.	HDFC MIP Long Term Plan	5.57	4.12
18.	HDFC Income Fund	2.46	1.91
19.	HDFC Short term plan	1.53	0.87
20.	HDFC Gilt fund	0.47	2.87
21.	FT India MIP	4.60	5.55
22.	Temp. India Inc. F-Growth	4.35	3.90
23.	Temp. India STIP	1.46	1.71
24.	Temp. India Govt Securities Fund - T Plan - Growth	0.83	0.006
25.	ICICI Prud. Balanced fund	25.5	21.05
26.	HDFC Prudence fund	30.79	20.47
27.	FT India Balanced Fund	28.97	23.96

Source: Computed from secondary data

Based on the above statement, if we observe the above table we can see that equity funds generally fall under high risk category. Out of the 12 equity funds, the standard deviations of 10 equity funds are very high. Only Templeton India equity income fund with a percentage of 12.70 has shown very low standard deviation when compared to the other equity funds. This means; this scheme is less risky when compared to the other schemes. In contrast to this scheme under the equity category, Templeton India Growth Fund has a very high standard deviation of 60.28 percent which shows the volatile nature of the scheme but high risk means high returns. So if an investor is willing to take high risk, a very good return can be expected.

On the debt front, it is interesting to note that almost all the schemes have shown a low standard deviation which implies that the schemes are less risky but a low standard deviation can affect the results. On the other hand if we observe the balanced schemes, ICICI Prudential Balanced fund has shown a Standard deviation of 25.5, while HDFC Prudence fund has shown a Standard deviation of 30.79 and India Balanced Fund has shown 28.97. Balanced funds generally are affected by market factors which affects both the equity market as well as debt market. From the investor's point of view, they prefer a balanced scheme because they are able to enjoy the benefits of both the debt and the equity schemes. Thus on the whole, it can be said that the debt schemes have managed to show moderate standard deviations when compared to the debt and the equity component. But the main objective of this chapter is to see what returns these schemes have managed to get after adjusting this risk element. So now in the following paragraph let us go ahead and compute the Sharpe Ratios of all the schemes.

8.5 Computation of Sharpe Ratios for the Mutual Fund Portfolio and the Benchmark Portfolio

Sharpe Ratio describes how much excess return investor receives for the extra volatility endured for holding a riskier asset. Sharpe Ratio tries to quantify how a fund performs relative to the risk it takes. It is one way of measuring a mutual fund's effectiveness. Sharpe Ratio reflects the returns generated by undertaking all possible risks. Now in this section, Sharpe Ratios for the sample mutual fund schemes returns and their benchmark returns have been computed using the main three evaluation parameters of the equation (Rp-Rf)/SD.

The three main evaluation parameters of the study required for the computation of Sharpe Ratio has been computed in the previous paragraphs. They are:

- Average Fund Return of the Schemes and the Bench mark return of the schemes
- Risk-Free Rate of Return
- Standard deviation of the fund and the benchmark

Applying the above parameters in the formulae to compute Sharpe Ratio, the results are derived in the following paragraphs.

8.5.1 Computation of Sharpe Ratios for the Mutual fund Schemes

The following table presents the Sharpe Ratios for all the 27 sample schemes, which includes 12 equity schemes, 12 debt schemes and 3 balanced schemes respectively from ICICI Prudential Mutual fund, HDFC mutual fund and Franklin Templeton mutual fund organisations. As mentioned earlier, the Sharpe ratio is based on the trade-off between risk and return. A high Sharpe ratio means that the fund delivers a lot of return for its level of volatility. The Sharpe ratio allows a direct comparison of the risk-adjusted performance of any two mutual funds, regardless of their volatilities and their correlations with a benchmark.

The table, shows us the risk, risk free return and the Sharpe Ratios of the schemes. As we all know that the Sharpe Ratio is a pure number and in isolation it has no meaning. It can be used only as a comparative tool when there is similarity in funds. This study uses a combination of debt,

Table 8.7
Sharpe Ratios of the Mutual Fund Schemes

Sr. No.	*Name Of The Sample Schemes*	*Average Fund Return of the MF Scheme (Percent) ARp*	*Average Risk Free Return Rf-5.4% Rp-Rf (Percent)***	*Standard Deviation of the FundSD*	*Sharpe Ratios of the MF Schemes (Rp-Rf)/ SD*
1.	ICICI Pr. G	41.00	35.6	42.65	0.83
2.	ICICI Pr.DY.	49.00	43.6	36.39	1.19
3.	ICICI Pr. Ind.F	34.00	28.6	37.25	0.76
4.	ICICI Pr. Tax S	55.00	49.6	42.19	1.17
5.	HDFC Gr. F	51.26	45.86	43.08	1.06
6.	HDFC Eq. Fund	53.60	48.2	49.7	0.97
7.	HDFC In. Fund	44.40	39	27.62	1.41
8.	HDFC Tax Sav.	56.00	5.06	47.5	1.06
9.	Temp. India GF	45.6	40-2	60.28	0.66
10.	Temp. I. Eq. IF	13.23	7.83	12.70	0.61
11.	Frank..I.Inddex	36.7	31.3	32.00	0.98
12.	Frank. I. Tax Sh	45.0	39.6	46.6	0.84
13.	ICICI Pr. MIP	10.0	4.6	3.33	1.38
14.	ICICI Pru Inc.F	5.82	0.42	3.89	0.10
15.	ICICI Pru STP	6.50	1.1	1.19	0.92
16.	ICICI Pr. Gilt F	5.80	0.4	1.95	0.21
17.	HDFC MIP LTP	13.00	7.6	5.57	1.36
18.	HDFC Inc. F.	4.40	-1.0	2.46	-0.41
19.	HDFC STP	6.89	1.49	1.53	0.97
20.	HDFC Gilt fund	4.87	-0.53	0.47	-1.13
21.	FT India MIP	11.24	5.84	4.60	1.27
22.	Temp.In. Inc. F	5.50	0.1	4.35	0.02
23.	Temp. India-STIP	6.15	0.75	1.46	0.51
24.	Temp.India. Govt. Se.-TP	5.38	-0.02	0.83	-0.02
25.	ICICI Pr.BAL.F	31.7	26.3	25.5	1.03
26.	HDFC Prud. F	40.6	35.2	30.79	1.14
27.	FT India Bal. F.	31.24	25.84	28.97	0.89

Source: Computed from secondary data
**Risk free return = Average fund return for the study period 2002-2007- Average risk free rate* for the study period 2002-2007

equity and balanced schemes from all the sample companies. So comparison is meaningless because funds have virtually nothing in common. Alternatively, Sharpe Ratio might be most meaningful when the second method is used where the Sharpe Ratio of the portfolio is compared against its relevant benchmark Sharpe Ratio. Therefore the authors have attempted to examine the performance of all the sample schemes based on the Sharpe Ratio results of both the portfolio returns and the benchmark returns. Table 8.7 presents the Sharpe Ratios of all the sample schemes. Now the following table presents the Sharpe Ratios of the benchmark returns. As mentioned earlier, Benchmark is a yardstick against which the return generated by an asset is evaluated. Now based on the schemes respective benchmarks, the Sharpe ratios were computed as follows:

8.5.2 Computation of Sharpe Ratios for the Benchmarks

Table 8.8
Sharpe Ratios for the Benchmarks

Sr. No.	*Name of the Sample Schemes*	*Average Bnechmark Return of the Portfolio*	*Risk Free Benchmark Return Rf-5.4% Rp-Rf (Percent)***	*Standard Deviation of the Benchmark*	*Sharpe Ratios of the Benchmark[3] (Rm-Rf) Sd*
1	2.	3.	4.	5.	6.
1.	ICICI Prud.G.Fund	32.36	26.96	35.66	0.75
2.	ICICI Pru.Dy.Plan	36	30.6	31.89	0.95
3.	ICICI Pru. Index Fund	33	27.6	39.47	0.69
4.	ICICI Prud Tax Saver	33	27.6	35.66	0.77
5.	HDFC Growth Fund	36.90	31.5	36.28	0.85
6.	HDFC Equity Fund	41.65	36.25	40.63	0.89

1	2.	3.	4.	5.	6.
7.	HDFC Index Fund	53.8	48.4	30.58	1.58
8.	HDFC-Tax Saver	41.65	36.25	36.1	1.00
9.	Temp.Ind. Growth	35.63	30.2	36.70	0.82
10.	Temp.Ind. Eq. in. Fund	9.19	3.79	8.67	0.44
11.	Franklin Ind. index	33.40	28.00	35.00	0.8
12.	Frank.Ind. Tax Shield	39.22	33.82	41.8	0.80
13.	ICICI Prud. MIP	8.89	3.49	5.51	0.63
14.	ICICI PR. Inc. Fund	5.38	-0.02	3.90	-0.005
15.	ICICI PRU STP	5.24	-0.16	1.66	-0.09
16.	ICICIPru. Gilt Fund	6.00	0.6	1.68	0.35
17.	HDFC-MIP LTP	8.19	2.79	4.12	0.68
18.	HDFC Inco.Fund	4.85	-0.55	1.91	-0.28
19.	HDFC STP	6.21	0.81	0.87	0.93
20.	HDFC Gilt fund	6.50	1.10	2.87	0.38
21.	FT India MIP	9.00	3.60	5.55	0.64
22.	Temp.Ind. Inc. Fund	5.35	-0.05	3.9	-0.01
23.	Templeton India-STIP	5.20	-0.2	1.71	-0.11
24.	Temp.In.Govt. Sec. F.TP- Gr	5.97	0.57	0.00	0.57
25.	ICICI PRU Balan fund	20.68	15.28	21.05	0.72
26.	HDFC Prud. fund	22.7	17.3	20.47	0.84
27.	FT India Balan.F	23.26	17.86	23.96	0.74

**Risk free return = Average fund return for the study period 2002-2007- Average risk free rate* for the study period 2002-2007

Source: Computed from secondary data

Now after having computed the Sharpe Ratios for the benchmark, the next step is to make a meaningful comparison in order to evaluate the performance of the sample schemes in comparison to its benchmark. The evaluation indicates the extent to which the portfolio has performed or outperformed or whether it has performed at par with the benchmark. Now in order to arrive at meaningful results let us have a look at the following table.

8.6 Results of Sharpe Ratios for the Mutual Fund Schemes and the Benchmarks

Table 8.9
Comparison of Results of Sharpe Ratios of the Schemes with their Benchmarks and the Ranks in the Order of Performance

Sr. No.	*Name of the Sample Schemes*	*Sharpe Ratios of the Mutual Fund Schemes*	*Sharpe Ratios of The Benchmarks*	*Rank*
1.	*2.*	*3.*	*4.*	*5.*
1.	ICICI PRU STP	0.92	-0.09	1
2.	ICICI Prudl MIP	1.38	0.63	2
3.	HDFC-MIP LTP	1.36	0.68	3
4.	FT India MIP	1.27	0.64	4
5.	Templeton India-STIP	0.51	-0.11	5
6.	ICICI Pru Tax Saver	1.17	0.77	6
7.	ICICI-PRU Balanced fund	1.03	0.72	7
8.	HDFC Pru. fund	1.14	0.84	8
9.	ICICI Pru.Dyn. plan	1.19	0.95	9
10.	HDFC Gr. Fund	1.06	0.85	10
11.	Franklin India index fund	0.98	0.8	11
12.	Temp.India Eq.Inc.Fund	0.61	0.44	12
13.	FT India Bal.F	0.89	0.74	13
14.	ICICI Prudential Income Fund	0.1	-0.005	14
15.	ICICI Pru. Gr. F	0.83	0.75	15
16.	HDFC-Eq. Fund	0.97	0.89	16

1.	2.	3.	4.	5.
17.	ICICI Prudential Index Fund	0.76	0.69	17
18.	HDFC-Tax Saver	1.06	1	18
19.	Franklin-India Tax Shield Fund	0.84	0.8	19
20.	HDFC STP	0.97	0.93	20
21.	Temp. Ind. Inc.F	0.02	-0.01	21
22.	HDFC Inc. F	-0.41	-0.28	22
23.	ICICI Prud. Gilt	0.21	0.35	23
24.	Temp. Ind. Gr.F	0.66	0.82	24
25.	HDFC Index F	1.41	1.58	25
26.	Temp. Ind. Gov. Sec. F- TP–G	-0.02	0.57	26
27.	HDFC Gilt fund	-1.13	0.38	27

Source: Computed from secondary data

After examining tables 8.7, 8.8 and 8.9, the authors have interpreted the results of Sharpe Ratio as shown below in paragraph 8.7.

8.7 Interpretation of the results of Sharpe Ratios of the mutual fund schemes and their benchmark ratios

Now, In order to identify easily the toppers and the laggards, the sample schemes have been ranked on basis of comparison with their benchmark ratios to facilitate understanding of the results. The total sample size is 27 schemes and the risk adjusted returns for each of the scheme based on the technique of Sharpe's ratio was computed. Like-wise, by using the same method of computation, the Sharpe Ratios for the benchmark portfolio was also computed. Out of the 27 sample schemes presented above 21 schemes have outperformed their benchmarks and 3 schemes have shown negative performance. The top 5 performing funds on the basis of Sharpe Ratio method are presented below in order of their ranks.

1. ICICI Prudential Short Term Plan
2. ICICI Prudential MIP

3. HDFC MIP Long Term Plan
4. FT India Monthly Income Plan
5. Templeton India-STIP

A look at the top ranking funds during the study period shows that ICICI Prudential Short Term Plan has emerged as the best performer among all the sample schemes. The fund manager has been very sensible in allocating the funds very carefully and managing the funds efficiently. If we observe the portfolio allocation strategy, that the fund manager has followed, it has mostly been in Private Corporate Securities only and the scheme has shown remarkable performance ever since its inception. The investment philosophy in debt securities with shorter term maturity has yielded satisfactory returns for this scheme as per Sharpe's technique.

Monthly Income Plans which are ideal investment options for investors seeking an alternate source of income have managed to grab the second (ICICI Prudential MIP), third (HDFC MIP Long Term Plan) and fourth (FT India Monthly Income Plan) ranks respectively. These funds are generally managed conservatively in terms of equity allocation and are also suitable for investors who neither may nor seek monthly income but would want to initiate investments in Equity but gradually through a product which bridges the gap between Equity and Debt. These funds have also managed to pay dividends consecutively to their investors since their inception and have always managed to outperform their benchmark returns since their inception which is evident from the results of Sharpe's ratio from the above table. Templeton India Short term income plan is in the fifth place. It is again a debt scheme that has showed good performance. A substantial proportion of the fund's portfolio constitutes corporate bonds. These bonds are not as frequently traded as government bonds, and are, hence, less volatile.

Among the 27 sample schemes, the schemes that showed margins of huge difference and displayed poor performance in their respective categories against their benchmarks are:

1. HDFC Income Fund
2. ICICI Prudential Gilt fund
3. Templeton India Growth Fund
4. HDFC Index Fund
5. Templeton India Govt. Sec. Fund TP - Growth
6. HDFC Gilt fund

We can see that all the above schemes have underperformed their benchmark ratios and the worst performer is HDFC Gilt fund. All these schemes which reflect negative Sharpe Ratios indicate that the funds have not performed satisfactorily. Examining schemes with negative ratios in a performance analysis of this nature is considered important because mutual funds are rated for risk with a greater emphasis on downward risk. That is, there is more emphasis placed on avoiding a negative outcome. Some of the important reasons for underperforming the benchmarks are:

- ➢ Tools
- ➢ High cost
- ➢ Incentives and
- ➢ Style limitations

Good funds should usually outperform their benchmarks and a five year study period is more appropriate to judge the performance of mutual funds and the disappointing performance of actively managed funds reflects the strategies of the fund managers or the high risk taken by them to yield returns in order to match the expectations of the investors. The other sample schemes have managed to outperform their benchmarks at least by marginal difference. Thus we can see that Sharpe Ratio provides an unbiased look into fund's performance.

Now after having measured the performance of the schemes using Sharpe Ratios, the authors have observed a huge difference in ranks of Sharpe's method and the five year Average return method (Table 8.4) of performance evaluation of schemes. According to Sharpe's method, ICICI

Prudential Short Term Plan stands in the first place whereas ICICI Prudential Tax Saver Plan has secured the first rank in the Average Return method. This explains the difference in results. The authors are not attempting here to compare two different methods where one considers risk and the other does not. The authors are only trying to present the results of both the methods to create awareness in the minds of the investors about the significance of risk - adjusted returns. Thus, it is evident in this chapter that the results computed based on Sharpe Ratios provides a deeper perspective on the performance of schemes to a mutual fund investor.

8.8 Testing of Hypothesis I

The authors have framed the following hypothesis and this hypothesis will be tested based on the results of Sharpe Ratios of the mutual fund schemes and their respective benchmark ratios.

The Sharpe Ratios of the sample schemes have outperformed the Sharpe Ratios of their respective benchmarks.

By framing this hypothesis, the authors have attempted to find out whether the Sharpe Ratios of the sample schemes have outperformed the Sharpe Ratios of the benchmark or have performed at par with that of the Sharpe Ratios of the benchmark. Since in this study the size of the sample is small, paired t test has been used to find the differences in means assuming the populations to be normal using one-tailed test. The Sharpe Ratios of the schemes and their respective benchmarks were computed in chapter 8 as shown in the tables 8.6 and 8.7. Based on this data the t-test is computed as given below:

Table 8.10
Statistical Computations of Sharpe Ratios of the Schemes

Schemes	X_1	$X_1 - A_1$ (A=.73)	$(X_1 - A_1)^2$
ICICI PRU STP	0.92	0.19	0.04
ICICI Prudential MIP	1.38	0.65	0.42
HDFC MIP Long Term Plan	1.36	0.63	0.40
FT India Monthly Income Plan	1.27	0.54	0.29
Templeton India-STIP	0.51	-0.22	0.05
ICICI Prudential Tax Saver	1.17	0.44	0.19
ICICI PRU Balanced fund	1.03	0.3	0.09
HDFC Prudence fund	1.14	0.41	0.17
ICICI Prudential Dynamic plan	1.19	0.46	0.21
HDFC Growth Fund	1.06	0.33	0.11
Franklin India index fund	0.98	0.25	0.06
Templeton India equity income fund	0.61	-0.12	0.01
FT India Balanced Fund	0.89	0.16	0.03
ICICI Prudential Income Fund	0.1	-0.63	0.40
ICICI Prudential Growth Fund	0.83	0.10	0.01
HDFC Equity Fund	0.97	0.24	0.06
ICICI Prudential Index Fund	0.76	0.03	0.00
HDFC Tax Saver	1.06	0.33	0.11
Franklin India Tax Shield Fund	0.84	0.11	0.01
HDFC Short term plan	0.97	0.24	0.06
Templeton India Income Fund	0.02	-0.71	0.50
HDFC Income Fund	-0.41	-1.14	1.30
ICICI Prudential Gilt fund	0.21	-0.52	0.27
Templeton India Growth Fund	0.66	-0.07	0.00
HDFC Index Fund	1.41	0.68	0.46
Templeton India Govt. Sec. Fund TP - Growth	-0.02	-0.75	0.56
HDFC Gilt fund	-1.13	-1.86	3.46
Total	19.78	0.07	9.28
		Mean 9.28	
		N = 27	
		Std. Deviation 0.59735	
		Std.Error Mean 0.11496	

Source: Computed and analysed from primary data

Table 8.11
Statistical Computations of Sharpe Ratios of the Benchmarks

Schemes	X_1	$X_2 - A_2$ (A=.73)	$(X_2 - A_2)^2$
ICICI PRU STP	-0.09	-0.69	0.48
ICICI Prudential MIP	0.63	0.03	0.00
HDFC MIP Long Term Plan	0.68	0.08	0.01
FT India Monthly Income Plan	0.64	0.04	0.00
Templeton India-STIP	-0.11	-0.71	0.50
ICICI Prudential Tax Saver	0.77	0.17	0.03
ICICI PRU Balanced fund	0.72	0.12	0.01
HDFC Prudence fund	0.84	0.24	0.06
ICICI Prudential Dynamic plan	0.95	0.35	0.12
HDFC Growth Fund	0.85	0.25	0.06
Franklin India index fund	0.80	0.20	0.04
Templeton India equity income fund	0.44	-0.16	0.03
FT India Balanced Fund	0.74	0.14	0.02
ICICI Prudential Income Fund	-0.01	-0.61	0.37
ICICI Prudential Growth Fund	0.75	0.15	0.02
HDFC Equity Fund	0.89	0.29	0.08
ICICI Prudential Index Fund	0.69	0.09	0.01
HDFC Tax Saver	1.00	0.40	0.16
Franklin India Tax Shield Fund	0.80	0.20	0.04
HDFC Short term plan	0.93	0.33	0.11
Templeton India Income Fund	-0.01	-0.61	0.37
HDFC Income Fund	-0.28	-0.88	0.77
ICICI Prudential Gilt fund	0.35	-0.25	0.06
Templeton India Growth Fund	0.82	0.22	0.05
HDFC Index Fund	1.58	0.98	0.96
Templeton India Govt. Sec. Fund TP - Growth	0.57	-0.03	0.00
HDFC Gilt fund	0.38	-0.22	0.05
	16.33	**0.13**	**4.42**
		Mean 0.6046	
		N = 27	
		Std. Deviation 0.41214	
		Std.Error Mean .07932	

Source: Computed and analysed from primary data

Table 8.12
Paired Sample Test Results of T-test

Results		T	df	P-value
		1.424	26	
Pair 1	Scheme - benchmark			.083

As we can see from the above tables-8.10, 8.11 and 8.12, t-test shows that the scheme-index is higher than the benchmark index . However the difference is not significant as the P-value is 0.083 (1-tail). In view of the above computed values the hypothesis of the study, Sharpe Ratios of the sample schemes have outperformed the Sharpe Ratios of the benchmark is rejected. In other words it can be said that Sharpe Ratios of the sample schemes have performed at par with that of the Sharpe Ratios of the benchmark or it can also be interpreted that there is only marginal difference in performance of the sample schemes with respect to their benchmarks.

Table 8.9 shows that 21 sample schemes have outperformed their benchmarks but when the schemes were put to statistical testing there was no significant difference in results. Even though the funds were selected in terms of their broad investment objectives, the reason for the results reported can be attributed to sampling fluctuations, volatility and market indices. Thus it can be concluded that statistically, difference in performance of the schemes in comparison with their respective benchmarks computed on the basis of Sharpe Ratio is not significant.

8.9 Conclusion

From this chapter it is evident that Sharpe's well acknowledged and widely quoted work on performance evaluation which considers risk-adjusted return provides a deeper perspective on the performance of schemes to a mutual fund investor. This is because they are based solely on quantitative measures. All mutual fund schemes have different objectives and therefore their performance also varies. This measure helps to identify the most "efficient" fund, namely the one with the highest return per unit of risk.

This study has found that ICICI Prudential Short Term Plan has emerged as the best performer among all the sample schemes on the basis of Sharpe's method. Evaluation of sample schemes based on Sharpe's ratio suggest that risk, return and performance measures are some of the important parameters to be kept in mind before investing in a fund. It is also observed that the funds which generally offer higher returns are more risky than those which offer lower returns. At the same time high returns are generally associated with a high degree of volatility. An investor accepts this volatility only because he wants higher returns. The Sharpe Ratio represents this trade-off between risk and returns. At the same time it also factors in the desire to generate returns, which are higher than those from risk free returns.

References

1. Amitabh Gupta,Mutual Funds in India, A study of Investment Management, pp. 143.
2. A benchmark is a market or sector index against which the performance of mutual fund can be measured.
3. The benchmark denotes the indices of the respective schemes

9

Comparison of Mutual Fund Sample Schemes Based on Sharpe's Ratios

9.1 Introduction

Mutual funds are often judged based on their performance compared to the respective benchmarks. Sharpe Ratio enables easy comparison of a fund's performance with its benchmark and peer group. Sharpe Ratio portrays for every unit of risk, how much the fund manager earned. Sharpe Ratios for the 27 sample mutual fund schemes and the benchmark ratios have been already computed in chapter 8. Based on the results derived, the performances of the schemes were evaluated against the benchmark. An investigation was made to check whether Sharpe Ratios of the schemes outperformed, underperformed or was at par with the benchmark ratios. A well-managed fund should be a consistent outperformer. In other words a fund can be called a good performer only if it has outperformed its benchmark indices continuously over a long period of time. Any portfolio which has performed better than the benchmark portfolio may be due to the portfolio being more risky than the benchmark portfolio. Therefore a simple investigation may not produce valid analysis of schemes. So the authors have attempted to further extend the investigation in this chapter by classifying the schemes which aims at grouping funds with comparable investment objectives and then compare and evaluate the performance of these schemes within the group to get meaningful results (Peer group comparison). The key objective of this chapter is to facilitate a transparent comparison of schemes. Now the following paragraphs will focus on peer group comparison of schemes.

9.2 Comparison of Sample Schemes of ICICI Prudential Mutual Fund, HDFC Mutual Fund and Franklin Templeton Mutual Fund

As discussed earlier, first the schemes were classified in to groups in terms of comparable investment objectives. On this basis all 27 sample schemes were further divided in to nine groups to facilitate peer group comparison. Each group comprised of three schemes - one scheme from ICICI Prudential mutual fund, one scheme from HDFC mutual fund and one scheme from Franklin Templeton mutual fund. An attempt is made in this study to evaluate and compare performance of these sample schemes which fall under the same investment objective category.

The objective of this performance evaluation is to find out the risk adjusted rate of returns of the schemes with the help of Sharpe Ratios that have been computed in the previous chapter both for the returns and their respective benchmarks. This method of performance evaluation and comparison is done in the following paragraphs and is important for three reasons. They are:

1. To understand the relative performance of the schemes.
2. Performance review provides data that helps the investor to assess their investments within the peer group.

3. This risk adjusted comparative performance, will give an insight into the fund manager's ability to outperform the peers and the benchmark over different periods of time.

9.3 Comparison of Equity-Oriented Schemes

An equity fund is a fund that invests primarily in equities. Such funds are typically held either in stock or cash. The objective of an equity fund is long-term growth through capital appreciation. Even if there is a decline in their value in the short- term these schemes deliver results in the long run. It is an ideal option for those in their prime earning years. As equity schemes invest in the equity markets, they have the potential to earn higher returns, but also carry higher risk. Research has shown that equities outperform all other asset classes in the long run. Based on the logic and using the computations derived using Sharpe's method of performance evaluation technique to find the risk adjusted returns from the previous chapter comparison is done. As we have seen earlier, 12 equity schemes were selected as samples - four schemes from ICICI Prudential mutual fund, four schemes from HDFC mutual fund and four schemes from Franklin Templeton mutual fund. Only the growth options are considered. This analysis is essential for the authors to understand how effective active management of the equity fund has been during the study period. This nature of comparison will also help the new breed of investors to understand the subject before making an investment decision.

Now let us examine the performance of first group of equity schemes as shown in the following table:

9.3.1 Comparison of Growth schemes

The following table and graph shows the performance of Growth funds calculated on the basis of Sharpe Ratio.

Table 9.1
Sharpe Ratios of the Mutual Fund Growth Schemes and their Benchmarks

Sr. No.	*Schemes*	*Sharpe Ratios of the Schemes*	*Sharpe Ratios of the Benchmarks*
1.	ICICI Prudential Growth Fund	0.83	0.75
2.	HDFC Growth Fund	1.06	0.86
3.	Templeton India Growth Fund	0.66	0.82

Source: Computed from secondary data

Table 9.1 shows the performance of Growth funds of all the sample mutual fund organizations, which has common investment objectives. Now if we look at the above table, we can see that out of the three growth schemes according to Sharpe's Risk to reward ratio method, both ICICI Prudential Growth Fund and HDFC Growth Fund have outperformed their bench mark ratios.

Graph 9.1
Sharpe Ratios of the Mutual Fund Growth Schemes and their Benchmarks

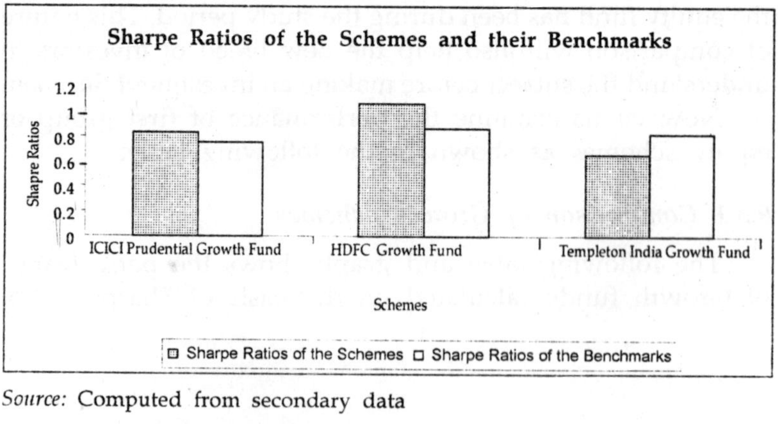

Source: Computed from secondary data

The fund's CAGR track records also shows a significant improvement in relative performance, compared to the preceding years. So it can be concluded that HDFC Growth fund is the best performer in this category and has comfortably grabbed the top position followed by ICICI Prudential Growth fund which has very moderately performed. An examination of the scheme profile in chapter 5 showed that this fund's performance was not satisfactory due to high inflation and volatility. Templeton India Growth fund has underperformed in this category when compared to its competitors and the Sharpe Ratio is below its benchmark ratio when compared to its competitors. The decline in performance is due to lack of diversification.

9.3.2 *Comparison of Equity schemes*

The following table and graph shows the performance of ICICI Prudential Dynamic plan, HDFC Equity Fund and Templeton India Equity Income Fund calculated on the basis of Sharpe Ratio.

Table 9.2

Sharpe Ratios of the Mutual Fund Equity Schemes and their Benchmarks

Sr. No.	*Schemes*	*Sharpe Ratios of the Schemes*	*Sharpe Ratios of the Benchmarks*
1.	ICICI Prudential Dynamic plan	1.19	0.95
2.	HDFC Equity Fund	0.97	0.89
3.	Templeton India equity income fund	0.61	0.44

Source: Computed from secondary data

Table 9.2 shows the performance of equity oriented schemes which falls under the same category. Here the risk adjusted returns computed with the help of Sharpe Ratios of all the three schemes have outperformed their benchmark ratios.

Graph 9.2
Sharpe Ratios of the Mutual Fund Equity Schemes and their Benchmarks

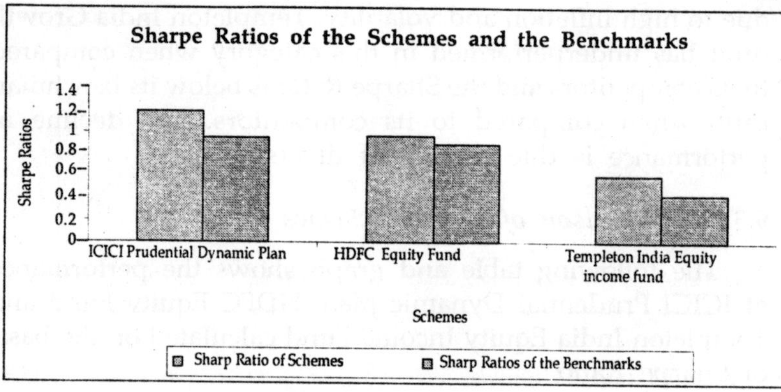

Source: Computed from secondary data

Again it is HDFC equity fund which has performed very well in this category and has surfaced to the top position followed by ICICI Prudential Dynamic plan. HDFC Equity, with its impressive track record, is a good investment option HDFC Equity has always opted for a compact portfolio without concentrated exposures in any single stock. On the other hand, ICICI Dynamic plan has managed steady rather than spectacular returns during bull runs as well as market corrections in 2007. Templeton India equity income fund is in the third place but still has managed to out perform its benchmark. So it can be concluded that this category on the whole has performed reasonably well.

9.3.3 Comparison of Index funds

The following table and graph shows the performance of Index funds calculated on the basis of Sharpe Ratio.

Table 9.3
Sharpe Ratios of the Mutual Fund Index Schemes and their Benchmarks

Sr. No.	Schemes	Sharpe Ratios of the Schemes	Sharpe Ratios of the Benchmarks
1.	ICICI Prudential Index Fund	0.76	0.69
2.	HDFC Index Funds	1.41	1.58
3.	Franklin India index fund	0.98	0.8

Source: Computed from secondary data

The authors have observed from the above table that the risk adjusted returns computed with the help of Sharpe Ratios of the portfolios ICICI Prudential Index Fund and Franklin India Index Fund have managed to outperform their benchmark ratios in this category. HDFC Index Fund has underperformed in this index category when compared to its competitors. This shows the fund managers disability and lack of proper sector allocation that has produced such low risk adjusted returns.

Graph 9.3
Sharpe Ratios of the Mutual Fund Index Schemes and their Benchmarks

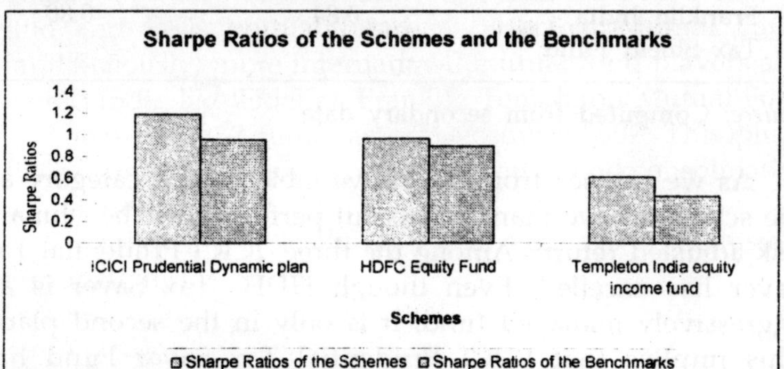

Source: Computed from secondary data

Another interesting observation the authorss would like to mention here is, without comparing with the benchmark, if the Sharpe Ratios of the scheme is examined in isolation, there is a chance of getting misguided with the fact that higher the ratio, better the returns in the case of HDFC Index Funds but when we compare it with the benchmarks, the actual risk-adjusted return is seen.

9.3.1 Comparison of Tax Saver Schemes

The following table and graph shows the performance of Tax Saver Funds calculated on the basis of Sharpe Ratio. The last group of sample schemes in the equity category is the Tax Saver Funds. Generally in this category of funds, investors would be able to avail of tax benefits and will also have the options including dividend payout, dividend reinvestment, growth and bonus options.

Table 9.4
Sharpe Ratios of the Mutual Fund Tax Saver Schemes and their Benchmarks

Sr. No.	*Schemes*	*Sharpe Ratios of the Schemes*	*Sharpe Ratios of the Benchmarks*
1.	ICICI Prudential Tax Saver	1.17	0.77
2.	HDFC Tax Saver	1.06	1.00
3.	Franklin India Tax Shield Fund	0.84	0.80

Source: Computed from secondary data

As we can see from the above table, in this category all the schemes have managed to out perform their benchmark risk adjusted returns.Among the three, ICICI Prudential Tax Saver has excelled. Even though HDFC Tax Saver is an aggressively managed fund, it is only in the second place. This implies that ICICI Prudential Tax Saver Fund has managed not only to time its market effectively but also has allocated its sector very carefully to get good returns. Franklin Tax Shield Fund is in the third place and it can be said that it has managed to get decent returns in spite of heavy competition.

Graph 9.4
Sharpe Ratios of the Mutual Fund Tax Saver Schemes and their Benchmarks

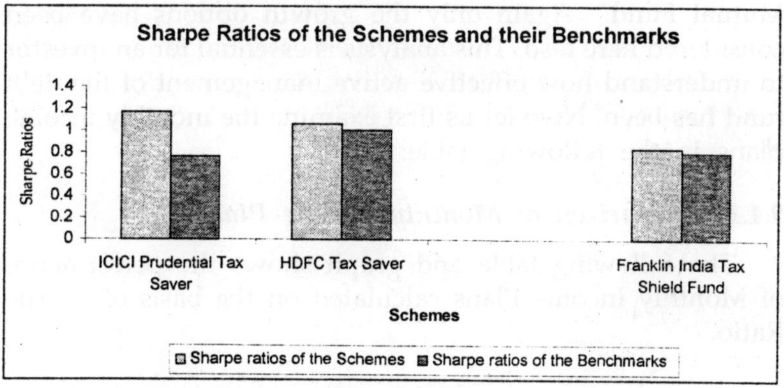

Source: Computed from secondary data

From the above paragraphs, it can be observed that out of 12 equity schemes, only two schemes have underperformed and the risk adjusted returns of the remaining ten schemes computed using Sharpe's technique is found to be satisfactory. Overall during the study period it can be said that analysis of risk adjusted returns of equity schemes reflects the high volatility in the last five years. Equity funds have outperformed the index in periods of boom in equity markets but have underperformed it in bear periods.

9.4 Comparison of Debt Schemes

After having examined the equity schemes selected for the purpose of the study, let us examine the Debt schemes. Generally the primary investment objectives of these schemes are to generate regular income in order to make regular dividend payments to unit holders and the secondary objectives are growth of capital. By using the computations derived using Sharpe's method of performance evaluation technique to find the risk adjusted returns from the previous chapter comparison is done in the following paragraphs. This study has twelve sample debt schemes - four schemes from ICICI Prudential Mutual Fund, four schemes from HDFC Mutual Fund and four schemes from Franklin Templeton Mutual Fund. Again only the growth options have been considered here also. This analysis is essential for an investor to understand how effective active management of the debt fund has been. Now let us first examine the monthly income plans in the following table:

9.4.1 Comparison of Monthly Income Plans

The following table and graph shows the performance of Monthly Income Plans calculated on the basis of Sharpe Ratio.

Table 9.5
Sharpe Ratios of the Mutual Fund MIP Schemes and their Benchmarks

Sr. No.	*Schemes*	*Sharpe Ratios of the Schemes*	*Sharpe Ratios of the Benchmarks*
1.	ICICI Prudential MI Plan	1.38	0.6
2.	HDFC MIP Long Term Plan	1.36	0.68
3.	FT India Monthly Income Plan	1.27	0.64

Source: Computed from secondary data

Graph 9.5
Sharpe Ratios of the Mutual Fund MIP Schemes and their Benchmarks

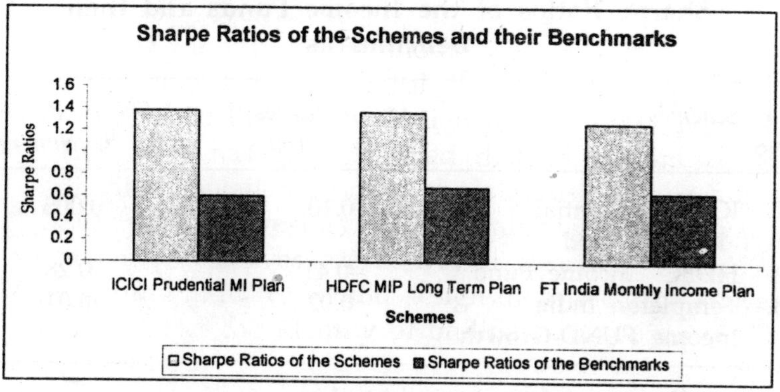

Source: Computed from secondary data

The monthly income plans are supposed to be a reasonably safe option with most of its corpus being invested in debt securities and the remaining in stocks. The objective is to give regular income to the schemes. From the above table, we can see that the funds have displayed its strength in both good and bad times, thus making it an attractive pick. This has been achieved by maintaining a good quality portfolio and through cautious duration management of the companies. As we can see from the above table this category has performed extremely well by matching the expectations of the investors. The Sharpe Ratios of all the schemes have outperformed the benchmark of the schemes. ICICI Prudential Monthly Income Plan which is a conservatively managed fund is in the first place within the group followed by HDFC MIP Long Term Plan. There is only marginal difference between HDFC MIP and FT India Monthly Income Plan which is in the third place. Overall the performance of these schemes are very satisfactory and the credit goes to the fund managers respectively.

9.4.2 Comparison of Income Funds

The following table and graph shows the performance of Income funds calculated on the basis of Sharpe Ratio.

Table 9.6
Sharpe Ratios of the Income Funds and their Benchmarks

Sr. No.	*Schemes*	*Sharpe Ratios of the Schemes*	*Sharpe Ratios of the Benchmarks*
1.	ICICI Prudential Income Fund	0.10	0.005
2.	HDFC Income Fund	-0.41	-0.28
3.	Templeton India Income FUND-Growth	0.02	-0.01

Source: Computed from secondary data

Graph 9.6
Sharpe Ratios of the Income Funds and their Benchmarks

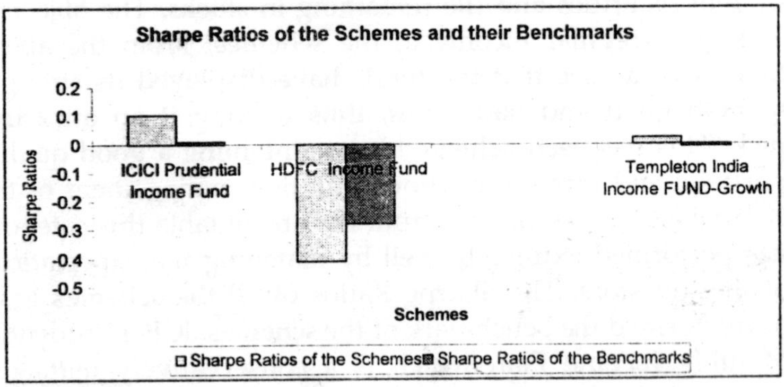

Source: Computed from secondary data

After adjusting risks, the performance of the income schemes is not satisfactory. Templeton India Income fund has generated lower returns per unit of risk than their benchmark. Even though ICICI Prudential Income Fund has managed to get more returns, the fact is, it has failed to notch higher returns to match risks is a negative factor. On the contrary HDFC Income Fund has shown a very poor performance. Both Sharpe returns and the benchmark returns have shown negative figures. Thus we can see that this category of funds which aims to give steady income has not kept its objective. The reason can be attributed to inflation and rising interest rates.

9.4.3 Comparison of Short Term Plans

The following table and graph shows the performance of Short term plans calculated on the basis of Sharpe Ratio.

Table 9.7
Sharpe Ratios of the Short Term Plans and their Benchmarks

Sr. No.	*Schemes*	*Sharpe Ratios of the Schemes*	*Sharpe Ratios of the Benchmarks*
1.	ICICI Prudential Short term plan	0.92	-0.09
2.	HDFC Short term plan	0.97	0.93
3.	Templeton India Short term income plan	0.51	-0.12

Source: Computed from secondary data

From the above table it can be observed that ICICI Prudential AMC has managed to out perform its benchmark ratios after adjusting risks significantly for the five year period and has grabbed the first place within the group. ICICI Prudential AMC has delivered a sustained out performance on a risk-adjusted basis across the fund line-ups in its category. Templeton India Short Term Income Plan which is in the second place has also managed to adjust risk

Graph 9.7
Sharpe Ratios of the Short Term Plans and their Benchmarks

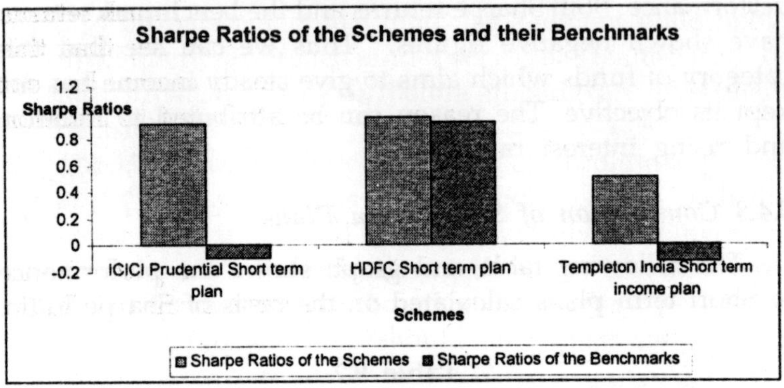

Source: Computed from secondary data

successfully and out perform its benchmark ratio with its consistent performance. HDFC Short Term Plan which has always promised an element of assured return and has managed to outperform the benchmark Sharpe Ratios for the five year period is in the third place within the group of sample schemes. Prudence in managing investors' hard earned money and process orientation are some of the reasons to generate confidence and trust in the minds of the investors and these schemes have managed this very effectively.

9.4.4 Comparison of Gilt Funds

Gilt Funds are mutual funds that predominantly invest in government securities (G-Secs). Unlike conventional debt funds that invest in debt instruments across the board, gilt funds target just a given category of debt instruments i.e. G-Secs. The latter are securities issued by the Reserve Bank of India (RBI) on behalf of the Government of India.

The following table and graph shows the performance of Gilt Funds calculated on the basis of Sharpe Ratio.

Table 9.8
Sharpe Ratios of the Gilt Funds and their Benchmarks

Sr. No.	*Schemes*	*Sharpe Ratios of the Schemes*	*Sharpe Ratios of the Benchmarks*
1.	ICICI Prudential Gilt fund	0.21	0.35
2.	HDFC Gilt fund	-1.13	0.38
3.	Templeton India Government Securities	-0.02	0.57

Source: Computed from secondary data

Graph 9.8
Sharpe Ratios of the Gilt Funds and their Benchmarks

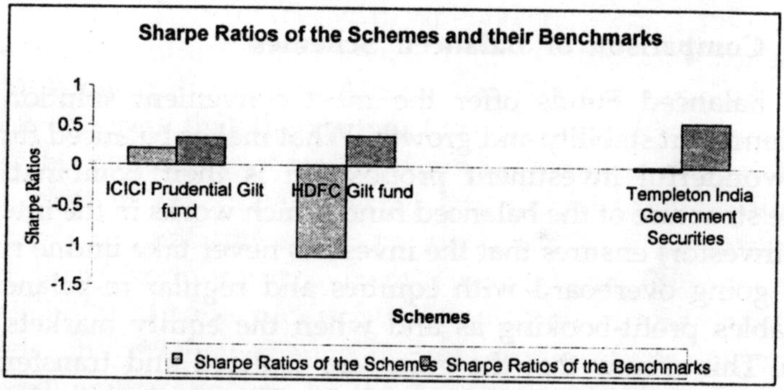

Source: Computed from secondary data

Gilt Funds are considered to be in the low risk category as they are invested in government securities. But it's important to recognize that higher safety does not mean elimination of all risks. While there's no credit risk, investments in gilt funds are vulnerable to interest rate risks. When interest rates rise, prices of government securities fall; this in turn has an adverse impact on the performance of gilt funds. Typically, higher the fund's average maturity, more it is prone to volatility. In the table above, the funds have languished in negative territory. Thus we can see that although the gilts market is largely liquid, it's also extremely volatile and price sensitive which has pushed the yields down. After carefully considering all these factors the authors have used the risk adjusted Sharpe Ratio method of performance measurement and the Sharpe Ratio results are as seen in the above table.

On this basis, if we observe the results of Sharpe Ratios, all the funds under this category have underperformed their benchmark ratios. This shows a negative picture on these funds. Therefore Investors should keep an eye on indicators that triggers a fall in interest rates, a slowdown in GDP growth, rising inflation, a decline in IIP (Index of Industrial Production) and expectations of a fall in corporate earnings.

9.5 Comparison of Balanced Schemes

Balanced Funds offer the most convenient solution to balance out stability and growth. What makes balanced funds a wonderful investment proposition is their combination. The structure of the balanced fund which works in the interest of investors ensures that the investors never take undue risks by going overboard with equities and regular re-balancing enables profit-booking as and when the equity markets go up. This means that the gains are realized and transferred to safer debt instruments regularly. This study has chosen one balanced scheme from each sample company which makes it three altogether. The following table shows the Sharpe Ratios of the sample balanced schemes and their benchmarks.

The above table shows that all the balanced schemes have performed extremely well after adjusting risk according to the method of Sharpe Ratios and have outperformed their benchmark ratios. HDFC Prudence Fund is the topper in this category, followed by ICICI Pru Balanced Fund and FT India Balanced Fund. HDFC Prudence Fund is a consistent 'above average' performer not only in terms of returns but also risk-adjusted returns. The funds' aggressive investing strategies were evident not only in their continuing to maintain a higher allocation to equities but also in their stock selection strategies. While HDFC Prudence has delivered returns superior to FT India Balanced, the former's bias for mid-caps and aggressive portfolio churning make the latter a better option for investors with low risk appetite.

Table 9.9
Sharpe Ratios of the Balanced Schemes and their Benchmarks

Sr. No.	*Schemes*	*Sharpe Ratios of the Schemes*	*Sharpe Ratios of the Benchmarks*
1.	ICICI Prudential Balanced fund	1.03	0.72
2.	HDFC Prudence fund	1.14	0.84
3.	FT India Balanced Fund	0.89	0.74

Source: Computed from secondary data

Graph 9.9
Sharpe Ratios of the Balanced Schemes and their Benchmarks

Source: Computed from secondary data

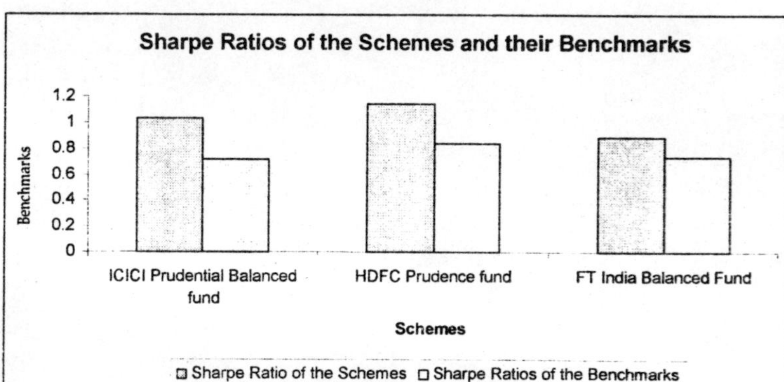

9.6 Conclusion

In this chapter an investigation was made to check whether Sharpe Ratios of the schemes outperformed, underperformed or was at par with the benchmark ratios and it can be concluded that peer comparisons of the sample schemes shows results that helps the investor to assess their investments within the peer group. The results are more meaningful as the schemes were classified by the authors to evaluate the performance of these schemes within the peer group. The authors are of the opinion that performance review of this nature provides data that helps the investor to assess their investments within the peer group. Thus it can be seen that Sharpe Ratio represents a well-accepted and highly useful statistic in the analysis of funds performance. It is a "compact" statistic for simultaneously considering risk and return. It is compact in that its calculation is (1) very straight-forward and (2) it does not involve unclear variables.

10

Comparison of ICICI Prudential Mutual Fund, HDFC Mutual Fund and Franklin Templeton Mutual Fund based on Investors Responses

10.1 Introduction

Investors respond differently to fund performance across fund types. They play a very important role and every decision an investor makes regarding holding or selling a mutual fund has an impact on the returns of that particular fund. So it is not sufficient for a research of this nature to focus only on the performance of the sample schemes alone. The investor behavioural aspect in this regard also has to be analysed. Generally an individual investor looks for three basic things, they are – growth of funds invested, liquidity, tax benefits, and safety. A mutual fund should satisfy all the above investor's "needs and expectations". In financial markets, "expectations" of the investors play a vital role. These expectations of the investors are influenced by their "perceptions" and humans generally relate perception to action. So in order to identify and understand the perceptions, behaviour, preferences among mutual fund organisations and preference among scheme types etc with regard to the sample schemes of ICICI Prudential Mutual Fund, HDFC Mutual Fund and Franklin Templeton Mutual Fund, a comprehensive survey was carried out.

The survey was based on direct personal interviews with the investors using the interview schedule method. The survey was conducted during the period December 2007 to January 2008. This section is devoted to present the observations of the survey which is further used to assess the perceptions of the investors regarding ICICI Prudential mutual fund, HDFC mutual fund and Franklin Templeton mutual fund. The results of the survey will serve as a benchmark for the fund managers to understand and focus more on the areas of their weakness and understand more about the perceptions of the investors.

Now the following paragraphs will examine the sample size, composition and observations of the survey and then the three sample mutual fund companies are compared based on the investor's response.

10.2 Sampling Procedure

In order to achieve the objectives of the survey as discussed earlier, pre-tested questionnaires were administered on a sample of 125 educated individual investors across Mumbai city and the questionnaires were administered on a combination of simple random and judgement sample. This careful selection of sample is not only due to the time and financial constraints but also to pick up only the investors who have invested in these three companies. The criterion that was kept in mind during the process of selection was - the investor should have invested at any point of time in all the above three sample companies or at least a minimum of two. Even though due care was taken by the authors in selecting the investors, the authors had to reject 34 filled up questionnaires and choose the final 125 respondents. So while starting the survey the sample size even though was decided as 125 respondents, actual interviews were conducted on 160 respondents. The remaining one was considered as invalid. The unit of observation and analysis of survey was only among educated individual investors. The meaning of individual investor in this context is "An individual who has invested in any mutual funds and this does not include institutional investors". The questionnaire had close-ended questions. The investors were screened and the inclusion was purely based on their knowledge about mutual funds. This was necessary, because the questionnaire presumed awareness of some basic terminology about mutual funds. But out of 125 respondents 11 respondents could not understand few questions to say for e.g. the expenses of mutual funds etc. In such cases, to facilitate understanding of the questionnaire the authors while interacting with the respondents explained the meaning wherever required because of its technical nature.

10.3 Profile of the Investors

10.3.1 Gender composition of the sample

There is always a general impression that men hold larger portfolios than women but the objective of this study is not to find out the size of the portfolio of the investors and since this nature of information is too personal that part has been ignored. But from a research perspective, understanding both types of investors will always give us a broader scenario. So the main sample of the survey covered both men and women.

In order to study the behaviour pattern of the investors, both men and women were selected as samples. Out of the total respondents 101 were men and 24 were women. While selecting the sample, due care was also taken that men and women do not come from the same household. The reason is- it is assumed that when both men and women are selected from the same household, who mostly fall under couple category, the pattern of investment will be the same and their objective of investment will also be the same. So to avoid this wide spread category of men and women were selected.

Table 10.1
Gender Composition of the Investors

Sr.No.	*Gender*	*No. of Investors*
1.	Male	101
2.	Female	24
	Total	**125**

Source: Compiled from primary data collected through questionnaires

Graph 10.1
Gender Composition of the Investors

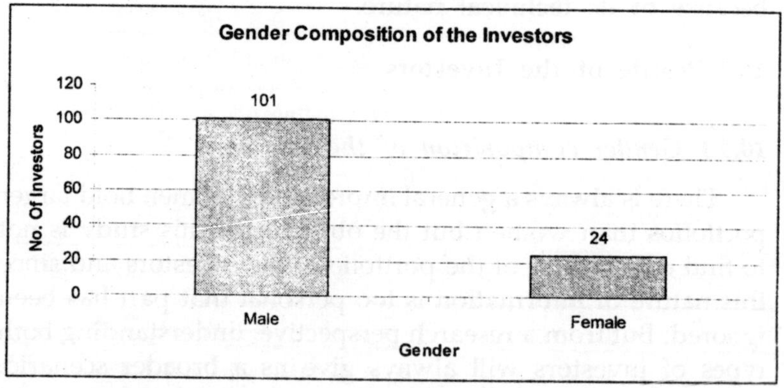

Source: Compiled from primary data collected through questionnaires

10.3.2 *Age-wise classification of investors*

When examining the perceptions of investors, age also plays a very crucial role. The following table shows the age-wise classification of the investors and their academic qualifications.

Table 10.2
Age-Wise Classification of the Investors

Sr.No.	*Age*	*No. of Investors*	*Percent*
1.	Up to 20	2	1
2.	21-40	78	63
3.	41-60	33	26
4.	Above 60	12	10
	Total	**125**	**100**

Source: Compiled from primary data collected through questionnaires

It can be seen from the above table, that the investors under 20 years have also been considered. These investors were college-goers who tried to invest their pocket money and multiply this income. Investors above the age of 60 years constitute 8 percent of the sample and mostly they belong to the category of pensioners. Of the total respondents, an overwhelming majority of respondents with the highest percentage of 62 percent investors belong to the working age group and were mostly aggressive investors. On the contrary about 26 percent of the respondents come from the prime earnings age group of 41- 60 and they were mostly conservative investors.

10.3.3 Academic Qualification of the investors

The following table shows the academic background of the investors.

It can be seen that 24 percent of the respondents were professional degree holders and majority of 38 percent were post graduates so we can safely conclude that majority of the respondents possess the necessary educational background and they were capable of understanding the return, risk and other important aspects of the schemes.

Table 10.3

Academic Qualification of the Respondents

Sr.No.	*Academic Qualification*	*No. of Investors*
1.	Under Graduate	8
2.	Graduate	39
3.	Post Graduate	48
4.	Professional Degree	30
	Total	**125**

Source: Compiled from primary data collected through questionnaires

10.3.4 Sources of information that helped the investors in making recent mutual fund purchases

Any direct or indirect influence on investors which prompts them to make an investment decision is very crucial from the company's point of view. Investors in mutual funds are generally motivated by different sources to make investment decisions. The following table indicates the influence of different agencies in influencing investor's investment decision.

Table 10.4

Sources of Information in Investment Decision Making

Sr. No.	*Information Sources*	*Percent*
1.	Financial Publication like newspapers and magazines	74
2.	Family and Friends	15
3.	Meetings and presentation of work	8
4.	Prospectus of the mutual funds company	49
5.	Information from the mutual funds distributor	62
6.	Internet	36

Source: Compiled from primary data collected through questionnaires

The above data indicates that the respondents just don't depend on a single source of information to make decisions. They depend on multiple sources. Even though the influence of financial publications is much higher by 74 percent, it is understood from the above table that 62 percent of the investors are considerably influenced by the distributors.

10.3.5 Objective of investment in mutual fund

Investor's objectives generally vary with the level of income. The respondents were asked to specify their objective of investment which is shown in the following table.

Table 10.5
Respondent's Objective of Investment in Mutual Funds

Sr.No.	*Primary objective*	*Percent*
1.	Preservation of Principal	22
2.	Current Income	17
3.	Growth and Income	32
4.	Conservation Growth	12
5.	Aggressive Growth	15
6.	No response	2

Source: Compiled from primary data collected through questionnaires

As can be seen from the above table, Investors mostly have multiple objectives. This study observes that 22 percent of the respondents were investing in mutual funds to preserve their principal while 17 percent of the investors were looking only at the current income. A majority of 32 percent investors came under the category whose objective of investment was both growth and income. So growth and income schemes were very popular among the respondents. Another interesting observation by the authors is that, the middle class educated investors were very much conscious about diversification of portfolios and house hold preferences for instruments generally matched their risk perceptions.

10.3.6 Knowledge of investment

Data regarding knowledge of investment is required for the simple reason to check whether the investor has any knowledge of investment or relies on the distributor's advice for investing.

Table 10.6
Respondent's Knowledge of Investment

Sr.No.	*Knowledge of investment*	*Percent of Investors*
1.	Nil	3
2.	Limited	27
3.	Good	47
4.	Extensive	23
	Total	**100**

Source: Compiled from primary data collected through questionnaires

From the above table, we can see that almost 47 percent of the investors were found to have good knowledge on investments and 23 percent of investors were found to have extensive knowledge on investments. These investors not only possessed good knowledge about mutual funds but also about other financial instruments.

10.3.7 Investment experience of the investors

In addition to finding out knowledge of investment, it is necessary to check about every individual investor's investment experience particularly mutual funds. Table 10.7 and table 10.8 shows the experience of investors.

Table 10.7
Respondent's Investment Experience in Mutual Funds

Sr.No.	*Investment experience*	*Percent*
1.	Extensive	38
2.	Average	53
3.	Limited	29
4.	Virtually nil	5
	Total	100

Source: Compiled from primary data collected through questionnaires

Graph 10.2
Respondent's Investment Experience in Mutual Funds

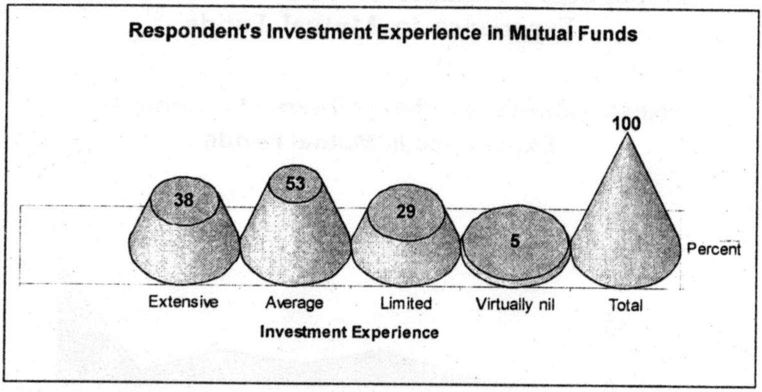

Source: Compiled from primary data collected through questionnaires

As we can see from table 10.7, 38 per cent of respondents had extensive investment experience. This category of investors mostly did not rely on the distributors and made investments on their own. 53 percent who had average experience mostly took the advice from the distributors and at the same time used their judgement to invest. Investors who virtually had nil experience completely relied on distributors for each and every investment.

Table10.8
Respondent's Number of Years of Investment Experience in Mutual Funds

Sr.No.	*Investment Experience*	*Percent*
1.	More than 10 years	9
2.	5 to 10 years	32
3.	3 to 5 years	18
4.	1 to 3 years	30
5.	Less than a year	11
	Total	100

Source: Compiled from primary data collected through questionnaires

Graph 10.3
Respondent's Number of Years of Investment Experience in Mutual Funds

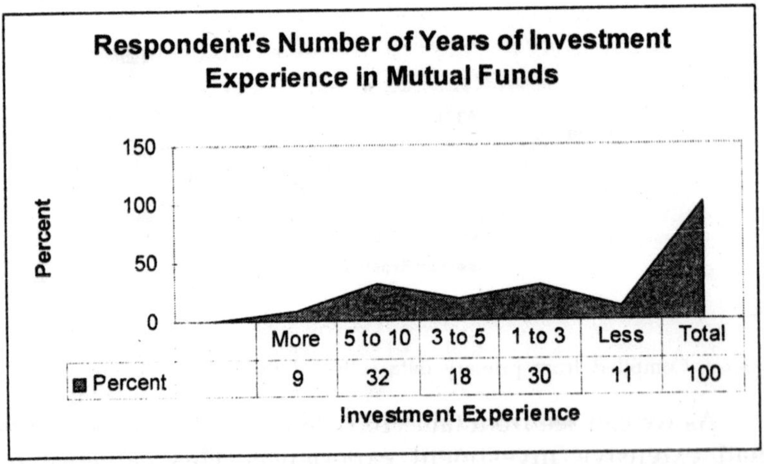

Source: Compiled from primary data collected through questionnaires

When the investor's number of years of experience in investing in mutual funds was observed, it was highly interesting to note that almost 32 percent respondents were investing between 5 to 10 years and 9 percent respondents were investing for more than 10 years. Generally these categories of investors were the ones who invested in other financial instruments also and their objective of investment was preservation of capital. Only 5 percent investors belong to the category of new investors mostly who were in the age group of 18 to 25 and have been investing in mutual funds for a year or so.

10.3.8 Qualities that affect the investor's selection of mutual funds

Table 10.9
Respondent's Expectations of Fund Qualities

Sr. No.	*Details*	*Highly Im, ortant %*	*Some-what Impor-tant%*	*Not Impor-tant %*	*Not at all Important %*
1.	Fund's performance record	88	115	-	-
2.	Fund's reputation or brand name	68	30	2	-
3.	Scheme's portfolio of Investment	77	20	3	-
4.	Withdrawal facilities	20	67	10	3
5.	Favourable rating by a rating agency	19	63	14	4
6.	Innovativeness of the scheme	48	46	5	1
7.	Products with tax benefits	37	55	7	1
8.	Entry and Exit Load	26	60	12	2
9.	Minimum initial investment	14	58	18	10

It is very important to find out the basic qualities that an investor expects from a mutual fund. An attempt has also been made by the authors to find out those qualities so that the sample companies can consider these qualities while designing the mutual fund products

From the above table it can be seen that the results are based on multiple responses and 88 percent of the respondents feel that the fund's performance record is the most important factor which has an impact or influences mutual fund selection. Next, the respondents give more importance to Scheme's portfolio of investment with 77 percent investors choosing the same. 48 percent of the investors feel that the scheme should be innovative and 37 percent feel that the products should come with tax benefits

10.4 Comparison of ICICI Prudential Mutual Fund, HDFC Mutual Fund and Franklin Templeton Mutual Fund based on Investors Response

The investor's profile discussed above gives us a brief idea about the respondent's objective of investments, risk perceptions, knowledge of investment and investment experience in mutual funds. It is very important to understand the profile of the respondents and then proceed with the comparisons of schemes based on investor's response in order to draw valuable conclusions. The authors would like to mention here that the objective of comparison is not to evaluate the performance of the schemes but only to understand the perceptions of the respondents about the sample mutual fund organisations. The following paragraphs will now try to compare the respondent's preference of the sample mutual fund organisations. In addition an attempt is also made to further probe the perceptions of the respondents of the sample mutual fund organisations.

10.4.1 Whether respondents Select Schemes based on the Performance of Schemes since Inception

This study has also made an attempt to examine the scheme selection behaviour of the individual investors for the existing schemes. Generally there are different criterions involved in scheme selection. One important consideration is performance since inception. Let us have a look at the following table:

Table 10.10
Whether Respondents select schemes based on the performance of schemes since inception

Sr. No.	*Name of the Company*	*Yes%*	*No%*
1.	ICICI Prudential Mutual Fund	57	43
2.	HDFC Mutual Fund	56	44
3.	Franklin Templeton Mutual Fund	61	39

Source: Compiled from primary data collected through questionnaires

As can be seen from the above table, we can see that a vast majority of respondents have said that they look at the performance of all the companies since inception before investing in an existing scheme of the company- 57 percent in the case of ICICI Prudential Mutual Fund, 56 percent in the case of HDFC mutual fund and 61 percent in the case of Franklin Templeton Mutual fund. It is generally believed that scheme performance seen on short terms or ignoring performance since inception will always dissuade investors. Active fund management involves too many factors that cannot be neglected. On the other hand the group of respondents who have said "No" believe that it is not necessary to look at the schemes performance since inception. It may be because of the market conditions, timing and the current performance of the scheme.

10.4.2 Response of Investors who feel that the funds offer higher returns

All mutual fund companies compete with each other to offer higher returns in the form of dividends etc., in order to attract and retain customers. In order to find out whether the sample companies offer good returns, the respondents were asked whether their funds in general offer good returns and the following observation was made.

Table 10.11
Response of Investors who feel that the funds offer higher returns

Sr. No.	*Name of the Company*	*Yes%*	*No%*
1.	ICICI Prudential Mutual Fund	60	40
2.	HDFC Mutual Fund	84	16
3.	Franklin Templeton Mutual Fund	56	44

Source: Compiled from primary data collected through questionnaires

Every mutual fund organisation strives to enhance the returns of their investors and if we observe the above table, we can see that HDFC mutual fund has to a certain extent managed to satisfy its investors in this regard. 84 percent of HDFC mutual fund investors have said that fund offers good or even high returns. They may fall in the risk-averse investor's category but returns are the main criterion for investment. ICICI Prudential Mutual Fund and Franklin Templeton Mutual Fund have occupied second and third positions respectively. These figures don't mean that the fund is not offering return at all. It depends on the scheme type and if we carefully observe the percentages it is a moderate figure where the respondents have said that some schemes of the fund offer good returns while some gives poor returns.

10.4.3 Whether Respondents think there is mismatch between expectations and reality

From the 10.12 table, it can be observed that all the three mutual fund companies have scored similarly with 76 percent of the respondents saying that ICICI Prudential Mutual Fund and HDFC Mutual Funds match their expectations and in reality only sometimes. But in the case of HDFC mutual fund, the figure stood at 68 percent. Further 15 percent, 18 percent and 24 percent of respondents of ICICI Prudential Mutual Fund, HDFC Mutual Fund and Franklin Templeton Mutual Fund respectively feel that there is never a mismatch between expectations and reality. These are the group of respondents who strongly believe in the respective funds and the funds should also always try and retain these investors.

Table 10.12
Whether Respondents think there is mismatch between expectations and reality

Sr. No.	*Name of the Company*	*Always %*	*Sometimes %*	*Never %*
1.	ICICI Prudential Mutual Fund	9	76	15
2.	HDFC Mutual Fund	6	76	18
3.	Franklin Templeton Mutual Fund	8	68	24

Source: Compiled from primary data collected through questionnaires

Graph 10.4
Whether Respondents think there is mismatch between expectations and reality

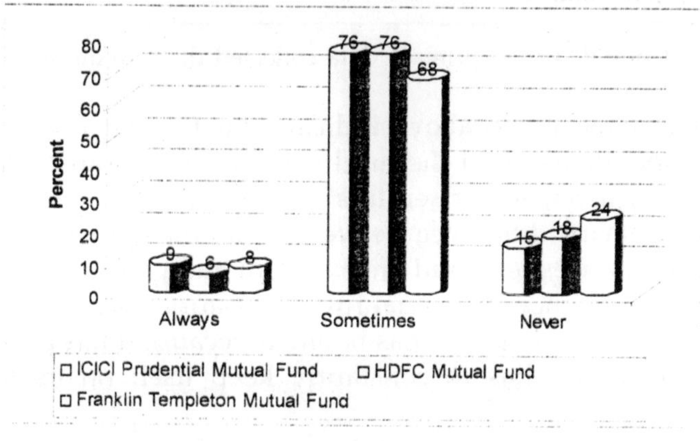

Source: Compiled from primary data collected through questionnaires

10.4.4 Whether Respondents think funds offer professional fund management services

Investing in mutual funds contains the same risk as investing in the markets; the only difference is professional management of the fund. This pooled income is professionally managed on behalf of the unit-holders, and each investor holds a proportion of the portfolio i.e. entitled not only to profits when the securities are sold, but also subject to any losses in value as well. Personal attention from the dedicated fund manager, combined with reasonable asset management fees and fund costs that are among the lowest in the industry, can result in extraordinary overall value for the portfolio. The following table shows the satisfaction levels of the respondents with regard to professional fund management services.

Table 10.13
Whether Respondents think Funds offer professional fund management services

Sr. No.	*Name of the Company*	*Excellent* %	*Very good* %	*Good* %	*Average* %
1.	ICICI Prudential Mutual Fund	10	54	29	7
2.	HDFC Mutual Fund	15	50	32	3
3.	Franklin Templeton Mutual Fund	23	46	26	5

Source: Compiled from primary data collected through questionnaires

The table given above indicates that about one half of the respondents of all the fund companies are satisfied with the fund management services of the respective companies. A fairly sharp difference between respondents who believe that the services rendered are excellent and good. The reason for this difference is; mutual fund investors insist on quality, and this industry, which has boomed because it has provided a great service has to constantly keep itself on its toes.

10.4.5 Whether Respondents invest in mutual fund companies even after a very bad investment experience

The following table shows us the investors response, to find out whether they will invest in one of the following funds even after a very bad investment experience.

Table 10.14
Whether Respondents invest in mutual fund companies even after a very bad investment experience

Sr.No.	*Name of the fund*	*Percent*
1.	HDFC Mutual Fund	34
2.	ICICI Prudential Mutual Fund	43
3.	Franklin Templeton Mutual Fund	33

Source: Compiled from primary data collected through questionnaires

As can be seen from the above table 43 percent of respondents have responded in favour of ICICI Prudential Mutual Fund, 34 percent for HDFC Mutual Fund and 33 percent have responded in favour of Franklin Templeton Mutual Fund. The reason they have stated is: - just because they had a very bad investment experience, they will not completely ignore the fund because fund performance depends on various factors like volatility, inflation, market timing etc. When the fund comes with a new scheme that matches their investment objectives and if they feel it is capable of producing the desired returns, they will definitely invest in those funds again.

10.4.6 Investors views on Funds that are better performers than other Private, Public and Foreign Mutual Funds

In order to find out whether the sample companies are better performers than other private, public and foreign mutual funds, the respondents were asked their opinion in this regard and the figures are shown below:

Table 10.15
Investors views on Funds that are better performers than other Private, Public and Foreign Mutual Funds

Sr. No.	*Name of the Company*	*Better%*	*Not Better%*
1.	ICICI Prudential Mutual Fund	92	8
2.	HDFC Mutual Fund	97	3
3.	Franklin Templeton Mutual Fund	56	44

Source: Compiled from primary data collected through questionnaires

From the respondents views, the authors observed that ICICI Prudential Mutual Fund and Franklin Templeton Mutual Fund have occupied 2nd and 3rd positions respectively but HDFC has comfortably topped with 97 percent of the respondents believing that HDFC mutual fund is the best performer among the three. Thus we can see an overwhelming situation where investors believe that these three companies are far better than other companies. But when the investors were asked to rate the best mutual fund company in India, invariably all the respondents chose Reliance mutual fund only, which is an important observation that was made.

10.4.7 Distributor's role

In order to find out the method of investment by the respondents in these companies, the respondents were asked to give us details about their investment methods and 32 percent respondents said that they prefer Online Investment, while 59 percent invest through brokers and the rest use both methods. Thus we can see that the distributors play an important role. Distributors have a large degree of influence over the investors. They are considered to be the middlemen who connect the investors and the mutual fund organisations. Distributors are the ones who explain the features, advantages and disadvantages of the funds. So they influence the investors to a great extent.

Table 10.16
Whether investors invest in Mutual Funds based on Distributor's recommendations

Sr.No.	*Name of the Company*	*Yes%*
1.	ICICI Prudential Mutual Fund	46
2.	HDFC Mutual Fund	54
3.	Franklin Templeton MF	47

Source: Compiled from primary data collected through questionnaires
*Each percent is against the total

The figures seen in the table given above shows us that 46 percent of respondents have purchased ICICI Prudential Mutual Funds, 54 percent of respondents have purchased HDFC Mutual Funds and 47 percent of them have bought Franklin Templeton Mutual Funds based on the recommendations made by the investor. Here one interesting observation made is; even though the respondents belong to the educated investor lot and among them, 38 percent of the investors have extensive investment experience and 53 percent have good investment experience, they have been influenced by the distributor's recommendations. Almost all the respondents felt that they were informed with right information about the companies while investing. But during the interaction with the investors, it was also observed that their decisions can be influenced by the distributors only when they fully believe that he has complete knowledge about the scheme they are distributing. Thus the authors found that the investors who invest through brokers have confidently invested based on the recommendations of the investor.

10.5 Testing of Hypothesis II

The authors framed the second broad hypothesis of the study as:

The individual investor's selection of mutual funds is

based on his perception about the funds in terms of brand image.

This hypothesis will be tested in the following paragraphs. Brand image plays an important role in building the confidence of the investors. An attempt has been made by the authors to find out what the respondents think about the brand image of the sample companies. In this framework, the authors have framed the above hypothesis and have applied Pearson's Chi-square test to assess whether the mutual fund investors have good brand image about the sample mutual fund companies or not. The primary survey results of investors based on brand image and investors who invest regularly in the sample companies are used to compute the Chi-square.

This broad hypothesis is further divided in to three categories as given in the following paragraphs.

1. The individual investor's selection of HDFC mutual funds is based on his perception about the funds in terms of brand image.

Now let us observe the following tables.

Table 10.17
Brand Image of HDFC Mutual Fund - Observed Frequencies

Investors opinion		*Details*	*Investors who invest regularly in – HDFC Mutual Fund*		*Total*
			Yes	**No**	
Good brand image - HDFC Mutual Fund	**Yes**	Count	**61**	**19**	**80**
		% within Good brand image - HDFC Mutual Fund	76.3%	23.8%	100.0%

Investors opinion		*Details*	*Investors who invest regularly in - HDFC Mutual Fund*		*Total*
	No	Count	**13**	**32**	**45**
		% within Good brand image - HDFC Mutual Fund	28.9%	71.1%	100.0%
Total		Count	74	51	125
		% within Good brand image - HDFC Mutual Fund	59.2%	40.8%	**100.0%**

Source: Compiled from Primary data

Table 10.18
Brand Image of HDFC Mutual Fund - Expected Frequencies

S. No.	*Investors Perceptions about brand image*	*Investors who invest regularly in HDFC mutual funds*	*Investors who do not invest regularly in HDFC mutual funds*	*Total*
1.	Number of Investors who have good brand image	47.36	32.64	**80**
2.	Number of Investors who do not have good brand image	26.64	18.36	**45**
	Total	**74**	**51**	**125**

Source: Computed from Primary data

Table 10.19
Computation of Chi- Square for Testing HDFC's Brand Image

Sr. No.	*Observed Frequencies*	*Expected Frequencies*	*(Oij-Eij)/Eij*
1	61	47.36	3.93
2	19	32.64	5.70
3	13	26.64	6.98
4	32	18.36	10.13
		2Chi Square (X)	**26.74**

Source: Computed and analysed from primary data

Table 10.20
Computation of Chi-Square test for HDFC Mutual Fund

	Value	*df*	*P*
Pearson Chi-Square	26.746(b)	1	.000
No. of Valid Cases	125		

Source: Computed and analysed from primary data
(a) Computed only for a 2x2 table
(b) 0 cells (0%) have expected count less than 5. The minimum expected count is 18.36.

Tables 10.17 shows the observed frequencies of mutual fund investors who invest regularly in HDFC mutual fund and their opinion about the brand image of the company. This table shows that 76.3 percent investors invest regularly in HDFC mutual fund and have good brand image of HDFC mutual fund as against 23.8 percent investors who do not invest in HDFC Mutual fund. 71.1 percent investors who do not invest in HDFC mutual fund do not view HDFC mutual fund as good brand image as against 28.9 percent investors of those who invest in HDFC. Table 10.18 shows that the calculated value of Chi-Square is 26.74. The degree of freedom in this case is 1 and P is < 0.001. The minimum expected count is 18.36. In view of the above values, it can be concluded that the difference is statistically significant and the results support the hypothesis. In view of the above computations it can be said that the individual investor's selection of HDFC mutual funds is based on his perception about HDFC mutual funds in terms of brand image.

2. The individual investor's selection of ICICI Prudential mutual funds is based on his perception about the funds in terms of brand image.

Now let us observe the following tables.

Table 10.21
Brand Image of ICICI Prudential Mutual Fund - Observed Frequencies

Investors opinion		*Details*	*Investors who invest regularly in - ICICI Prudential Mutual Fund*		*Total*
			Yes	**No**	
Good brand image - ICICI Prudential Mutual Fund	Yes	Count	50	30	80
		% within Good brand image - ICICI Prudential Mutual Fund	62.5%	37.5%	100.0%
	No	**Count**	**24**	**21**	**45**
		% within Good brand image - ICICI Prudential Mutual Fund	53.3%	46.7%	100.0%
Total		**Count**	**74**	**51**	**125**
		% within Good brand image - ICICI Prudential Mutual Fund	59.2%	40.8%	100.0%

Source: Compiled from Primary data

Table 10.22
Brand Image of ICICI Prudential Mutual Fund - Expected Frequencies

S. No.	*Investors Perceptions about brand image*	*Investors who invest regularly in ICICI mutual funds*	*Investors who do not invest regularly in ICICI mutual funds*	*Total*
1.	Number of Investors who have good brand image	47.36	32.64	**80**
2.	Number of Investors who do not have good brand image	26.64	18.36	**45**
	Total	**74**	**51**	**125**

Source: Computed from primary data

Table 10.23
Computation of Chi-Square for testing ICICI Prudential Mutual Fund's Brand Image

Sr. No.	*Observed Frequencies*	*Expected Frequencies*	*(Oij-Eij)/Eij*
1	50	47.36	0.147
2	30	32.64	0.213
3	24	26.64	0.262
4	21	18.36	0.379
		2Chi Square (X)	**1.002**

Source: Computed and analysed from primary data

Table 10.24
Computation of Chi-Square test for ICICI Prudential Mutual Fund

	Value	*df*	*P*
Pearson Chi-Square	1.002 (b)	1	.317
No. of Valid Cases	125		

Source: Computed and analysed from primary data
(a) Computed only for a 2x2 table
(b) 0 cells (0%) have expected count less than 5. The minimum expected count is 18.36.

Table 10.19 shows the observed frequencies of mutual fund investors who invest regularly in ICICI Prudential mutual fund and the opinion they have about the brand image of the company. This table shows that 62.5 percent investors who invest regularly in ICICI Prudential mutual fund have good brand image of ICICI Prudential mutual fund as against 37.5 percent investors who do not invest regularly in ICICI Prudential mutual fund. 46.7 percent investors who do not invest in ICICI Prudential mutual fund do not view ICICI Prudential mutual fund as good brand image as against 53.3 percent of those who invest in ICICI Prudential mutual fund. Table 10.20 shows that the calculated value of Chi-Square is 1.002. The degree of freedom in this case is 1 and the value of P is 0.317. It is observed that there is no significant difference between investors and non-investors about their opinion on ICICI Prudential mutual fund. So the hypothesis stands rejected. In view of the above computations, it can be said that the individual investor's selection of ICICI Prudential mutual funds is not based on his perception about ICICI Prudential mutual funds in terms of brand image.

3. The individual investor's selection of mutual funds is based on his perception about the funds in terms of brand image.

Now let us observe the following tables.

Table 10.25
Brand Image of Franklin Templeton Mutual Fund - Observed Frequencies

Investors opinion		*Details*	*Investors who invest regularly in – Franklin Templeton Mutual Fund*		*Total*
			Yes	**No**	
Good brand image - Franklin Templeton Mutual Fund	Yes	Count	60	36	96
		% within Good brand image - Franklin Templeton Mutual Fund	62.5%	37.5%	100.0%
	No	**Count**	**14**	**15**	**29**
		% within Good brand image - Franklin Templeton Mutual Fund	48.3%	51.7%	100.0%
Total		**Count**	**74**	**51**	**125**
		% within Good brand image - Franklin Templeton Mutual Fund	59.2%	40.8%	100.0%

Now let us observe the following tables.

Table 10.26
Brand Image of Franklin Templeton Mutual Fund - Expected Frequencies

S. No.	*Investors Perceptions about brand image*	*Investors who invest regularly in FT mutual funds*	*Investors who do not invest regularly in FT mutual funds*	*Total*
1.	Number of Investors who have good brand image	56.88	39.17	**96**
2.	Number of Investors who do not have good brand image	17.17	11.8	**29**
	Total	**74**	**51**	**125**

Source: Computed from primary data

Table 10.27
Computation of Chi-Square for testing Franklin Templeton Mutual Fund's Brand Image

Sr. No.	*Observed Frequencies*	*Expected Frequencies*	*(Oij-Eij))/Eij*
1	60	56.88	0.17
2	36	39.17	0.25
3	14	17.17	0.58
4	15	11.83	1.97
		2Chi Square (X)	2.97

Source: Computed and analysed from primary data

Table 10.28
Results of Chi-Square test for Franklin Templeton Mutual Fund

	Value	*df*	*P*
Pearson Chi-Square	2.97 (b)	1	.172
No. of Valid Cases	125		

Source: Computed and analysed from primary data
(a) Computed only for a 2x2 table
(b) 0 cells (0%) have expected count less than 5. The minimum expected count is 11.83.

Table 10.21 shows the observed frequencies of mutual fund investors, who invest regularly in Franklin Templeton mutual fund and the opinion they have about the brand image of the company. This table shows that 62.5 percent investors who invest regularly in Franklin Templeton mutual fund have good brand image of Franklin Templeton mutual fund as against 37.5 percent investors who do not invest in Franklin Templeton MF. 51.7 percent investors who do not invest in Franklin Templeton mutual fund do not view Franklin Templeton mutual fund as good brand image as against 48.3 percent of those who invest in Franklin Templeton. Table 10.22 shows that the calculated value of Chi-Square is 2.97. The degree of freedom in this case is 1 and the value of P is 0.172. . It is observed that there is no significant difference between investors and non-investors about their opinion on Franklin Templeton mutual fund. So the hypothesis stands rejected. In view of the above computations, it can be said that the individual investor's selection of Franklin Templeton mutual funds is not based on his perception about the Franklin Templeton funds in terms of brand image.

10.6 Conclusion

This chapter has made an attempt to understand the

behaviour and perceptions of mutual fund investors with reference to the scheme preference, scheme selection and their perceptions in terms of various important factors. Based on these factors a comparison has been made among the three companies.. This chapter observes that the Indian investor is highly risk averse as he looks for the safety of funds, reasonable returns and liquidity. The survey also reveals that the investors are basically influenced by the brand image in their selection of schemes followed by fund qualities and efficient fund management. The Fund houses should therefore keep these factors in mind while designing products to meet the investors' needs and should be alert to capture the changing market moods and be innovative. They should focus on product innovation and development continuously to capture this segment.

The comparison among the three companies based on investors response is also very close because the investors have responded in a similar manner for all the companies. But if we go as per the results of the study, HDFC mutual fund can be concluded as the best among the three from the investors point of view. Next, in order is ICICI mutual fund and Franklin Templeton mutual fund. It is hoped that the survey findings will have some useful managerial implications and these companies should keep in mind important qualities that an investor expects out of a mutual fund.

11

Comparison of ICICI Prudential Mutual Fund, HDFC Mutual Fund and Franklin Templeton Mutual Fund based on Distributors Responses

11.1 Introduction

With the capital market riding on the back of a booming Indian economy, mutual funds have emerged as an important financial intermediary for the investing public. There is a need for the investors to understand how a mutual fund works and how complex investment options are.

The agent or distributor assumes the role of a financial advisor and is the key channel for bringing mutual funds to a large number of investors all over the country. Thus a mutual fund distributor is responsible for selling the mutual fund shares directly to the public. He helps the mutual fund companies to reach a larger number of investors by providing them a large wholesale market. In a big country like India which is geographically diversified, there is a need to have a large network of distribution and the tally of distributors registered with AMFI, the association formed by mutual funds, is hovering near the 45,000-mark[1]. As discussed earlier, the next important objective of this study is to identify and understand the distributor's perceptions, strategies and the influence they have on the investor's decision making which also enables us to understand the distributor's views on investor's perception regarding the sample companies and their performance chosen for the purpose of the study.

In order to achieve these objectives, a separate survey as in the case of investors was conducted. For this a separate set of questionnaire was prepared for the sample mutual fund distributors. The unit of observation and analysis of survey was only among AMFI registered distributors. By using the random sampling method, 50 distributors were selected who were geographically spread across Mumbai city.

The questionnaire had close-ended questions. The questionnaire was very carefully designed so that both the investor questionnaire and distributor questionnaire partially overlapped and were administered by different means for accuracy. The distributor questionnaire was then pre-tested and administered on the sample.

The methodology for the survey was similar to that of the investor questionnaire. They were based on direct personal interviews with distributors using the interview schedule method. The survey was conducted during the period December 2007 to January 2008.

The analysis of distributors has been carried out in order to find out the role played by them in influencing an investor's investment decision. This aspect of study is very important in order to find out the strategies used by the distributors which affects the investor's choice of mutual fund organisation. Now in the following paragraphs, we will first examine the distributor's profile and then compare the sample mutual fund companies based on distributors response.

11.2 Profile of the Distributors

Now the following paragraphs will first discuss the profile of the distributors.

1. Gender composition of the sample

The authors before selecting the sample first collected the list of distributors registered with AMFI across Mumbai city. Mumbai is a very large city and since it is practically not possible to collect the complete list due to geographical and financial constraints, the authors narrowed down the sample from an exhaustive list which is shown below:

Table 11.1
Gender composition of Distributors

Sr.No.	*Gender*	*No. Of Distributors*
1.	Male	43
2.	Female	7

Source: Compiled from primary data collected through questionnaires

As we can see from the above table, based on the random sampling method, 43 male distributors and 7 female distributors were selected. Since SEBI has made it mandatory for distributors to register themselves with AMFI, some of the distributors were even willing to give their registration numbers. Among the above list, there were big aggressive distributors like SBI, HDFC, ICICI etc. and big time private distributors like Kotak securities, Share khan, Bajaj Capital etc. There were also many small private distributors. Infact the authors observed that these were the ones who were doing a tremendous job with limited infrastructure.

2. Age Group

The age of the distributor plays an important role because while giving recommendations to an investor or while planning the portfolio of an investor, maturity which comes with age is very crucial.

Table 11.2
Age of Distributors

Sr.No.	*Age*	*No. of Distributors*
1.	Up to 20	1
2.	21-40	26
3.	41-60	19
4.	Above 60	4
	Total	**50**

Source: Compiled from primary data collected through questionnaires

The above table shows that 4 distributors fall under the category of above 60. They were the most experienced lot who had extensive experience in financial planning and advice. The investors who came to them for advice and dealings had complete trust and confidence in them. There were 26 distributors in the age group of 21-40. These were the group of distributors who had mostly 3-5 years experience in mutual fund distribution. These distributors were aggressive and were mostly marketing new schemes and trying to capture the attention of the investors who look for growth and income. There were 19 respondents in the age group of 41-60. These distributors seemed to possess good knowledge about the different schemes, market timing and the investor's expectations. Based on these qualities, they made recommendations to the investors and convinced them in buying those funds. There was one interesting respondent who was 19 years old. This distributor was a college goer and had cleared the AMFI Distributor's certification and was trying to market the schemes along with his father who was a successful distributor.

3. Academic Background and Distribution experience of the Respondents

Even though SEBI and the Association of Mutual Funds

in India (AMFI) has made the certification process mandatory for any agents as well as those employed in distribution companies and banks engaged in selling mutual funds it is important to find out the academic background of the distributors. The following table shows us the academic qualifications of the distributors.

Table 11.3
Academic Qualification of Distributors

Sr.No.	*Academic Qualification*	*No. of Distributors*
1.	Graduate	28
2.	Post Graduate	16
3.	Professional Degree	6
	Total	**50**

Source: Compiled from primary data collected through questionnaires

From the above table the authors observe that the respondents were mostly well educated with 25 percent of them holding graduation. 16 percent were post graduates and 6 percent were professionals. This indicates that the level of knowledge of the respondents is very satisfactory and all the respondents were technically equipped to influence the investors with their skills.

Table 11.4
Experience in Distribution

Sr.No.	*Years*	*Percent*
1.	Less than 3 years	20
2.	3 to less than 5 years	34
3.	5 to less than 10 years	38
4.	10 years or more	8
	Total	**100**

Source: Compiled from primary data collected through questionnaires

Table 10.4 shows that 8 percent respondents had more than 10 years of distribution experience and 38 percent of the respondents had 5 – 10 years of distribution experience. It was also observed that majority of the respondents were offering most of the financial services like Life Insurance solutions, Other Investment counselling /portfolio management, Securities broker or dealer services and tax advice apart from mutual funds.

4. Methods currently used to attract clients

The distributors were asked to explain the methods they use to attract new clients and retain existing clients for which they have responded as follows. The different methods an agent uses to attract the investors are given below in table 11.5. If we observe the above table we can see that the agents do not use just one method to attract the clients but two or more methods not only to attract but also to retain the customer. 49 respondents have said that they use the most popular technique of aggressive advertising and 43 respondents have chosen media profile to attract new clients and to retain them.

Table 11.5
Methods currently used to attract clients

Sr. No.	*Methods currently used to attract new clients*	*No of Respondents*
1.	Cold calls	15
2.	Telemarketing	13
3.	Personal newsletters	32
4.	Corporate newsletters	35
5.	Seminars with outside speakers	28
6.	Seminars with distributors as speakers	26
7.	Advertising	49
8.	Media	43
9.	Direct mail	26
10.	E-mail	14
11.	Community involvement	18
12.	Referrals	45

Source: Compiled from primary data collected through questionnaires

Another interesting observation is, 45 respondents have reported referrals which indicate that when a client is satisfied with the services of an agent, they refer him to their friends and neighbours. Next in order comes corporate news letters with 35 respondents and then comes personal news letters with 32 respondents. The agents also use the technique of mailing directly to the clients and many of them resort to method like seminars and community involvement. It was also observed that 92 percent of the respondents have segmented their client base by segregating their clients on the basis of different criteria like commission potential, centre of influence, level of attention required and affinity.

Another interesting observation made during the survey is about the segmentation of clients. About 92 percent of the distributors have segmented their clients in to categories such as A+, A, B+, gold, silver, etc., which is generally done on the following criteria and offer different levels of service to the investors.

- Assets
- Level of attention required
- Commission potential
- Affinity
- Center of influence etc.

5. Recommendations by the distributor

Another important aspect which the authors wanted to investigate was to find out whether distributors recommend funds to the investors. This aspect of the study is very important because the level of influence the distributor has on the investor can be determined. Let us observe the following graphs on next page:

The graphs shows that in addition to being the main purchase channel for the investors, distributors are a widely consulted source for advice. Infact, when the distributors were asked whether investors consult them for investment, it was found that about 80 percent of the investors who purchased mutual funds through the distributor consulted them for their advice. Like wise, when the distributors were

Graph 11.1
Whether Investors consult Distributors

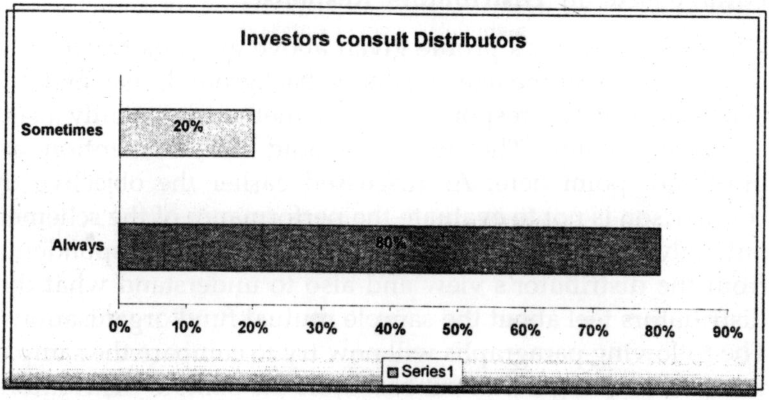

Source: Compiled from primary data collected through questionnaires

Graph 11.2
Whether Distributors recommend Funds to Investors

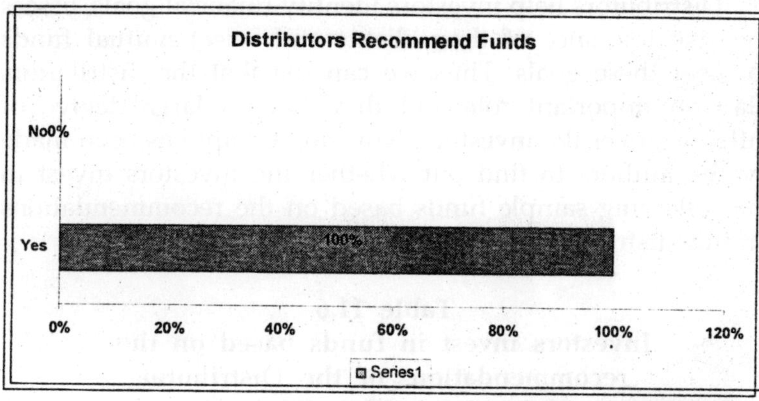

Source: Compiled from primary data collected through questionnaires

asked whether they only sell funds or recommend also, it was found that all the 50 respondents recommended funds to the investors. Thus we can conclude that distributors have considerable influence in inducing them to make investment decisions.

11.3 Comparison of ICICI Prudential Mutual Fund, HDFC Mutual Fund and Franklin Templeton Mutual Fund based on Distributors Response.

The distributor's profile given above gives us reasonably a fair idea about the age, academic background, distribution, experience of the respondents and methods currently used to attract clients. The authors would like to mention an important point here; As discussed earlier the objective of comparison is not to evaluate the performance of the schemes but only to understand the perceptions of the respondents from the distributor's view and also to understand what the distributors feel about the sample mutual fund organisations. The following paragraphs will now try to compare the sample mutual fund organisations based on the sample distributors response.

1. Whether investors invest in Funds based on the recommendations of the distributor

Distributors help investors identify financial goals, assess the risk tolerance of their clients and select mutual funds to meet these goals. Thus we can see that the distributors play an important role and they have a large degree of influence over the investors. Now an attempt has been made by the authors to find out whether the investors invest in the following sample funds based on the recommendations of the distributor.

Table 11.6
Investors invest in funds based on the recommendations of the Distributor

Sr. No.	*Name of the Company*	*Always* %	*Sometimes* %	*Never* %
1.	ICICI Prudential Mutual Fund	52	46	2
2.	HDFC Mutual Fund	51	46	2
3.	Franklin Templeton Mutual Fund	48	50	2

Source: Compiled from primary data collected through questionnaires

The above table shows that one half of the distributors have said that the investors who invest in the funds invest based on their recommendations only. The figure shows that 52 percent of the distributors have said that the investors always invest in sample funds, 46 percent have said that they invest only sometimes and only 2 percent respondents have said that they never invest based on their recommendations in the case of ICICI Prudential mutual fund. In the case of HDFC mutual fund 51 percent respondents have said investors always invest, 46 percent have said the investors sometimes invest and 2 percent respondents have said they never invest and the figures are 48 percent, 50 percent and 2 percent respectively in the case of Franklin Templeton mutual fund. So it can be concluded that comparison on this basis is difficult because half the respondents feel that their recommendations are accepted in the case of all the companies and the other half feels that even though they give recommendations the investors use their own judgement.

Table 11.7
Whether investors redeem/sell funds based on the recommendations of the Distributor

Sr. No.	*Name of the Company*	*Always* %	*Sometimes* %	*Never* %
1.	ICICI Prudential Mutual Fund	42	49	8
2.	HDFC Mutual Fund	45	46	9
3.	Franklin Templeton Mutual Fund	46	46	6

Source: Compiled from primary data collected through questionnaires

Advice on when an investor must invest in a mutual fund is available from many sources but it takes a certain degree of expertise and proficiency to sell or redeem the mutual fund investment at the right time. Since this is the dilemma that many investors face with, the authors have attempted to find out whether the investors sell their funds based on the recommendations of the distributor when they go through him. From the above table we can see that here also, all the three companies have scored fairly equal except for a very minor difference. Those respondents who have opted for always sell or redeem (42 percent in the case of ICICI Prudential mutual fund, 45 percent in the case of HDFC mutual funds and 46 percent in the case of Franklin Templeton mutual funds) are the group of distributors who have an influence over the investors and are able to convince the investors and they have greater influence over them.

Table 11.8

Whether Investors invest in the same Mutual Funds in spite of a very bad investment experience

Sr. No.	*Name of the Company*	*Always* %	*Sometimes* %	*Never* %
1.	HDFC Mutual Fund	34	62	4
2.	ICICI Prudential Mutual Fund	32	64	4
3.	Franklin Templeton Mutual Fund	34	62	4

Source: Compiled from primary data collected through questionnaires

The above table shows that even after a very bad investment experience, investors have approached the distributors and consulted them whether to invest again in the same fund or not. This shows us that the investors have a good opinion on these companies which has made them go back to the distributors they trust, to help them to invest in these companies even after a very bad investment experience. Only 4 percent of distributors have said that the investor never invests again in all the three companies after a bad investment experience. On a comparative note, the authors feel that all the three companies are equally good.

2. *Whether Distributors have Good Brand Image about the Company*

Creating a brand identity is the process of differentiating a product/company in the minds of its customers. Many fund companies have attempted to attach trust and confidence in the fund company to the brand identity. Brand image is the linking of favourable associations to the brand in customer memory. The distributor is a person who plays a major role in linking both the parties and enhances the brand image of the company. Even though this duty is one of their obligations towards the company, individually every distributor will have some perception about the brand image of the company. So an attempt has been made by the authors to find out 'what the respondents think about the brand image of the sample companies'.

Table 11.9
Whether Distributors have Good Brand Image about the Company

Sr. No.	*Name of the Company*	*Good Brand ImageYes-%*	*Good Brand Image No-%*
1.	ICICI Prudential Mutual Fund	63	37
2.	HDFC Mutual Fund	76	24
3.	Franklin Templeton Mutual Fund	52	48

Source: Compiled from primary data collected through questionnaires

The data collected from the respondents is shown in the table above. 76 percent distributors feel that comparatively HDFC mutual fund has a very good brand image and is very popular among the investors. An interesting observation has to be mentioned here. When the respondents were asked the same question, the response was the same. This shows HDFC mutual fund has managed to win the confidence of both the distributors and the investors. Next in ranking comes ICICI Prudential mutual fund with 63 percent followed by Franklin Templeton mutual fund with 52 percent distributors feeling that the company has a good brand image.

Graph 11.3
Whether Distributors have Good Brand Image about the Company

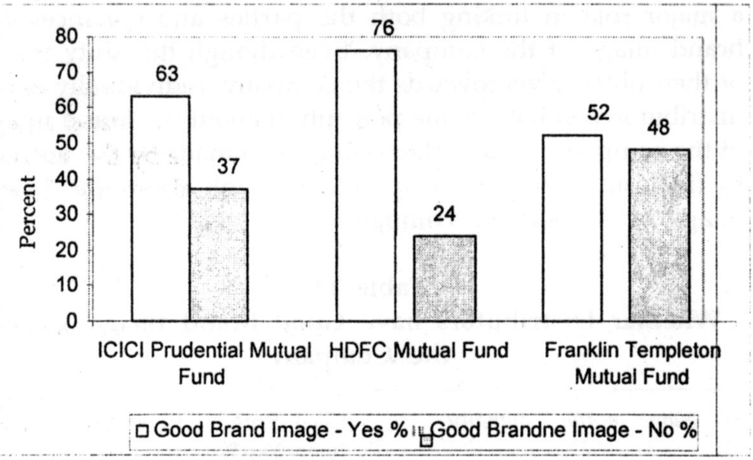

Source: Compiled from primary data collected through questionnaires

Table 11.10
Whether the funds offer high returns - Response of Distributors

S. No.	*Name of the Company*	*Yes%*	*No%*
1.	ICICI Prudential Mutual Fund	21	79
2.	HDFC Mutual Fund	22	78
3.	Franklin Templeton Mutual Fund	25	75

Source: Compiled from primary data collected through questionnaires

When the distributors were asked whether the funds offer high returns, 79 percent of the distributors in the case of ICICI Prudential mutual fund, 78 percent of the distributors in the case of HDFC mutual fund and 75 percent of the distributors in the case of Franklin Templeton mutual fund have said that the funds do not offer high returns but reasonable returns that match the expectations of the investors. Funds which promise higher returns generally have higher risks. The distributors in this case appeared very loyal to the company and said only schemes which claim to offer high returns have shown high returns which is 21 percent in the case of ICICI mutual funds, 22 percent in the case of HDFC mutual funds and 25 percent in the case of Franklin Templeton mutual funds.

3. *Response of Distributors who feel that the funds perform consistently*

The distributors appeared very diplomatic in giving feed back about the funds that offer high returns. So the authors wanted to find out in the survey about the consistency of fund performance and whether past performance can be interpreted as a reliable indicator of future performance.

Table 11.11
Response of Distributors who feel that the funds perform consistently

Sr. No.	*Name of the Company*	*Always%*	*Sometimes%*
1.	ICICI Prudential Mutual Fund	21	79
2.	HDFC Mutual Fund	29	71
3.	Franklin Templeton Mutual Fund	25	75

Source: Compiled from primary data collected through questionnaires

The distributors felt that all the fund managers of the above companies have the ability to perform consistently better than others. 79 percent of the distributors feel that funds perform consistently only sometimes while 21 percent have felt that the fund is always a consistent performer. In the case of HDFC mutual fund, 29 percent have said that the funds always perform consistently and 71 percent perform only sometimes. On the other hand 25 percent respondents have felt that Franklin Templeton has performed consistently always and 75 percent have felt, it performs consistently only sometimes. One part of this research has already examined the track records of funds for a five year period so the figures shown above are the perceptions of the distributors and not the findings of the performance analysis carried out by the authors.

4. Response of Distributors who think Funds offer professional fund management services

Mutual funds are managed by individuals or groups who monitor investments continuously and have access to research and resources that most individual investors do not. They are experts in monitoring economic conditions and their impact on the fund's holdings. The experienced professionals work to pursue the fund's objectives in the best interest of the fund's shareholders. In order to find out the satisfactory level of the fund management services from the distributors point of view the respondents were asked about it and the responses are given below:

Table 11.12
Response of Distributors who think Funds offer professional fund management services

Sr. No.	*Name of the Company*	*Good%*	*Fair%*
1.	ICICI Prudential Mutual Fund	16	82
2.	HDFC Mutual Fund	20	80
3.	Franklin Templeton Mutual Fund	24	76

Source: Compiled from primary data collected through questionnaires

Almost 82 percent of the distributors in the case of ICICI Prudential mutual fund, 80 percent in the case of HDFC Mutual funds and 76 percent in the case of Franklin Templeton Mutual funds have said that the companies reasonably offer fair professional fund management services and the investors are in general satisfied with this aspect of the company.

Not only that almost 84 percent respondents have said that ICICI Prudential mutual fund is an investor friendly company, 88 percent feel the same about HDFC mutual and 86 percent have said the Franklin Templeton is very investor friendly. So even on these grounds the companies have scored similarly. Apart from the companies making sincere effort in designing investor friendlyproducts, continuous regulatory reforms and oversight by SEBI has no doubt been instrumental in making mutual funds more transparent and investor friendly.

Table 11.13
Distributors views on funds that are better performers than other Private, Public and Foreign Mutual Funds

Sr.No.	*Name of the Company*	*Better%*	*Not Better%*
1.	ICICI Prudential Mutual Fund	92	8
2.	HDFC Mutual Fund	92	8
3.	Franklin Templeton Mutual Fund	89	11

Source: Compiled from primary data collected through questionnaires

In order to find out whether the sample companies are better performers than other private, public and foreign mutual funds, the respondents were asked their opinion in this regard and the figures given above very clearly convey the fact that the 92 percent distributors both in the case of HDFC mutual fund and ICICI mutual fund are of the opinion that these companies are better performers than other private, public and private mutual funds .Franklin Templeton is only slightly behind the above two companies with 89 percent. At the same time when the respondents were asked to express their views on the current state and future state of mutual fund industry, 90 percent and 88 percent of the respondents

Graph 11.4
Distributors views on funds that are better performers than other Private, Public and Foreign Mutual Funds

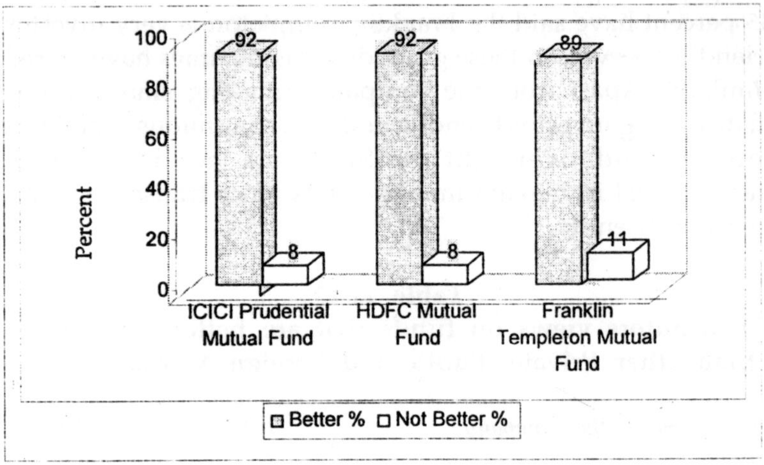

Source: Compiled from primary data collected through questionnaires

respectively have expressed full satisfaction and foresee a very bright future for Indian mutual funds.

11.4 Conclusion

From this chapter the authors have observed that HDFC mutual fund has scored better than other two companies on all grounds from the respondents opinion. The success mantra of HDFC Mutual Fund according to the distributor's opinion is that it works for the benefit of the investor and at the same time keeping in mind the new market trends, designs products to suit the needs of the investors. ICICI prudential mutual fund is only slightly behind HDFC mutual fund. With little effort, this company can easily overtake HDFC mutual fund. Franklin Templeton on the other hand with its foreign experience has the capacity to excel with its sound infrastructure.

After examining the distributor's perceptions and behaviour, the authors are of the opinion that SEBI should ensure that the concentration of the market operations should not be in the hands of select brokers. SEBI should also frame guidelines with regard to sales practices for the distributors. SEBI should ban distributors who offer mutual fund advice based on subjective or arbitrary information and make stringent norms for mutual fund brokers, researchers and analysts. It should also seek complete information of both the brokers and the clients they are servicing.

Reference

1. Source AMFI Web site.

12

Conclusions and Findings

12.1 Introduction

The Indian Mutual Fund Industry has witnessed unprecedented developments and innovations since its inception in 1966. This book aims at evaluating the performance of Indian mutual fund industry with special reference to Franklin Templeton, HDFC and ICICI Prudential mutual funds. A good research work has to draw valid conclusions and findings of the study in a systematic manner.

In a broader sense, this chapter presents the conclusions and findings of the study based on the examination that was carried out to find the growth and the development of the Indian mutual fund industry in terms of resources mobilised, assets under management and the different products existing in the country. The authors have also made a sincere attempt to examine the profile of Franklin Templeton, HDFC and ICICI Prudential Mutual Funds, their products and performance. The conclusions and the findings based on the performance evaluation of the sample schemes using Sharpe ratio and the observations made from the investors and distributors' survey is presented in the following paragraphs in a logical and systematic manner.

12.2 Objective-Wise Conclusions

Sr. No.	*Objectives*		*Conclusions*
1.	To understand and examine the growth of the Indian mutual fund industry.	a.	This study observes that the Indian mutual fund industry has witnessed major transformation and has evolved out of four distinctive phases. Initially the industry started with UTI as its only player. However, with the entry of public, private and global players, India has not only emerged as a major investment destination but also has some of the best international practices in terms of performance and investor services.
		b.	The Indian financial market is now becoming more sophisticated and complex and the industry has started opening up many exciting investment opportunities for Indian investors.
		c.	The industry has not only grown in terms of number of funds but also in terms of number of schemes, investor base and the range of products offered to the investors, which has eventually made them emerge as a strong financial intermediary and the fastest growing segment of the

Sr. No.	*Objectives*		*Conclusions*
			financial services sector in India.
		d.	The study also observes that many average middle income investors have relied on mutual funds as the one place in the securities industry where their interests were likely to get fair consideration.
2.	To study the organisation, management and regulation of mutual funds in India.	a.	This study observes that in India, mutual funds can be set up as trust only and the legal structure is mandated by the Securities Exchange Board of India. As per these regulations, mutual funds are required to have a three-tier structure of Sponsor, Trustee and Asset Management Company.
		b.	The Asset Management company manages the money of the unit holders and the custodian holds the funds securities in safe keeping. The units are then sold to the investors by the distributors.
		c.	The regulatory framework is very comprehensive and matches with other countries in terms of standards, practices and procedures. It is also observed that there is wide innovation in the

Sr. No.	*Objectives*		*Conclusions*
			different categories of mutual funds and they offer a wide variety of schemes to suit the various needs of investors. The government has also liberalised the policies relating to the setting up of mutual funds.
3.	To study the services offered by mutual funds.	a.	The present study observes that the mutual funds offer a wide variety of services to the investors. Investors have benefited greatly over the years from the opportunity mutual funds offer by gaining broad diversification and professional fund management.
		b.	Some of the leading companies also offer specialised services like Portfolio Management Services, Redemption of units within 24 - 48 hours, switching between units and plans and options. Investor statements, web based services, phone services, call centres, online calculators, and online account servicing.
4.	To examine the development of Indian mutual funds in terms of resource mobilisation and assets under management.	a.	The present study which examined the Indian mutual fund industry found that during the study period, the mutual fund industry registered a significant growth and grew in size in terms of both resource

Sr. No.	*Objectives*		*Conclusions*
			mobilisation and assets under management. Overall the study reveals that the development was found to be satisfactory. The study has found that new avenues have been opened up and the industry is witnessing a transition to a better future.
		b.	The industry is also witnessing consolidation and aggressive expansion of the foreign owned mutual fund companies and the decline of the companies floated by smaller private sector players and nationalized banks.
5.	To understand the inception and growth of Franklin Templeton, HDFC and ICICI Prudential Asset management companies.	a.	The study observes that Franklin Templeton, HDFC mutual fund and ICICI Prudential mutual funds were launched during different phases of the industry. From the time of their launch, these companies have grown significantly in terms of assets under management and variety of products, superior technology and a powerhouse of the best talent in the Industry and have generated long term returns for their investors.
		b.	The study reveals that in terms of size of the funds, among the sample companies,

Sr. No.	Objectives		Conclusions
			ICICI Prudential is in the first position, followed by HDFC mutual fund and Franklin Templeton mutual fund.
6.	To evaluate the performance of the sample schemes of Franklin Templeton, HDFC mutual fund and ICICI Prudential mutual using Sharpe's ratio.	a.	From this study it is found that performance evaluation of sample schemes using the technique of Sharpe's ratio is a better technique than the Average Rate of Return measure as it considers the risk adjusted rate of returns. It also provides an unbiased look into the sample schemes performance. All mutual fund schemes have different objectives and therefore their performance also varies. This resulting measure helps to identify the most "efficient" fund, namely the one with the highest return per unit of risk.This study has found out that top 5 performing funds on the basis of Sharpe ratio method are : 1. ICICI Prudential Short Term Plan 2. ICICI Prudential MIP 3. HDFC MIP Long Term Plan 4. FT India Monthly Income Plan 5. Templeton India-STIP

Sr. No.	Objectives	Conclusions
		b. A look at the top ranking funds during the study period shows that ICICI Prudential Short Term Plan has emerged as the best performer among all the sample schemes.

12.3 General Conclusions of the Study

1. The present study observes that mutual funds are collective investments which gather money from different investors to invest in stocks, short-term money market financial instruments, bonds and other securities and distribute the proceeds as dividends. The mutual funds in India has grown tremendously in terms of number of funds, number of schemes, resources mobilised, range of products being offered to the investors and service offerings in recent years.
2. The present study has found the following as the advantages of mutual funds:
   - In India, the mutual funds offer flexibility by means of dividend reinvestment, systematic investment plans and systematic withdrawal plans.
   - These funds are available in small units, so they are affordable to the small investors.
   - The fees charged for custodial, brokerage and other services are very low in case of mutual funds in India.
   - These funds have the option of redeeming or withdrawing money at any point of time.
   - The mutual funds in India are managed professionally.
3. The market regulator, Securities and Exchange Board of India, has already brought about sweeping changes regarding disclosure norms for the industry. As the

regulatory framework moves towards a platform of greater transparency, in a move to safeguard the integrity and viability of this industry, investors would increasingly have a greater degree of comfort.

4. After examining the Indian mutual fund industry, this study has found that the industry has evolved over four distinct phases. There was a period when investor confidence in mutual funds eroded but now with a stable government in place and a conducive investing atmosphere, the growth seems to be satisfactory.
5. With the entry of more and more mutual funds, the number of mutual fund schemes has increased tremendously and competition has also intensified. This has forced product innovation and the private sector mutual funds and foreign mutual funds are coming forward with tailor made products to meet the needs of the investors.
6. The present study has found that the industry has designed variety of schemes to suit the needs of the investors. They are:
   - ➢ Open-ended scheme that does not have fixed units and which is not listed on stock exchanges.
   - ➢ Close-ended scheme with limited capitalisation and a fixed number of units which are traded at a stock exchange.

   On the basis of investment objectives, there are two basic types of schemes:
   - ➢ Equity funds which primarily invest in listed equity to give a higher rate of return.
   - ➢ Debt fund which invest in the fixed income securities like bonds and debentures to provide a reasonable rate of return to investors at minimal risk.

   Some of the popular schemes tailored to meet varying investor needs are:
   - ➢ Income schemes which seek to maximise yearly income
   - ➢ Growth schemes which try to achieve both, capital and income growth.

- Tax-saving schemes which contain various options like income, growth or capital appreciation.
- Balanced schemes that attempt to earn an acceptable return with a low-risk strategy of investing in a mix of equity and debt.
- Money market mutual funds are funds that operate in short-term money market securities like certificates of deposits, commercial papers and government short-dated securities and call money markets.
- Gilt fund is a debt fund investing in government-specified gilt securities.
- On the basis of charges levied on investors, load schemes are ones which charge a fee to cover various expenses like commission.

7. The study found that the robust growth in mobilisation by mutual funds has been due to the following factors:
   - The private sector mutual funds generated good returns.
   - Increased liquidity as industry players have focused on product innovation.
   - The industry players have devised innovative channels of delivery to gain and strengthen their market share.
   - The tax incentives offered by the government have helped mutual funds gain popularity with investors.
   - Growing risk appetite, rising income and high savings rate.
   - An appropriate regulatory environment.
8. The study observes that financial assets show a clear declining trend. More and more investors are shifting towards mutual funds.
9. The fund houses have also launched many new innovative schemes such as power, energy, natural resources and Gold ETFs. Another long-standing innovation – global funds, also debuted in the industry.
10. The study observes that technology has made the mutual fund industry more efficient, cost effective and transparent so the companies are trying to build

technology, infrastructure and quality control processes to provide convenience and customer satisfaction. The mutual fund companies have also developed Portfolio Management Services.

11. The close-ended schemes were always the preferences of the fund managers until three years back. Now the growth pattern shows that the scenario has completely changed. Open-ended schemes that provide liquidity to the investors and their easy entry and exit options have become very popular among the investors.
12. Fund managers are now offering schemes that have features of re-investment plans, systematic withdrawal plans and switchover facilities between the schemes that suit the preferences of the investors.
13. The Asset Management Companies have come out with sector specific schemes also targeting sectors such as information technology, pharmaceutical, brand value and fast moving consumer goods. These innovations are widely being accepted by the investors.
14. Another long-standing innovation - global funds, debuted in the industry. Fund houses adopted different strategies. Some invested directly in global equities; others opted for the Fund of Funds (FoF) route by investing in global funds.
15. Gilt fund envisaging 100 percent investment in government securities were launched making the gilt market accessible to small investors.
16. Another innovative product was to invest solely in dematerialized securities and exchange of any security in dematerialized segment, instead of cash, for the units of the scheme.
17. Just as individual investors in India have started to accept mutual funds as viable saving options, mutual funds have started warming up to an unorthodox category of bulk investor, the foreign institutional investor.
18. The fund managers find it very difficult to understand the expectations, perceptions, beliefs and the sources of

motivation of the individual investors since it varies from one person to the other. This is where the fund managers fail miserably.

19. The Association of Mutual Funds in India (AMFI) which sets the industry standards for all funds operating in India has a certification process and SEBI has made it mandatory for anyone engaged in selling mutual funds – agents as well as those employed in distribution companies and banks to obtain this AMFI Registered Mutual Fund Advisor (ARMFA).
20. The study observes that expectations of the investors play a vital role. These expectations of the investors are influenced by their "perceptions" and humans generally relate perceptions to action.
21. The role of investors is also changing as they become more selective about schemes. This new breed of customers could be called e-customers. Technology advancement via the internet has reduced distribution and transaction costs and speeded up document processing online. The internet also provides instantaneous access to information and enables a switchover in investment decisions, and handling of investors' grievances and so on. As a result, it will improve efficiency and decrease costs.
22. The study reveals that the pattern of investment in India has changed tremendously. The growth oriented schemes and tax saving schemes are increasingly becoming popular among the investors.
23. Many mutual funds organisations believe that the agent's play an important role in influencing the investor.
24. The future of Indian mutual fund market depends to a large extent on the various initiatives taken and the policies framed by the government and the regulators towards the development of this market, but one thing is sure that in future mutual funds are here to stay, sustain and grow.

12.4 Specific Conclusions about the profile of ICICI Prudential Mutual Fund, HDFC Mutual Fund and Franklin Templeton Mutual Fund

1. This study observes that ICICI Prudential Asset Management Company Limited is a joint venture between ICICI Bank and Prudential Plc. set up with the key objective of providing mutual fund products to suit a variety of investment needs of Indian investors.
2. ICICI Prudential Asset Management Company is the largest asset management company in the private sector and the second largest in the mutual fund industry in India.
3. ICICI Prudential Asset Management Company has forged a position of pre-eminence in the Indian Mutual Fund industry as one of the largest companies in the country with its consistent long term performance, innovative products, superior technology and a powerhouse of the best talent in the Industry and has generated long term returns for its investors.
4. It has been observed that ICICI Prudential's bottom up and rigorous process driven approach to managing funds coupled with strict control measures has ensured consistent product performance over the years.
5. The study reveals that ICICI Prudential mutual fund has emerged as the most popular brand in the country. The advertisement campaign launched by the company on several well-known and popular channels of television has also been well acknowledged by the investors, and its advertising in the past has won numerous accolades and mentions, such as the 2001 Abby Award for Best Internet Advertising.
6. The study reveals that ICICI Prudential mutual fund has established a multi-channel approach in order to distribute its various products and the company's operations have been fine-tuned to meet competition. The company also educates and trains the agents and distributors to understand customer requirements and counsel them accordingly.

7. The study also reveals that ICICI Prudential mutual fund follows the customer- centric approach and for this the company gives more importance to understand customer requirements. The company also commenced the Portfolio Management Services (PMS) on a discretionary and non-discretionary basis.
8. The company has institutionalized real time brand awareness monitors and has undertaken usage and attitude studies on investment options. Using various media effectively has been the hallmark of ICICI Prudential's advertising campaigns.
9. The company is also tapping new investor segments to boost business such as daily wage earners and other unorganized sector workers – by offering them SIPs for very nominal amounts in their debt and liquid fund schemes.
10. This study observes that HDFC Limited and Standard Life Investments Limited are the sponsors of HDFC Mutual Fund and is one of the dominant players in the mutual funds space recognized for its high level of ethical and professional conduct and a commitment towards enhancing investors' interest.
11. The study reveals that HDFC Mutual Fund has solid infrastructure and the company also does the required research and analysis, based on which the investors can invest profitably and need not worry about the market swings.
12. From the examination of the profile of HDFC Mutual Fund, it is observed that HDFC Mutual fund is called as a Star Performer. It has been a consistent performer and the age-old brand image has helped them find trustworthiness in the minds of the investors.
13. The study reveals that the company also commenced portfolio management activities and believes that the employees are important stakeholders in the growth and development of the organization.
14. The study observes that HDFC Mutual Fund recognizes their distributors as the most important link between

the investors and the company. It has also launched country's first-ever mutual fund service to enable investors to buy and sell mutual fund units through automatic teller machines (ATMs). The company has also tied up with Union Bank of India to distribute its products across India.

15. HDFC Mutual Fund has witnessed significant growth in the past few years. An important reason for HDFC Mutual fund's success is that the company always tries to give the investors long-term benefits by constantly reviewing the markets for new trends and by identifying new growth sectors and by offering innovative products.
16. This study which examined the profile of Franklin Templeton Asset Management Company sponsored by Templeton International Inc., has found that even though this company is not among the top five best funds of the country, it is very popular among the investors because of the consistent returns delivered by their schemes.
17. It has been found that after acquiring Pioneer-ITI, to expand its operations, Franklin Templeton has been launching new schemes and it is also one of the biggest players on the equity side in the Indian mutual fund industry.
18. Franklin Templeton follows a rigorous risk management process, which includes a dedicated risk manager who works closely with the investment teams in monitoring and evaluating the performance of the schemes.
19. Templeton mutual fund has also established a multi-channel approach to the distribution of its various products it has been regularly tying-up with banks for the distribution of its mutual fund products. This has given the company products accessibility across the country.
20. The study reveals that most important reason for the success of Franklin Templeton can be attributed to the talented local management across all functions of the organisation in India. Not only that it has adapted its

international products, processes and practices to suit Indian investors.

21. Another important observation of sample schemes of the companies shows that sector allocation plays a major role. The fund managers who have cautiously selected the sectors have shown good performance.
22. On examination of the profile of the sample schemes in chapter 5,6 and 7, the following interesting observations were made by the authors.
    - ICICI Prudential Dynamic Plan - A look at the allocation strategy clearly indicates that the strategy is generally based on liquidity in the market, return potential and market valuation at that time.
    - ICICI Prudential Growth plan-Due to high inflation and volatility, the schemes performance was not satisfactory.
    - ICICI Prudential Index fund- serves the investors by holding a portfolio comprised of well-managed diversified equity funds with proven track records across parameters and time frames.
    - ICICI Prudential Tax plan has under-performed its category only few times and during those times it has also recovered very quickly.
    - ICICI MIP has continuously outperformed its bench mark and has shown a satisfactory performance.
    - ICICI STP has shown remarkable performance since its inception.
    - ICICI Balanced fund has consistently been delivering an above average return.
    - HDFC Growth fund despite having a decent corpus size, active fund management style and a good brand name has failed to match the expectations of the investing people.
    - HDFC Index fund has underperformed its benchmark returns. Even the peer average has been very unsatisfactory. During the study period, the five year return has continuously shown underperformance which reflects the market scenario.

- ➢ HDFC Equity has not only outpaced the indices, but also a host of peer funds. This remains one of the best performing funds in its category. The portfolio is characterized by concentrated stock and sectoral holdings.
- ➢ HDFC MIP has always stood on the top across all selected time frames.
- ➢ Templeton India Growth Fund has outperformed its benchmark for two years during 2004 and 2005. But 2006 and 2007 has not been a satisfactory year because of the sudden fall in returns.
- ➢ Franklin India Tax shield is an average performer and has consistently outperformed its benchmark.
- ➢ Templeton India Government Securities Fund has under performed the benchmark and has not matched the expectations of the investors.
- ➢ The fund manager of FT India Balanced Fund has succeeded in striking an optimum balance between growth and stability, by maintaining a diversified portfolio of equities and managing interest rate movements and credit risk on the fixed income component.

23. On examination of the ICICI Prudential, HDFC and Franklin Templeton's sample schemes which includes four equity schemes, four debt schemes and one balanced scheme from each company, where only the growth options were considered, the performance of the schemes on the basis of Rate of Return method in comparison with its benchmark without considering risk differed from the results that was computed on the basis of Sharpe ratio which considered risk adjusted returns.
24. On examination of the performance of the sample companies on the basis of simple comparison of average returns against their average benchmark returns, where the risk factor is not considered during the five year study period, the following results were observed across the different categories of schemes.

- An observation of the sample schemes from the equity category shows that ICICI Prudential Tax Saver is the topper and has outperformed its benchmark consistently.
- The worst performer in the Equity category is HDFC Index fund.
- An observation of the sample schemes from the Debt category shows that ICICI Prudential Short Term Plan is the best performer.
- The worst performer in the Debt category is ICICI Prudential Gilt Fund.
- An observation of the sample schemes from the balanced scheme category shows that all the three schemes of the sample companies have performed satisfactorily.

12.5 Specific Conclusions relating to the Sharpe's performance evaluation technique

1. Higher returns or a rapidly appreciating NAV do not necessarily mean that the fund is a good performer. A well-managed fund should be a consistent performer and it should have the ability to outperform the peers and the benchmarks over different periods of time.
2. This study observes that a good performance evaluation technique for mutual funds should always consider the risk adjusted returns and not the returns alone. For this purpose, the performance evaluation of the sample schemes were carried out using the Sharpe Ratio in this study and it was observed that on an average the risk adjusted return computed on the basis of Sharpe ratio for majority of the sample schemes outperformed their benchmark ratios.
3. This study observes that the speciality of Sharpe ratio is that it brings different schemes on an even level, and it helps the investors to find out whether the excess returns earned are due to smart investment decisions, or due to excess risk undertaken by the fund manager. If investors only look at the return and volatility figures

given by the standard deviation of the scheme, the decision-making process becomes tough, as it is difficult to interpret how the various schemes stand with respect to each other

4. This study has found that by using the technique of Sharpe's ratio, when the performance of the sample schemes was computed ICICI Prudential Short Term Plan surfaced to the top position.
5. The study observes that there is no statistical difference in performance of the Sharpe ratios of the sample schemes and Sharpe ratios of their respective benchmarks.
6. Out of the 27 sample schemes, the best five performers based on Sharpe's measure on the basis of their ranks are:
   a. ICICI Prudential Short Term Plan
   b. ICICI Prudential MIP
   c. HDFC MIP Long Term Plan
   d. FT India Monthly Income Plan
   e. Templeton India-STIP
6. The Monthly Income Plans of all the three sample companies have also performed very satisfactorily and the Sharpe ratios of these funds have outperformed their benchmark ratios with a decent margin.
7. Among the 27 sample schemes, the schemes that showed margins of huge difference and displayed poor performance against their benchmarks are:
   1. HDFC Income Fund
   2. ICICI Prudential Gilt fund
   3. Templeton India Growth Fund
   4. HDFC Index Fund
   5. Templeton India Govt. Sec. Fund TP - Growth
   6. HDFC Gilt fund
8. ICICI Prudential Growth Fund and HDFC Growth Fund have outperformed their bench mark ratios in the growth fund category. Templeton India Growth fund has underperformed in this category when compared to its competitors and the Sharpe ratio is below its benchmark ratio when compared to its peers.

9. HDFC equity fund is the best performer in the Equity category followed by ICICI Prudential Dynamic plan. Templeton India equity income fund is in the third place but still has managed to outperform its benchmark. So it can be concluded that this category on the whole has performed reasonably well.
10. ICICI Prudential Index Fund and Franklin India Index fund have managed to outperform their benchmark ratios in Index fund category. HDFC Index fund has underperformed in this index category when compared to its competitors.
11. ICICI Prudential Tax saver fund has excelled in the Tax saver category and this scheme has managed not only to time its market effectively but also has allocated its sector very carefully to get good returns.
12. The monthly income plans are supposed to be a reasonably safe option with most of its corpus being invested in debt securities and the remaining in stocks. The Sharpe ratios of all the schemes have outperformed the benchmark ratios of the schemes in this category and ICICI Prudential Monthly Income Plan which is a conservatively managed fund is in the first place.
13. The performance of the sample income schemes is not satisfactory. Templeton India Income fund has generated lower returns per unit of risk than their benchmark and HDFC Income fund has shown a very poor performance.
14. Prudential AMC has delivered a sustained outperformance on a risk-adjusted basis across the fund line-ups in the short term plan category followed by Templeton India Short term income plan and HDFC short term plan which has also managed to adjust risk successfully and outperform their benchmark ratios with their consistent performance.
15. Gilt funds are considered to be in the low risk category as they are invested in government securities but the study observes that Sharpe ratios of all the funds under this category have underperformed their benchmark ratios. This shows a negative picture on these funds.

16. All the balanced schemes have performed extremely well after adjusting risk according to the method of Sharpe ratios and have outperformed their benchmark ratios. HDFC prudence fund is the topper in this category, followed by ICICI Prudential balanced fund and FT India Balanced fund.
17. The study also found that there is difference in results of performance of schemes based on Sharpe's reward to variability method and Average Rate of Return method.
18. Some of the important reasons for underperformance of funds are:
    - Tools
    - High cost
    - Incentives and
    - Investment style limitations.

12.6 Specific Conclusions based on the Investors response

In order to identify and understand the perceptions, behaviour, preferences among mutual fund organisations and preferences among scheme types etc. with regard to the sample schemes (ICICI Prudential mutual funds, HDFC mutual funds and Franklin Templeton mutual funds), a comprehensive survey was carried out by the authors and the conclusions drawn based on the observations made are presented below:

1. The present study observes that a mutual fund should satisfy the investor's "needs and expectations". Generally an individual investor looks for the basic things, they are – growth of funds invested, liquidity, tax benefits, and safety. These expectations of the investors are influenced by their "perceptions" which in turn influence their decision making.
2. The investors play a very important role and their investment decision making affects the returns of the

fund. They also respond differently to fund performance across fund types.

3. The survey reveals that the investors are very cautious about their investment decisions. They have diversified their investments and the most preferred investment vehicles are bank deposit and mutual funds.
4. The survey reveals that investors give importance to fund qualities so the fund managers must keep in mind the following qualities which the investor expects while designing the products:
   - Fund's performance record
   - Fund's reputation or brand name
   - Scheme's portfolio of investment
   - Withdrawal facilities
   - Favourable rating by a rating agency
   - Innovation of the scheme
   - Products with tax benefits
   - Entry and exit load
   - Minimum initial investment
5. Investors in mutual funds are generally motivated by different sources to make investment decisions. This survey reveals that a majority of investors are influenced by the financial publications and the mutual fund distributors in making investment decisions.
6. With respect to investment objectives, it was observed that a majority of the respondents invest in growth and income schemes only. Next, they give importance to preservation of principal. Keeping in mind the investors objective of investing, the mutual fund companies can launch schemes to match their expectations.
7. Investors give importance to brand image, so the fund managers must always keep in mind that brand image and market goodwill generated out of past performance of mutual fund should be maintained at the same level if the company wants to be successful all the time. This study observes that HDFC mutual fund has a good brand image.
8. This study observes that mutual fund investors seem

to have extrapolative expectations. They are optimistic in bull markets and pessimistic in bear markets. They always expect the continuation of past returns. However, many times their expectations are not matched. They do not get the desired returns.

9. When the hypothesis "Individual investor's selection of mutual funds is based on his perception about the funds in terms of brand image" was put to statistical testing, the following results were observed:
   - ➢ The results support the hypothesis in case of HDFC Mutual Fund.
   - ➢ The results do not support the hypothesis in case of ICICI Prudential Mutual Fund and Franklin Templeton Mutual Fund.
10. A majority of the investors are of the view that ICICI Prudential Mutual Fund, HDFC Mutual fund and Franklin Templeton Mutual Fund are better performers than other private, public and foreign mutual funds.

12.7 Specific Conclusions based on the Distributors response

In order to identify and understand the distributors influence and their perceptions about investor behaviour with regard to the sample schemes (ICICI Prudential mutual funds, HDFC mutual funds and Franklin Templeton mutual funds), a comprehensive survey was carried out by the authors and the conclusions drawn based on the observations made are presented below:

1. The present study observes that the agent or distributor assumes the role of a financial advisor and is the key channel for bringing mutual funds to a large number of investors all over the country. A mutual fund distributor is responsible for selling the mutual fund shares directly to the public. He helps the mutual fund companies to reach a larger number of investors by providing them a large wholesale market.
2. SEBI has made it mandatory for distributors to register themselves with AMFI.

3. Distributors have a large degree of influence over the investors. They are considered to be the middlemen who connect the investors and the mutual fund organisations. Distributors are the ones who explain the features, advantages and disadvantages of the funds. This survey reveals that distributors influence the investors to a great extent.
4. The present study reveals that the agents do not use just one method to attract the clients. They use two or more methods not only to attract but also to retain the customers.
5. The methods generally followed by the distributors are given below:
   - Cold calls
   - Telemarketing
   - Personal newsletters
   - Corporate newsletters
   - Seminars
   - Advertising
   - Media
   - Direct mail
   - E-mail
   - Community involvement
   - Referrals

   Among the methods given above, the most popular method used by the distributors to attract the investors is advertising.
6. This study reveals that in addition to being the main purchase channel for the investors; distributors are a widely consulted source for advice.
7. This study also reveals that distributors recommend funds to the investors. Infact the investors even consult the distributors for buying, selling and switching between funds. Thus we can conclude that distributors have considerable influence in inducing them to make investment decisions.
8. This study observes that a majority of the distributors are of the view that ICICI Prudential Mutual Fund,

HDFC Mutual fund and Franklin Templeton Mutual Fund are better performers than other private, public and foreign mutual funds.

12.8 General Findings about the Indian Mutual Fund Industry

1. This study observes that the Indian mutualfund industry which started with UTI as its only player in 1964, officially called as the first phase had 8 funds during its second phase and now has 32 funds comprising of Public sector mutual funds, private sector mutual funds and joint ventures predominantly both Indian and foreign.
2. The industry has not only grown in terms of number of funds but also in terms of Assets Under Management which stood at Rs. 1, 00,594 crores during 2002 rose to Rs. 3.26.292 crores as on December, 2007.
3. Net resources mobilised by bank-sponsored and FI-sponsored mutual funds stood at Rs. 7,258 crores during the period 2006-2007.
4. Resource mobilisation in the private placement market stood at Rs. 1,45,866 crores during the year 2007.
5. The Total Net resources mobilised by mutual funds which stood at Rs. 6 crores during 1972 touched Rs.13, 021crores during 1992-93 and reached Rs. 1,83,917crores during 2007-2008.
6. The Category Wise Assets under management as on December 31,2007 stood as follows
   - Income- Rs. 1,97,342 crores
   - Growth- Rs. 1,92,129 crores
   - Balanced- Rs. 19,937 crores
   - Liquid/Money Market- Rs. 1,12,349 crores
   - Gilt- Rs. 1,975 crores
   - ELSS- Rs. 19,063 crores
   - Gold ETFs- Rs. 467 crores
   - Other ETFs- Rs. 6,674 crores
7. During 1993 the first Mutual Fund regulation came in

to existence. The 1993 SEBI (Mutual Fund) Regulations were substituted by a more comprehensive and revised Mutual Fund Regulations in 1996. The industry now functions under the SEBI (Mutual Fund) Regulations 1996.

8. The Association of Mutual Funds in India (AMFI) which was incorporated in 1995 reassures the investors in units of mutual funds that the mutual funds function within the strict regulatory framework.
9. With mergers taking place among different private sector funds, the mutual fund industry has entered the phase of consolidation and growth. There were totally 32 funds as on December 31, 2007.
10. During the last few years, India's position as a market having potential for long-term growth has really been noteworthy as the Indian economy is being ranked among the top 10 globally (in terms of GDP), and as the fourth-largest (in terms of purchasing power parity (PPP)].
11. Another good thing to note about Indian mutual funds industry is that it has grown at a rapid pace of 16.4 percent during the last 8 years as compared to global growth rate of 13 percent during the same period and the trend is expected to go up further.
12. SEBI's involvement in the financial sector has been a great boost for investor confidence which has resulted in an increase in the total number of individual investors but according to Invest India Economic Foundation survey, there are around 34 million people with the potential and capacity to invest in mutual funds and over 57 percent of such people live in rural areas and this segment is yet to be tapped.
13. However, when it comes to AUM of the global mutual fund industry, India's rank is only 19 which is not very satisfactory. AS per AMFI figures at the end of November '06, India forms just 0.4 percent of the world's global Mutual funds assets under management which is very less as compared to other developed countries.

12.9 Specific Findings relating to ICICI Prudential Mutual Fund, HDFC Mutual Fund and Franklin Templeton Mutual Fund

1. ICICI Prudential mutual fund began in the year 1998, with an AUM of Rs. 160 crores, has since expanded its Assets Under Management to Rs. 56772.58 crores as on December 31, 2007 spread over 40 funds thus making the Company the largest asset management company in the private sector and the second largest in the mutual fund industry in India.
2. ICICI Prudential mutual fund has a wide range of schemes in order to meet the different investment objectives of the investors. The total number of schemes of the company as on December 31, 2007 stood at 358 including options.
3. ICICI Prudential mutual fund has established a multi-channel approach to the distribution of its various products and has today an extensive network of customer service centres in 26 cities and over 12,000 customer contact points.
4. ICICI Prudential mutual fund has been allowed by SEBI to spend up to 6% of a scheme as marketing expense, and the company typically spends part of this allocation on distributors.
5. ICICI Prudential AMC is the first private MF player in the country – and the second overall in the MF industry – to cross the five figure mark (Rs 10,000 crores) in terms of AUM)
6. The total asset under management of HDFC mutual funds on December 31, 2007 stood at Rs.48560.60 crores, and is one among the top three mutual funds of the country.
7. HDFC mutual fund has a wide range of schemes and the total number of schemes stood at 287 including plans and options in order to meet the different investment objectives of the investors.
8. HDFC mutual fund is one of the largest mutual funds in India with an investor base of over 25 lakh.

9. As per SEBI rule, HDFC mutual fund is allowed to spend up to 6 percent of a scheme as marketing expense, and the company typically spends part of this allocation on distributors.
10. The total assets under management of Franklin Templeton AMC stood at Rs.31175.54 crores as on December 2007 and over the years, Franklin Templeton has emerged as one of the largest and renowned mutual funds in the country.
11. Franklin Templeton AMC has a wide range of schemes in order to meet the different investment objectives of the investors. The total number of schemes of the company as on December 31, 2007 stood at 201 including options.
12. An overwhelming majority of 86 percent investors believed that the sample companies HDFC, ICCI Prudential and Franklin Templeton are better performers than the other mutual fund companies.

12.10 Specific Findings relating to Performance evaluation of Mutual Funds based on Sharpe ratios

1. The study observes that by using Sharpe's Ratio method of performance evaluation, 21 sample schemes have outperformed their respective benchmark ratios and 3 schemes have shown negative performance.
2. The average rate of return of all the sample equity schemes shows that out of 12 equity schemes, 11 schemes have out-performed their benchmark indices. The only scheme that has under-performed is HDFC Index fund.
3. The average rate of return of all the debt schemes shows that out of 12 debt schemes, 11 schemes have out-performed their benchmark indices. The only scheme that has underperformed is ICICI Prudential Gilt Fund.
4. The average five year annualised yield shows the average risk free rate which is **5.4** in this study.
5. Out of the 12 equity funds, the standard deviations of 10 equity funds are very high. Only Templeton India

equity income fund with a percentage of 12.70 has shown very low standard deviation when compared to the other equity funds. This means this scheme is less risky when compared to the other schemes.

6. The study observes that Templeton India Growth Fund has a very high standard deviation of 60.28 which shows the volatile nature of the scheme.
7. By using the Sharpe ratio method of performance evaluation technique, it was found that ICICI Prudential Short term plan has emerged as the best performing scheme with a Sharpe ratio of 0.92 against its benchmark ratio of -0.09.
8. The study found that ICICI Prudential MIP has emerged as the second best performer among the schemes with a Sharpe ratio of 1.38 as against 0.63 benchmark ratio.
9. By using the Sharpe ratio method of performance evaluation technique, the study observes that HDFC MIP Long Term Plan ranks third with a Sharpe ratio of 1.36 as against 0.68 benchmark ratio.
10. It was found in this research that HDFC Gilt fund has emerged as the worst performing scheme with a Sharpe ratio of -1.13 against its benchmark ratio of 0.38.
11. The study observes that there is a huge difference in performance of the schemes in both the methods. According to Sharpe's method, ICICI Prudential Short Term Plan stands in the first place whereas ICICI Prudential Tax Saver Plan has secured the first rank in the Average Rate of Return method. This explains the difference in results.
12. The authors made an attempt to test the first hypothesis of the study. The statistical computation of t-test shows that the scheme-index (0.7326) is higher than the benchmark index (0.6046). However the difference is not significant as the P-value is 0.083 (1-tail). In view of the above computed values the hypothesis of the study, Sharpe ratios of the sample schemes have outperformed the Sharpe ratios of the benchmark is rejected.

12.11 Specific Findings based on the Investors response

1. In order to study the behaviour pattern of the investors, both men and women were selected as samples. Out of the total respondents 101 were men and 24 were women.
2. The investor survey carried out covered all age groups and it was found that 46 percent of the investors belong to the service class, 13 percent from business class, 23 percent were professionals, 13 percent from the retired class and rest from other classes.
3. It has been found out that 8 percent of investors have been investing in mutual funds for more than 10 years, 32 percent of investors for a period of more than 5 to 10 years and 29 percent for a period 1 to 3 years. These figures also show the period of their holdings in mutual funds.
4. When questioned about their investment experience in mutual funds, it was found that 52 percent of investors had good experience in investing in mutual funds while 37 percent had extensive investment experience in mutual funds. 29 percent agreed that their knowledge was very limited and they rely on other sources. Three percent of investors were very new and had virtually nil experience in mutual funds and had to depend on brokers.
5. The investment behaviour of the young investors was very different from that of the older ones. The young investor's investment objective was mostly current income or aggressive income and about 30 percent of investors who belong to the middle age group preferred growth and income.
6. The survey also shows that contrast to the old belief, investing starts at a younger age. About 3 percent of the respondents were between the age group 19 and 20.
7. The investors were asked about their perception of safety

of mutual fund investments and it was found that 71 percent investors feel that mutual funds are reasonably safe.

8. Since the respondents believe in diversification, only the investors who have invested in the sample companies are taken into consideration. 75 percent of respondents have invested in Franklin Templeton, 77 percent in ICICI and 72 percent in HDFC.
9. When the hypothesis "Individual investor's selection of mutual funds is based on his perception about the funds in terms of brand image" was put to statistical testing, the following results were observed:
   - The calculated value of Chi-Square is 26.74 and the value of P is < 0.001. In view of the above values it can be concluded that the difference is statistically significant and the results support the hypothesis in case of HDFC Mutual Fund.
   - The calculated value of Chi-Square is 1.002 and the value of P is 0.317. It is observed that there is no significant difference between investors and non-investors about their opinion on ICICI Prudential mutual fund. So the hypothesis stands rejected.
   - The calculated value of Chi-Square is 2.97 and the value of P is 0.172. . It is observed that there is no significant difference between investors and non-investors about their opinion on Franklin Templeton mutual fund. So the hypothesis stands rejected.
10. From this survey, it has been found out that the investors use multiple sources to gain awareness about investing in mutual funds. About 73 percent of the respondents have used multiple sources like financial publications, newspapers; internet etc. 15 percent have relied only on family and friend's advice.
11. With regard to the qualities, which affect the mutual funds/scheme selection the response from the investors, was mixed. 88 percent felt that fund's performance record is "Highly important", while 68 percent felt that the funds brand name is important. Innovation of the scheme

stood at 47 percent for "Highly important" and 46 percent for "Some what" important respectively. But withdrawal facilities and favourable rating by an agency were considered as only "Some what important".

12. With respect to consistency in the performance of the sample companies, 59 percent of the respondents in the case of HDFC mutual fund, 69 percent in the case ICICI Prudential AMC and 51 percent in the case of Franklin Templeton felt that these companies perform consistently only sometimes.
13. About 32 percent of investors prefer Online Investment.
14. About 62 percent Investors view the current state of the mutual fund industry in India as excellent.
15. As regards the professional fund management services offered by the sample companies, 49 percent of the respondents in the case of HDFC mutual fund, 53 percent in the case of ICICI Prudential AMC and 46 percent in the case of Franklin Templeton felt that these companies offer very good services.
16. About 81 percent of the investors in the case of HDFC mutual fund, 85 percent in the case of ICICI Prudential AMC and 76 percent in the case of Franklin Templeton have said that there is mismatch between expectations and reality in the sample companies. This shows us that the fund managers are not able to match the investor's expectations.
17. When the respondents were asked whether they would invest in the sample companies in spite of a bad investment experience, 59 percent of the respondents in the case of HDFC mutual funds, 69 percent in the case of ICICI Prudential AMC and 51 percent in the case of Franklin Templeton have said they will invest.
18. About 34 percent of the investors in the case of HDFC mutual funds, 42 percent in the case of ICICI Prudential Mutual fund and 61 percent in the case of Franklin Templeton have said that they would choose to invest again in the schemes of these companies even after a bad investment experience.

12.12 Specific Findings based on the Distributors response

1. It was observed from the study that 94 percent of the investors convey their objectives very clearly to the distributors. Only 73 percent of the investors ask for the background of the company before investing. This shows that the remaining investors have confidence in their distributors.
2. Further mutual fund distributors were asked to indicate the funds that are popular among their clients and it was found out that Reliance was the most popular fund house, which was very closely followed by ICICI, Franklin Templeton, Fidelity and HDFC mutual funds.
3. When the distributors were asked about their idea of a good performance evaluation, 84 percent distributors have said that all variables are important. The variables that were considered for a good performance evaluation framework are as follows:
   a. The horizon of the investment
   b. The benchmark for the evaluation
   c. Avenues of investment and associated risks
   d. The disclosure polices and the objectives of the investment
4. About 92 percent of the respondents have segmented their client base by segregating their clients on the basis of different criteria like commission potential, centre of influence, level of attention required and affinity.
5. The present study observes that 19 respondents were in the age group of 41-60 years. These distributors seem to possess good knowledge about the different schemes, market timing and the investor's expectations.
6. The present study observes that in addition to being the main purchase channel for the investors, distributors are a widely consulted source for advice. Infact when the distributors were asked whether investors consult them for investment, it was found that about 80 percent of the investors who purchased mutual funds through the distributor consulted them for their advice.

7. This study reveals that only 4 percent of distributors have said that the investor never invests again in all the three companies after a bad investment experience.
8. The study shows that 52 percent of the distributors have said that the investors always invest in sample funds, 46 percent have said that they invest only sometimes and only 2 percent respondents have said that they never invest based on their recommendations in the case of ICICI Prudential mutual fund. In the case of HDFC mutual fund 51 percent respondents have said investors always invest, 46 percent have said the investors sometimes invest and 2 percent respondents have said they never invest and the figures are 48 percent, 50 percent and 2 percent respectively in the case of Franklin Templeton mutual fund.
9. 42 percent in the case of ICICI Prudential mutual fund, 45 percent in the case of HDFC mutual funds and 46 percent in the case of Franklin Templeton mutual funds are the group of distributors who have an influence over the investors and are able to convince the investors and they have greater influence over them.
10. The study shows that 76 percent distributors feel that comparatively HDFC mutual fund has a very good brand image and is very popular among the investors.
11. When the distributors were asked whether the funds offer high returns, 79 percent of the distributors in the case of ICICI Prudential mutual fund, 78 percent of the distributors in the case of HDFC mutual fund and 75 percent of the distributors in the case of Franklin Templeton mutual fund have said that the funds do not offer high returns but reasonable returns that match the expectations of the investors.
12. Almost 82 percent of the distributors in the case of ICICI Prudential mutual fund, 80 percent in the case of HDFC Mutual funds and 76 percent in the case of Franklin Templeton mutual funds have said that the companies reasonably offer fair professional fund management services and the investors are in general satisfied with this aspect of the company.

13. About 92 percent distributors both in the case of HDFC mutual fund and ICICI mutual fund are of the opinion that these companies are better performers than other private, public and foreign mutual funds. Franklin Templeton is only slightly behind the above two companies with 89 percent.
14. When the respondents were asked to express their view on the current state and future state of mutual fund industry, 90 percent and 88 percent of the respondents respectively have expressed full satisfaction and foresee a very bright future for Indian mutual funds.

12.13 Conclusions

It is evident from this chapter that with the growing risk appetite, rising income, and increasing awareness, mutual funds in India are becoming a preferred investment option compared to other investment vehicles. It can also be said that mutual funds have opened up a different dimension of investment opportunities that lead to wealth creation for investors.

There are mutual funds sponsored by public sector banks, institutions, private sector (including wholly foreign owned) and joint sector with foreign participation. The regulatory framework is very comprehensive and matches with the best in terms of standards, practices and procedures. The industry is passing through a phase of consolidation. AMFI, which is a trade body, supports these developments and on its own takes several initiatives in putting in place best standards and practices. The regulator plays a very active role in promoting and ensuring strict compliance of the regulations as well as in developing the industry on healthy lines. The industry also registered a significant growth and grew in size in terms of both resource mobilisation and assets under management. On examination of the performance of ICICI Prudential Mutual Fund, HDFC Mutual Fund and Franklin Templeton Mutual Fund, it can be well concluded that these companies follow a disciplined approach to investing with a strong process orientation that serves as a common thread running through their schemes. Competition has also intensified with the entry of new players. Tailor made products to meet the needs of the investors are being designed by the AMC's. Sector/Specialised funds have become the main attraction of mutual funds. On the whole it is found that in terms of performance also most funds have provided market related returns, many schemes have outperformed benchmark indices and investors started appreciating the performance of mutual funds.

13

Suggestions and Recommendations

13.1 Introduction

The Indian Mutual fund industry has opened up many exciting investment opportunities for Indian investors. The industry has started witnessing the phenomenon of savings now being entrusted to the funds rather than in banks alone. The Indian mutual fund industry has seen dramatic improvements not only in terms of quality but also in terms of quantity. The private sector and foreign mutual funds can be credited with introducing many new practices such as new product innovation, sharp improvement in service standards and disclosure, usage of technology, broker education and support etc. In fact, they have forced the industry to upgrade itself and service levels of organizations.

Competition has been very stiff but still the last five years has been very exciting for the industry. There were some interesting mergers and acquisitions also. Product innovation has taken a new dimension and the focus now has shifted completely to delivery of performance in terms of matching investor's expectations and reality. Even the distributors, registrars and transfer agents, and the regulators have become more mature and responsible and the current scenario in our country has brought with it a fresh wave of opportunities.

For the purpose of exploring these opportunities, few suggestions and recommendations are given below for the different parties associated with the industry such as the sponsors, fund managers of the different asset management companies, regulators, registrars, custodians, agents and the distributors and most importantly the retail investors.

13.2 Suggestions and Recommendations

The present study has made a sincere attempt in evaluating the performance of the mutual fund industry with special reference to ICICI Prudential mutualfund, HDFC mutual fund and Franklin Templeton mutual fund. Based on the observations made from the study, the following suggestions have been made:

a. For Regulators

1. SEBI has, undoubtedly, undertaken a large amount of work on the development of mutual fund regulation in recent years and has worked with AMFI on this and other areas but SEBI should further ensure for better corporate governance, and should bring about transparency in the operations of the mutual fund to safe guard the interests of the investors.
2. Appropriate measures should be taken for funds to make fair and truthful disclosures of information to the investors, so that subscribers know what risk they are taking by investing in funds.
3. Uniform co-ordinated regulations by a single authority should be framed to provide shelter to the investors.
4. Regulations should require firms to maintain and retain records of all complaints received, report how and when they were resolved and report to the regulatory authorities regarding the same.
5. SEBI should ensure that the market concentration activities should be eliminated.

6. SEBI should ensure that the AMC's do not involve in any speculative activities and regular monitoring is required in this regard.
7. It is evident from the study that some mutual funds have not been performing well during the reference period and have incurred losses. The poor performance can be attributed to many reasons such as poor planning, improper fund management, bad market timing, weak distribution network etc. The regulatory bodies should intervene and seek justification from these companies for poor performance and if the poor performance continues for more than two years, they should not be allowed to continue with the weak scheme since they are running business with the hard-earned money of the investors. The regulatory agencies should ensure that the inexperienced and new investors receive a fair treatment and are safeguarded properly.
8. SEBI should also frame guidelines with regard to sales practices for the distributors. SEBI should ban distributors who offer mutual fund advice based on misguiding information and make strict norms for mutual fund brokers, researchers and analysts. It should also seek complete information of both the brokers and the clients they are servicing.
9. SEBI needs to get the distributors under the regulatory scanner. The regulations should also include the distributor getting convicted if the nature of misconduct demands it.
10. Another area that requires to be addressed seriously is quick redressal of grievances and promptness in response to queries. This would infuse greater confidence in the retail investor community.
11. AMFI should ensure that apart from the distributors, all the employees of mutual fund organisation should take up AMFI's mandatory test.
12. Due to operators of many mutual funds, there should be appropriate guidelines for self-regulation in respect of publicity/advertisement and inter-scheme transactions within each mutual fund.

13. Financial illiteracy is one major weakness in our system. AMFI can play a very crucial role by educating investors and by creating awareness about the different mutual fund products.
14. SEBI can also issue guideline to the AMC's and help them in focussing more on investment research.
15. From this study it is evident that Sharpe's performance evaluation technique is most effective when it is used in conjunction with several other parameters and is logically more accurate. The Sharpe ratio can also be considered for schemes across a range of categories to check whether any scheme is revealing any abnormal behaviour. So AMFI can take initiative and insist that these techniques are widely used by the concerned parties to help the investors in choosing the right scheme.
16. SEBI should also bring some performance indicators that will reveal the quality of stock selection of various AMC's.

b. For Mutual Fund Companies /Industry

1. The changes in the financial and economic scenario in our country have brought with it a fresh wave of opportunities. The mutual fund organisations should exploit these opportunities.
2. Mutual Funds need to offer products, which are affordable as well as competitive against low risk assured returns of government sponsored saving schemes like post office saving deposits.
3. From the investor's perspective, mutual funds have emerged as the most appropriate investment vehicle. The expectations of investors have touched the sky with respect to profitability factor. So the sector will now be required to meet the expectations of the investors even as the markets expand, deepen and integrate with the rest of the world.
4. The Indian mutual fund industry needs to widen its range of products with affordable and competitive

schemes to tap the semi-urban and rural markets in order to attract more investors.

5. The AMC's should also ensure that they provide separate fund managers for every individual fund. This will definitely enhance the performance of the funds.
6. The individual investors can be divided in to various segments such as young families with or without small children, middle-aged people saving for retirement and retired people looking for steady income. By this kind of proper segmentation and by targeting the right product to the right customer, mutual fund companies can win the confidence of their customers.
7. Indian mutual funds must trade more actively in the secondary markets.
8. The companies should create an awareness about the SIP options which is always a good investment option for the investors when the market is volatile.
9. The AMC's should focus more on the advertising strategy and also the marketing of the product.
10. The AMC's should disclose information on their investment style, strategies and performance indicators clearly in their offer documents and annual reports. The risks associated with the schemes, risk adjusted return, the costs and expenses of the schemes, the management fees, and the Sharpe ratios with their related benchmarks should also be disclosed. This would help the investors in choosing the right scheme.
11. The fund houses can design innovative products where attractive insurance and investment benefits are clubbed to pull the moderate risk averse investors towards mutual funds.
12. The small retail investors should be better informed about the benefits of investment in mutual funds as compared to alternative investment avenues and they should be offered a choice between low-cost, low-risk and low-return standardised products by fund houses.
13. The AMC's should take the initiative of training the advisors about the new funds from time to time.

14. The company should come up with innovative ways of offering service to the investors at their door steps. This may be a costly affair but will surely give positive results in the long run.
15. Any direct or indirect influence on investors which prompts him to make an investment decision is very crucial from the company's point of view. The study says that 62 percent of the sample investors are influenced by the distributors. The mutual fund companies should ensure that the distributors are well trained to handle an intelligent investor.
16. Another important observation that was made during the survey is 32 percent of investors prefer online investment. Therefore the companies should introduce a more user friendly program to attract online investors.
17. The AMCs must consider reducing the expenses to reduce the burden of the investors.
18. The mutual fund companies should mount an awareness campaign to bring investors into equity funds.
19. Investors must be given a standard prospectus in simple language and also in regional languages prior to investing. The document should include all risks associated with the specific fund, the measures taken to mitigate them, and their potential impact.
20. The NRI market is required to be tapped as the potential for growth is strong. Semi-urban and rural areas can also be tapped for investors residing in very small towns and villages. The objective of these schemes should be to provide liquidity and the mechanism of sale; resale etc. should be simplified.
21. Another area that requires to be addressed seriously is to focus more on the semi-urban areas of India, as mutual funds are currently confined to some of India's major cities only.
22. The product differentiation and quality standards are the key factors to attract an investor. Hence more research is required in this area.
23. The portfolio allocation of the benchmark – proportion

invested in government securities, corporate securities or the proportion invested in securities that fall under various rating grades – needs to be available instantly.

24. The mutual fund companies should device strategies to retain experienced fund managers and address the issues of pressures on margins, pressure of consolidation, innovation and product differentiation and meeting the issues of governance.
25. Mutual fund industry should gear up to face stiff competition from the global players which is expected to go up further in the Indian mutual fund industry.
26. The study has also observed that 15 percent of the distributors fail to convey the objective of the funds clearly to the investors. So the companies should ensure that the objectives are conveyed clearly.
27. The fund industry should design those security devices that protect the identity of on-line transactions of the investors.

c. For Mutual Fund Managers

Fund management is not a science but an art of decision making. Thus the fund managers are the backbone for the mutual funds and they should concentrate on the following areas to improve the performance of mutual funds.

1. Fund Scan - In-depth analysis should be carried out before investments are made.
2. Market positioning is very important. So the fund managers should focus more on market positioning to satisfy the needs of the investors.
3. The fund managers should educate the investors and make them well aware of the characteristics, risk-return trade off in investments in a mutual fund scheme.
4. The long delays in investor servicing and inadequate response to the investor queries should be rectified.
5. Success of mutual funds in the long run would be bright only if the fund managers understand the needs of the investors while designing the schemes. The

schemes should offer flexibility, liquidity and risk adjusted rate of return that suits all categories of investors. They should also upgrade their skills and technology. Hence, more research is required in this area.

6. Since the investors need for liquidity is found to be very high, fund managers can launch more open-ended schemes.
7. The fund managers can think of having tie-ups with organisations where a portion of their salary gets invested automatically in funds. This will increase the popularity of systematic investment planning.
8. With respect to the mutual fund managers, they should identify 'opportunity zone' to rebuild investor confidence.
9. Mutual fund managers should monitor the activities of their agents/distributors to ensure that they do not indulge in any kind of malpractice or unethical practice while selling/marketing mutual funds units. If any intermediary does not comply with the code of conduct, the mutual funds should report it to AMFI and SEBI.
10. It was found in the survey that few investors had stated that they would invest again in the sample companies even after a bad investment experience. This is an important issue that the fund managers have to consider. In order to retain these investors, innovative schemes have to be designed to satisfy their needs and a healthy relationship has to be developed by offering quality post sales services.

d. For Mutual Fund Distributors

1. Distributors should strictly stop recommending inappropriate products solely because the intermediary is getting higher commissions.
2. Distributors should strictly discontinue practices like encouraging, over transacting and churning of mutual fund investments to earn higher commissions, even if

they mean higher transaction costs and tax for investors.

3. Also, when marketing various schemes, distributors are advised to remember that a client's interest and suitability to their financial needs should be kept in mind. The study has observed that 77 percent of the distributors give different levels of attention to the investor's base on segmentation. The investors should be fairly treated. The distributors should give the same level of attention to all the investors in order to attract and retain the customers.

e. For Mutual Fund Investors

1. If the investors are thinking of investing in a mutual fund, they should remember to follow these rules diligently before they set out to invest their hard-earned money.

   Simple Rules of Investing

   - In choosing mutual funds, the first task of the investors is to formulate their investment objectives and identify the time frame.
   - The next step is to identify which type of mutual funds match their investment goals and risk tolerance.
   - Diversify among different asset classes to help reduce risk and potentially increase the rate of return of the portfolio.
   - Diversify among different investment styles to potentially reduce risk and increase returns.
   - Understand the relationship between risk and reward.
   - Maintain realistic expectations about investment performance.
2. The investor should carefully decide on which mutual fund to opt for and to ascertain whether the fund house has a process-driven approach to identify the right investment opportunity.
3. The comparative performance, both absolute and risk-

adjusted, will give the investor an insight into the fund manager's ability to outperform the peers and their benchmarks over different periods of time.

4. The investors should remember not to trust any one fund manager. So it is important that the investor evaluates the fund manager carefully before investing. It is crucial for investors to evaluate the fund house also on parameters like fund management philosophy, investment approach and processes (team-based or individualistic process), before making an investment decision.
5. The comparative performance, both absolute and risk-adjusted, over various time periods vis-a-vis both the benchmark index and its peers will give the investors an insight into the fund manager's ability to outperform the peers and the benchmark over different periods of time. So the investors should take great care in this aspect.
6. Investors must be cautious while investing in a fund that gives higher returns or a rapidly appreciating NAV. There is a lot more to performance than just the headline NAV return number.
7. The investor should look at returns over a period of time and take into account the performance of the scheme not just during the bull phase but also during bear phase.
8. Before entering in to a mutual fund transaction based on mutual fund distributor's advice, the investors should remember that they should not trust anyone blindly as it is their hard earned money.

f. For Researchers

The researcher is of the opinion that there is lot of scope for research in this subject with regard to the various relevant aspects of mutual funds. Some of them are:

- Study on Ethical mutual funds
- Study on Mutual fund investment styles

- Study on Fund manager's decision making
- Portfolio preferences of urban mutual fund investors
- Portfolio preferences of rural mutual fund investors
- Techniques of disclosure and cost reduction
- An empirical study on agency costs
- Investor orientation in designing mutual fund products
- Investment behaviour of rural investors
- Investment behaviour of urban areas
- Various other techniques for evaluating mutual fund performances.

13.3 Conclusion

This book tries to evaluate the performance of Indian mutual fund industry with special reference to ICICI Prudential mutual fund, HDFC mutual fund and Franklin Templeton mutual fund. After a detailed examination, this book observes that the mutual fund industry has exploded and the popularity of mutual fund investing is undeniable. The shift in the preferences of the mutual fund investors towards mutual funds can be attributed to many reasons like increase in returns from mutual fund investments, availability of solid products tailored to meet their financial needs, the gradual change in risk profile of the investors as well as the attempts by the Association of Mutual Funds of India (AMFI) to put in place an appropriate regulatory environment. Thus the tremendous success the fund industry has enjoyed is due to the fact that it has done more than any other financial services industry but in the long run to be successful mutual fund organisations requires complete understanding of the peculiarities of the Indian stock market and the expectations of the investors. Transparency should be followed like a religion in every mutual fund because malpractices, inefficiency and poor performances are usually rooted in lack of transparency.

A major challenge posed before the mutual fund industry would be that of dealing with the decreasing talent pool of the fund managers, pressures of consolidation, margins, innovation and product differentiation and meeting the governance issues, as it is the responsibility of the trustees to ensure that the operations of the funds are managed to the full benefit of the unit holders.

In line with the industry requirements and to match with the best of standards and practices available elsewhere in the world, the regulatory framework and guidelines are constantly updated and made sensitive to the market realities. The regulator plays a very active role in promoting and ensuring strict compliance of the regulations as well as in developing the industry on healthy lines. This has helped to see Indian mutual fund companies/sector from a broader prospective. India now has virtually every possible type of mutual fund product. Indian stock markets have broken all-time records. Investors have been pouring into funds and have been reaping handsome returns.

Undoubtedly, the Indian mutual fund industry which has evolved out of four distinctive phases has come a long way and has never had it so good and there is still enormous scope for growth. Going forward, the researcher also believes that with increasing maturity of the Indian investors, more and more investors would be drawn to the mutual fund sector; investors would increasingly have a greater degree of comfort, fund managers would continuously innovate and deliver relevant products to attract investors and the consumer demand is expected to boom in line with the growing economy. FIIs are more likely to remain dominant participants. Also the quality of financial advice, product diversification, distribution and greater transparency will give positive growth rates for the industry. This certainly portrays plenty of opportunity and there is huge growth potential for the Indian mutual fund industry. Overall the study has found the development and growth of the Indian mutual funds to be satisfactory.

Annexures

ANNEXURE - I
MUTUAL FUND
INVESTOR QUESTIONNAIRE

1. Gender M ☐ F ☐
2. Age ____________
3. Academic Qualification
   1. Under Graduate ☐ 2. Graduate ☐
   3. Post Graduate ☐ 4. Professional Degree ☐
4. Occupation
   1. Service ☐ 2. Business ☐
   3. Professional ☐ 4. Government ☐
   5. Retired ☐ 6. Others ☐
5. Where does your knowledge of investment fall?
   1. Nil ☐
   2. Limited ☐
   3. Good ☐
   4. Extensive ☐
6. Which of the following statements best describes your investment experience?
   a. Extensive. I have invested in a variety of vehicles including stocks, bonds, and mutual funds.

b. Average. I have some experience in mutual funds and stocks. I do my own research but sometimes use the advice of others.
c. Limited. I have invested in mutual funds and a few stocks, but my expertise is limited and I rely on a financial professional to guide me.
d. Slight. I mostly stick with savings vehicles such as certificates of deposit, although recently I have begun to participate in a tax-deferred retirement plan through work.
e. Virtually nil. I am new to the area of investing.

7. For how long have you been investing in mutual funds?

1. More than 10 years	☐	4. 1 to 3 years	☐
2. 5 to 10 years	☐	5. Less than a year	☐
3. 3 to 5 years	☐		

8. What is your risk perception of mutual funds? (Pls. rank the same. (Rank 1-5, 1 being First Choice and 5 being the last)

1. Absolutely Safe	☐	4. Unsafe	☐
2. Reasonably Safe	☐	5. Do not know	☐
3. Somewhat Safe	☐		

9. What is your primary objective for your investment in mutual funds?

1. Preservation of Principal	☐
2. Current Income	☐
3. Growth and Income	☐
4. Conservative Growth	☐
5. Aggressive Growth	☐

10. You prefer investment in mutual funds due to (Rank from 1 to 8 down)

1. Safety ☐
2. Liquidity ☐
3. Flexibility ☐
4. Good Return ☐
5. Capital appreciation ☐
6. NAV ☐
7. ProfessionalManagement ☐
8. Tax Benefit ☐
9. Diversification Benefit ☐

11. How do you invest in mutual funds? - Tick in the box
    1. Online Investment ☐
    2. Investment through brokers/agents ☐
    3. Direct Investment ☐

12. There are many qualities that could affect your selection of mutual funds and specific schemes. (Please indicate importance of the following in your decision.)

Sr. No.	*Name of the Company*	*Highly Important*	*Somewhat Important*	*Not very Important*	*Not at all Important*
1.	Fund performance record				
2.	Funds reputation or brand name				
3.	Scheme's portfolio of Investment				
4.	Reputation of the fund manager / scheme				
5.	Withdrawal facilities				

Sr. No.	*Name of the Company*	*Highly Important*	*Somewhat Important*	*Not very Important*	*Not at all Important*
6.	Favourable rating by a rating agency				
7.	Innovativeness of the Scheme				
8.	Products with tax benefits				
9.	Entry & exit load				
10.	Minimum initial investment				

13. Which of the following are the best sources of information to you that have helped you make your recent mutual fund purchase?
    1. Financial Publications like newspapers and magazines ☐
    2. Family and friends ☐
    3. Meetings and presentations at work ☐
    4. Prospectus of the mutual funds company ☐
    5. Information from the mutual funds distributor ☐
    6. Internet ☐

14. Do you invest regularly in any of the following funds?

	YES	NO
1. H.D.F.C. Mutual Fund	☐	☐
2. ICICI Prudential Mutual Fund	☐	☐
3. Franklin Templeton Mutual Fund	☐	☐
4. None of the above	☐	☐

15. Which of the following mutual fund company do you think has a good brand image?

    1. H.D.F.C. Mutual Fund ☐

    2. ICICI Prudential Mutual Fund ☐

    3. Franklin Templeton Mutual Fund ☐

    4. Other funds (Name them) ____________
    Name any three

16. Which of the following funds do you think offer higher returns?

    1. H.D.F.C. Mutual Fund ☐

    2. ICICI Prudential Mutual Fund ☐

    3. Franklin Templeton Mutual Fund ☐

17. In which of the following mutual fund company do you select schemes based on their performance

    1. H.D.F.C. Mutual Fund ☐

    2. ICICI Prudential Mutual Fund ☐

    3. Franklin Templeton Mutual Fund ☐

18. Which of the following mutual fund companies have been performing consistently?

Sr. No.	*Name of the company*	*Always*	*Sometimes*	*Never*
1.	H.D.F.C. Mutual Fund			
2.	ICICI Prudential Mutual Fund			
3.	Franklin Templeton Mutual Fund			

19. Which of the following mutual fund company do you think offer professional fund management services?

Sr. No.	Name of the Company	Excellent	Very good	Good	Average	Poor
1.	H.D.F.C. Mutual Fund					
2.	ICICI Prudential Mutual Fund					
3.	Franklin Templeton Mutual Fund					

20. In which of the following mutual fund company do you think there is a mismatch between expectations and reality?

Sr. No.	Name of the company	Always	Sometimes	Never
1.	H.D.F.C. Mutual Fund			
2.	ICICI Prudential Mutual Fund			
3.	Franklin Templeton Mutual Fund			

21. Which of the following funds are better performers than other private, public and foreign mutual funds?

Sr. No.	Name of the company	Better	Not Better
1.	H.D.F.C. Mutual Fund		
2.	ICICI Prudential Mutual Fund		
3.	Franklin Templeton Mutual Fund		

22. Which of the following do you think your distributor recommends more?
(Please rank 1 to 3 based on the order of recommendation).
1. H.D.F.C. Mutual Fund ☐
2. ICICI Prudential Mutual Fund ☐
3. Franklin Templeton Mutual Fund ☐

23. In which of the following mutual funds do you think your distributor offers better services?

    1. H.D.F.C. Mutual Fund ☐
    2. ICICI Prudential Mutual Fund ☐
    3. Franklin Templeton Mutual Fund ☐

24. Inspite of a very bad investment experience, which of the following mutual funds will you choose to invest again?

    1. H.D.F.C. Mutual Fund ☐
    2. ICICI Prudential Mutual Fund ☐
    3. Franklin Templeton Mutual Fund ☐
    4. None of the above ☐

25. What is your idea of a good performance evaluation framework of a mutual fund?

    1. The horizon of the investment ☐
    2. The benchmark for the evaluation ☐
    3. Avenues of investment and associated risks ☐
    4. The disclosure polices and objectives of the investment ☐
    5. All the above ☐

26. What are your views on the current state of the mutual fund industry in India?

    1. Excellent ☐ 4. Satisfactory ☐
    2. Very good ☐ 5. Poor ☐
    3. Good ☐

27. What are your views on the future state of the mutual fund industry in India?

    1. Excellent ☐ 4. Satisfactory ☐
    2. Very good ☐ 5. Poor ☐
    3. Good ☐

ANNEXURE - II
MUTUAL FUND
DISTRIBUTOR QUESTIONNAIRE

1. Gender ☐ M ☐ F
2. Age Below 20 ☐ 21-40☐ 41-60☐ Above 60☐
3. Educational Qualification

   Undergraduate ☐ Graduate ☐ Post Graduate ☐

   Professional
4. Which services do you currently offer? Select all that apply.
   1. Financial planning ☐
   2. Life insurance solutions ☐
   3. Other Investment counseling / portfolio management ☐
   4. Mutual Fund dealer/distributors ☐
   5. Securities broker or dealer ☐
   6. Tax advice (no tax returns) ☐
   7. Other Services ☐
5. For how many years have you been a mutual fund distributor?
   1. Less than 3 years ☐
   2. 3 to less than 5 years ☐
   3. 5 to less than 10 years ☐
   4. 10 years or more ☐
6. Are you an AMFI registered agent?
   1. Yes ☐ 2. No ☐
7. Do you distribute all mutual fund products?
   1. Yes ☐ 2. No ☐
8. Have you segmented your client base by segregating your clients into categories (such as A+, A, B+, gold, silver, etc).
   1. Yes ☐ 2. No ☐

9. What criteria do you use to segment your client base? Select all that apply.
   1. Assets ☐
   2. Commission potential ☐
   3. Center of influence ☐
   4. Level of attention required ☐
   5. Affinity ☐
   6. Other ☐
10. Do you offer different levels of service to clients based on your segmentation?
    1. Yes ☐ 2. No ☐
11. Do your clients convey his/her objective clearly to you?
    1. Always ☐
    2. Sometimes ☐
    3. Never ☐
12. Do your clients ask for background of the mutual fund company?
    1. Always ☐
    2. Sometimes ☐
    3. Never ☐
13. Do your clients seek your advice for investing?
    1. Always ☐
    2. Sometimes ☐
    3. Never ☐
14. Do you recommend any mutual funds to your clients?
    1. Yes ☐ 2. No ☐
15. Have you recommended any of the following mutual funds to your clients? (Please rank 1 to 3 based on the order of recommendation)
    1. H.D.F.C Mutual Funds ☐
    2. ICICI Prudential Mutual Funds ☐
    3. Franklin Templeton Mutual Fund ☐

16. In which of the following mutual fund companies investors invest based on your recommendation?

	Always	Some-times	Never
1. H. D. F. C. Mutual Funds	☐	☐	☐
2. ICICI Prudential Mutual Funds	☐	☐	☐
3. Franklin Templeton Mutual Fund	☐	☐	☐

17. In which of the following mutual fund companies investors have sold based on your recommendations?

	Always	Some-times	Never
1. H.D.F.C Mutual Funds	☐	☐	☐
2. ICICI Prudential Mutual Funds	☐	☐	☐
3. Franklin Templeton Mutual Fund	☐	☐	☐

18. In which of the following mutual fund companies investors have invested again in a fund's scheme even after a bad investment experience based on your recommendations?

	Always	Some-times	Never
1. H.D.F.C Mutual Funds	☐	☐	☐
2. ICICI Prudential Mutual Funds	☐	☐	☐
3. Franklin Templeton Mutual Fund	☐	☐	☐

19. Which of the following do you think offer high returns?

Sr. No.	*Name of the company*	*YES*	*NO*
1.	H.D.F.C. Mutual Fund		
2.	ICICI Prudential Mutual Fund		
3.	Franklin Templeton Mutual Fund		

20. Which of the following according to you have been performing consistently?

Sr. No.	*Name of the company*	*Always*	*Some-times*	*Never*
1.	H.D.F.C. Mutual Fund			
2.	ICICI Prudential Mutual Fund			
3.	Franklin Templeton Mutual Fund			

21. Which of the following do you think offer professional fund management?

Sr. No.	*Name of the company*	*Good*	*Fair*	*Poor*
1.	H.D.F.C. Mutual Fund			
2.	ICICI Prudential Mutual Fund			
3.	Franklin Temp. Mutual Fund			

22. Which of the following funds are investors friendly?

Sr. No.	*Name of the company*	*Very friendly*	*Some what friendly*	*Not friendly*
1.	H.D.F.C. Mutual Fund			
2.	ICICI Prudential Mutual Fund			
3.	Franklin Templeton Mutual Fund			

23. In which of the following Funds do you think there is a mismatch between expectations and reality?

Sr. No.	Name of the company	Always	Sometimes	Never
1.	H.D.F.C. Mutual Fund			
2.	ICICI Prudential Mutual Fund			
3.	Franklin Templeton Mutual Fund			

24. Which of the following Funds are better performers than other private, public and foreign players in the market?

Sr. No.	Name of the company	YES	NO
1.	H.D.F.C. Mutual Fund		
2.	ICICI Prudential Mutual Fund		
3.	Franklin Templeton Mutual Fund		

25. What is your idea of a good performance evaluation frame work?
    1. The horizon of the investment ☐
    2. The benchmark for the evaluation ☐
    3. Avenues of investment and associated risks ☐
    4. The disclosure policies and objectives of the investment ☐
    5. All the above ☐

26. What are your views on the current state of the Mutual Fund industry in India?

    1. Excellent ☐ 4. Satisfactory ☐
    2. Very good ☐ 5. Poor ☐
    3. Good ☐

27. What are your views on the future state of the Mutual Fund Industry in India?

1. Excellent	☐	3. Satisfactory	☐
2. Very good	☐	4. Poor	☐

ANNEXURE - III

INDICES FOR BENCHMARKING PORTFOLIOS

1. Benchmarks for Equity Portfolios

1. BSE Sensex
2. BSE 100
3. BSE 200
4. BSE 500
5. S&P CNX Nifty
6. CNX Nifty Junior
7. S&P CNX 500

2. Benchmarks for Debt Portfolios

1. Crisil composite bond fund index
2. Crisil Short term fund index
3. Crisil liquid fund index
4. I -Sec Si-Bex
5. I-Sec Mi-Bex
6. I-Sec Li-Bex

3. Benchmarks for Balanced Portfolios

1. Crisil balanced index
2. Crisil MIP blended index

Bibliography

1. Books

1. Apte P.G., International Financial Management, New Delhi, McGraw Hill, Co., 1998.
2. Auerbach D. Robert, Money, Banking and Financial Markets, New York, Macmillan Publishing Company, 2002.
3. Baid Rachna, Mutual Funds Products and Services, New Delhi, TaxMann Publications (P.) Ltd., 2007.
4. Bansal Lalit K., Mutual Funds - Management and Working, New Delhi, Deep and Deep Publicat.ions, 1997.
5. Batra G.S., Financial Services and Markets, New Delhi, Deep & Deep Publications, 2002.
6. Bhalla V.K.., Investment Management-Security analysis and portfolio management, New Delhi, S. Chand and co publishers, 2005.
7. Bhole, L.M., Financial Institutions and Markets - Structure, Growth and Innovations, New Delhi, Tata McGraw- Hill Publishing Company Limited, 2002.
8. Chandra Prasanna, The investment Game: How to Win, 3rd ed., New Delhi, Tata McGraw- Hill Publishing Company Limited, 1992.
9. Dave S.A., The Challenges of the Mutual Fund Industry, (Edited volume 'The Future of Fund Management in

India' Editor Tushar Waghmare), New Delhi, Tata McGraw Hill Publishing Company Ltd., 1998 pp.15-17.

10. Fischer, Donald E., Jordon, Ronald J., Security Analysis and Porfolio Management, New Delhi, Prentice - Hall of India Pvt. Ltd., 2002.

11. Fisher, Black, Myson Scholes and Michael Jensen C., The Capital Asset Pricing Model: Some Empirical Tests, in Studies in the Theory of Capital Markets, New York, Praeger, 2000.

12. Fredman Albert J. and Russ Wiles, How Mutual Funds Work, New York Investment of Finance, Chicago, Morningstar Inc., 2003.

13. Gala Jitendra, Gala Ankit, Guide to Mutual Fund, Mumbai, Buzzing Stock Publishing House, 2007.

14. Grieffeth, Bill, The Mutual Fund Master, Chicago, PROBUS Publishing, 2001.

15. Gupta, L.C., Mutual Funds and Asset Preference Household Investors Survey, New Delhi, Society for Capital Market Research and Development, 1994.

16. Gupta O.P. and Sanjay Sehgal, Investment Performance of Mutual Funds: The Indian experience in Trends and Dimensions, New Delhi, Tata McGraw- Hill Publishing Company Limited, 2000.

17. Gupta, O.P. and Sehgal, S., Investment Performance of Mutual Funds - The Indian Experience: Indian Capital Market - Trends and Dimensions, Tata McGraw Hill Publishing Company Ltd., 1997, pp.1-41.

18. Haslem J.A., Investor's Guide to Mutual Funds USA, Prentice Hall International, 1988.

19. Haslem John A., Mutual Funds - risk and performance analysis for decision making, Blackwell Publishing, 2003.

20. Haughen, Robert, A Modern Investment Theory, New Jersey, Prentice Hall, Englewood Cliffs, 2003.

21. Hiremath, C. V, 'Directory of Mutual Funds in India - 1997', AMFI & UTI Institute of Capital Markets,Mumbai, 1997 (Compiled)

22. Hooda, R.P. Statistics for Business and Economics, New Delhi, Macmillan India Limited, 2000.

23. Hudson Julie, Issues in Performance Evaluation- (Edited volume 'The Future of Fund Management in India' Editor Tushar Waghmare), Tata McGraw Hill Publishing Company Ltd.,New Delhi,1998 pp. 37-43.

24. Khan M.Y., Financial Service, New Delhi, Tata McGraw Hill Publishing Company Limited, 1997.

25. Kothari C.R., Research Methodology-Methods and Techniques, New Delhi, New age international Publisher, 2006.

26. Kulkarni Vivek, Fund Evaluation at CRISIL, Edited volume 'The Future of Fund Management in India' Editor Tushar Waghmare, Tata McGraw Hill Publishing Company Ltd., New Delhi, 1998, pp. 33-35.

27. Kumaraswamy Naidu G. and Sravana Kumar B., The Gold ETFs-The Nitty Gritty, Mutual Fund Industry in India-An Introduction, ICFAI university press.

28. Kumar Shishir and Sisodiya Amit Singh, Evolving Distribution Models, Mutual Fund Industry in India-An Introduction, ICFAI university press.

29. Jain, P.K., Financial Institution in India – A Study of Unit Trust of India, New Delhi, Triveni Publication, 1982.

30. Jeunemaitre A., Financial Market Regulation-A Practitioner's Perspective', New Delhi, Macmillan Ltd., 1997.

31. "Mutual Fund Year Book-2000", Joint Publication of Association of Mutual funds in India and UTI Institute of Capital Markets, 2001.

32. Ramesh Chandra, Performance Appraisal of Mutual Funds in India, New Delhi, Excel Books, 2002.

33. Rao Mohan p., Working of Mutual Fund organizations in India, New Delhi, Kanishka Publishers and Distributors, 1998.

34. Raju Venkatapathi, Mutual funds in India-Investor's perceptions, New Delhi, Quality publishing company, 2000.

35. Rutherford Ronald K., The Complete Guide to Managing A Portfolio of Mutual Funds, Tata McGraw-Hill Publishing Ltd., 1998.

36. Rowland Mary, The new commonsense guide to mutual funds, New Delhi, Vision Books.

37. Sadhak H., Mutual Funds in India -Marketing Strategies and Investment Practices, New Delhi, Response Books, 2003. Research Methodology in Social Sciences.

38. Sadhu A.N and Singh, Research Methodology in Social Sciences, Bombay, Himalaya Publishing house, 1980.

39. Sahadevan and Raju, M.T., Mutual Funds, Data, Interpretation and Analysis, New Delhi, Prentice Hall of India Pvt. Ltd., 1996.

40. Sankaran Sundar, Indian Mutual Funds Handbook, New Delhi, Vision Books, 2003.

41. Saroj, S., Emerging trends in the Capital Markets in India, New Delhi, Global Business Press, 1991.

42. Scott David Logan, David Scott's Guide to Investing in Mutual Funds, Houghton Mifflin, 2004.

43. SEBI - NCAER, Survey of Indian Investors, SEBI, Mumbai, 2000.

44. Securities and Exchange Board of India, Indian Securities Market: Agenda for Development and Reform, Bombay, 1994.

45. Seth Anderson C. and Parvez Ahmed," Mutual Funds: Fifty Years of Research Findings", Springer, 2005,Vol. 16, 2005, IX, 165 p., Hardcover, ISBN: 978-0-387-25307-7.

46. Sharp, W.F., and Alexzender Gorden J., Investments, New Delhi, Prentice - Hall of India, 2000.

47. Singh, Preeti, Investment Management Security Analysis and Portfolio Management, New Delhi, Himalaya Publishing House, 1996.

48. Sisodiya Amit Singh, Mutual Fund Industry in India- An Introduction, ICFAI university press.

49. Sondhi, H., 2004, Financial Performance of Indian Mutual Funds, an unpublished doctoral dissertation, IIT, New Delhi.

50. Sujit Sikidar and Amrit Pal Singh, 1996, Financial Services: Investment in Equityand Mutual Funds – A Behavioural Study, in Bhatia B.S., and Batra G.S., ed.,Management of Financial Services, Deep and Deep Publications, New Delhi, Chapter 10, 136-145.

51. Tandon B.C., Research Methodology in Social Sciences, Allahabad, Chaitanya Publishing House, 1979.

52. Thomas Susan, "Performance evaluation of Indian Funds" (Edited volume 'The Future of Fund Management in India' Editor Tushar Waghmare), Tata McGraw Hill Publishing Company Ltd., New Delhi 1998, pp. 23-31.

53. Vaid Seema , Mutual Fund Operations in India, Varanasi, Rishi Publications, 1994.

54. Verma J.C., Mutual Funds and Investment Portfolio, New Delhi, Bharat Publishing House, 2002.

55. Verma J.C., Mutual of Merchant Banking – Concept, Practice Procedures, 4th Edition, New Delhi, Bharat Law House, 2004.

56. Verma J.C., Bharat's Guide to Mutual Fund and Investment Portfolio, New Delhi, Bharat Publishing House, 1997.

57. Vivek Kulkarni, Fund Evaluation at CRISIL- Edited volume' The Future of Fund Management in India' Editor Tushar Waghmare, New Delhi, Tata McGraw Hills, 1998.

2. Journals

1. Arumugam, S., "Day of the Week Effects in Stock Returns: An Empirical Evidence from Indian Markets", Prajnan, Vol. XXVII (2), July - September, 1998.
2. Baks, Klaas, Metrick, Andrew, Wachter and Jessica, "Should Investors Avoid All Actively Managed Mutual Funds? A Study in Bayesian Performance Evaluation", Journal of finance, Vol. 56, No.1, February 2001, pp. 45-85.
3. Biswadeep Mishra "Selectivity and Timing Skills of Mutual Funds in India: An Empirical Analysis", The ICFAI Journal of Applied Finance, Vol. 8, No. 5, September 2002, pp. 5-16.
4. Blake, Elton and Gruber, "The Performance of Bond Mutual Funds", Journal of Business, 1993.
5. Blake, Elton and Gruber, "The Persistence of Risk-Adjusted Mutual Fund Performance", Journal of Business, 1996.
6. Chakrabarti Anjan and Harsha Rungta "Mutual Funds Industry in India: An In-depth Look into the Problems of Credibility, Risk and Brand" The ICFAI Journal of Applied Finance, Volume 6, No. 2, April 2000, pp. 26-46.
7. Chang, E.C. and Lewellen W., (1984), 'Market Timing and Mutual Fund Investment Performance', Journal of Business, January 1984, pp.57-72.
8. Chevalier and Ellison, "Are Some Mutual Fund Managers Better Than Others? Cross-Sectional Patterns in Behaviour and Performance", Journal of Finance, 1999.
9. Gupta Amitabh, "Mutual Funds in India: A study of Investment Management" Finance India Vol. XV- No. 2, June 2001, pp. 631-637.
10. Fama E., "Efficient Capital Market: A Review of theory and Empirical work" Journal of Finance, Vol.25, No. 5, 1970.

11. Fama, Eugene F., "Efficient Capital markets: A review of Theory and Empirical Work", The Journal of Finance, Vol. 25, No. 3, pp.383-417.

12. Graciela Kaminsky L., Richard Lyons K. and Sergio Schmukler L., "Mutual Fund Investment in Emerging Markets : An Overview", The World Bank Economic Review, Vol. 15, No. 2, 315-340,2001.

13. Grinblatt, Titman, Wermers and Daniel, "Measuring Mutual Fund Performance with Characteristic-Based Benchmarks", Journal of Finance, 1997.

14. Henriksson, R.D., "Market Timings and Mutual Funds Performance: An Empirical Investigation", Journal of Business, January 1984, pp.73-96.

15. Jain Abhinav," The Consolidation Spree", Mutual Fund Industry in India-An Introduction, ICFAI University press.

16. Jain and Wu, "Truth in Mutual Fund Advertising: Evidence on Future Performance and Fund Flows", Journal of Finance, 2000.

17. Jayadev M., "Mutual Fund Performance: An Analysis of Monthly Returns" Finance India Vol. X, No. 1, March 1996, pp.73-84.

18. Jensen M. C., "The performance of Mutual Funds in the period 1945 - 1964" Journal of Finance, Vol. 23, No 2, 1968 pp. 389 - 416.

19. Kaura and JayaDev, "Performance of Growth Oriented Mutual Funds: An Evaluation", The ICFAI Journal of Applied Finance, Vol. 1, No.1, January 1995, pp. 1-14.

20. Kon, S.F., "The Market Timing Performance of Mutual Fund Managers", Journal of Business, July 1983, pp. 323-347.

21. Malhotra and McLeod: "An Empirical Analysis of Mutual Fund Expenses", Journal of Financial Research, 1997.

22. Malkiel, "Returns from Investing in Equity Mutual Funds 1971 to 1991", Journal of Finance 1995.

23. Markowitz, "Portfolio Selection", Journal of Finance, 1952.
24. McDonald, J.G., "Objectives and Performance of Mutual Funds: 1960-67", Journal of Financial and Quantitative Analysis, June 1974, pp.311-333.
25. Michael C. Jensen," The Performance of Mutual Funds in the period 1945-1964", Journal of Finance, Vol. 23, No. 2,1967, 389-416.Mohanty, P., "Efficiency of the Market for Small Stocks", 2001, NSE Research Paper Series (nseindia.com).
26. Muneesh K. and Sehgal S., "Company Characteristics and Common Stock Returns: The Indian Experience", Vision, July- December 2004, pp 33-45.
27. Narasimhan and Vijayalakshmi S., "Performance Analysis of Mutual Funds in India" Finance India Vol XV No. 1, March 2001, pp. 155-174.
28. Panchali and Jinesh N., "Ownership Structure and Financial Performance: An inquiry into Corporate Governance in Indian Corporate Sector", The ICFAI Journal of Applied Finance, July 1997.
29. Panchali and Jinesh N., "Defense Mechanism in Corporate Control Battle", The Journal of Corporate Restructuring, Vol. 2. (1), 1997.
30. Pendaraki, K., "On the construction of mutual fund portfolios: A Multi- criteria methodology and an application to the Greek market of equity mutual funds", European Journal of Operational Research, Vol. 163, June 2005.
31. Philip Davis E. and Benn Steil, " Institutional Investors", MIT Press, 2001.
32. Raja Rajan, "Investment size based segmentation of individual investors", Management Researcher, 3 (3 & 4), 1997, pp.21-28.
33. Raja Rajan, 1998, "Stages in life cycle and investment pattern", The Indian Journal of Commerce, 51 (2 & 3), 1998, pp.27 - 36.

34. Rajeshwer and Jutur Sharat, "Gold Exchange Traded Funds-Enter India", Mutual Fund Industry in India-An Introduction, ICFAI university press(publication division)

35. Raychaudhuri Arjun," Persistence in the Indian Mutual Fund Market", The ICFAI Journal of Financial Economics, Vol. III, Issue 1, 2005, pp 6-25.

36. Russ Wermers, "Mutual Fund Herding and the Impact on Stock Prices", The Journal of Finance, Volume 54 Issue 2, April 1999, pg. 581.

37. Sarkar Jaideep and Majumdar Sudip, "Performance Evaluation of Mutual Funds in India", NMIS Management Review, Vol. VI, No. 2, July-December 1994, pp. 64-78.

38. Sarkar, J. and Mazumdar S., "Weak Form of Efficient Market", Hill Publishing Company Ltd., 1997, pp.1-41.

39. Sarkar A.K., "Mutual Funds in India: Emerging Trends", Management Accountant, Vol.26, No.3, 171-194, 1991.

40. Sethu, G. "State of the Indian Capital Market" TASMAC Management Review, October 2003.

41. Sethu, G. & Baid, Rachana "Valuation of Asset Management Companies - A free cash flow approach", ICFAI Journal of Applied Finance, August 2003.

42. Shah Ajay and Susan Thomas, "Performance Evaluation of Professional Portfolio Management in India", A paper prepared by CMIE, 10 April, 1994.

43. Sharpe, William F., "Mutual fund performance", Journal of Business 39(1), 1966, pp. 119-138.

44. Sharpe, William F., "Mutual fund performance and the theory of capital asset pricing" , Journal of Business, 1968, pp. 235-236.

45. Sharpe, William F., "Adjusting for risk in performance measurement. Journal of Portfolio Management", 1975, pp. 29-34.

46. Sharpe, William F., "Likely gains from market timing", Financial Analysts Journal, 1975, pp. 60-69.

47. Sharpe, W. F., "Asset allocation: management style and performance measurement.", Journal of Portfolio Management, 1992.

48. Sharpe, W.F., "Determining a Fund's Effective Asset Mix," Investment Management Review, December 1988, pp. 59-69.

49. Shashikant and Uma, "Are Emerging Market Correlations Stable?", The ICFAI Journal of Applied Finance, Vol. 4(2), July 1998.

50. Shashikant, Uma and Ramesh B., "Risk and Return in Emerging and Developed Markets: Some Stylized Facts", The ICFAI Journal of Applied Finance, Vol. 3 (2), 1997.

51. Shashikant, Uma and Ramesh B., "Benefits From Diversification into Emerging Markets: Theories and Evidence", The Journal of Foreign Exchange and International Finance, Vol. 3 (2), 1997.

52. Sisodiya Amit Singh and Bala Bharathi Y., "Arbitrage Funds in India: Leveraging the Derivatives Markets", Mutual Fund Industry in India-An Introduction, ICFAI university press

53. Sisodiya Amit Singh, Reddy Aala Santosh and Zaheer Feroz, "On a Growth Trail", Mutual Fund Industry in India-An Introduction, ICFAI university press.

54. Statman M.,"Socially responsible mutual funds", Financial Analysts Journal 56, 2000, pp.30-38.

55. Treynor J.L. and Mazuy K.K., "Can Mutual Funds outguess the Market" Harvard Business Review, 44, 1966, pp. 131-13.

56. Turan M.S., Bodla B.S., and Mehta Sushil Kumar, "Performance Evaluation of Listed Schemes of Mutual Funds" Management Researcher, Vol. VIII, No. 1 & 2 July-December 2001, pp.38- 66.

57. Value Research India Pvt. Ltd.," Mutual Fund Survey-2000-2001", New Delhi, 2001.

58. Verma J.R., "Indian Money Market: Market Structure, Covered Parity and Term Structure", *ICFAI Journal of Applied Finance,* 3(2), July 1997, pp. 1-10.

59. Verma J.R. and Raghunathan., " What Does Your Capital Cost?", Chartered Financial Analyst, March 1996.

60. Verma J.R. and Raghunathan, "Mutual Funds: Product Innovation", Chartered Financial Analyst, January 1996.

61. Wenchi Kao G., Louis Cheng T. W., Kam Chan C., "International mutual fund selectivity and market timing during up and down market conditions", The Financial Review, Volume 33 Issue 2, May 1998, Page 127.

62. Wermers, "Mutual Fund Performance: An Empirical Decomposition into Stock-Picking Talent, Style, Transactions Costs, and Expenses", Journal of Finance, 2000.

63. Wong, K.A., and Lye, "Market Values, Earnings Yields and Stock Returns", Journal of Banking and Finance, 1990, 14, pp.311-326.

64. Zakri Bello Y.,"Socially Responsible Investing and Portfolio Diversification", The Journal of Financial, Research, Vol. XXVIII, No. 1, 2005, pp.41-57.

65. Zheng, "Is Money Smart? A Study of Mutual Fund Investors' Fund Selection Ability", Journal of Finance, 1999.

3. News papers

1. Agarwal Akhil, "Shock and awe", Your Money, The Economic Times, May 2006.

2. Jhaveri Mitra,"Investing Through Mutual Funds", Times Personal, July 27, 2004.

3. Mulraj J., "Master Shares : A Critical Evaluation", The Economic Times, September 28, 1992.

4. Mundat Johan, "Spread the Good Word", The Economic Times, June 2006.
5. Pai Gaurav, "For Better or for Worse", The Economic Times, June 2006.
6. Punjabi Joanna, "A Basic Guide to Mutual Funds", Your Money Simplified, The Times of India presentation, October 4, 2005.
7. Sachin Khedekar, "SEBI to Curb Mis-Selling of Mutual Funds", The Economic Times, June 13, 2006.
8. Sachin Khedekar, "Mutual Fund Muscle", The Economic Times, June 7, 2005.
9. Sanyal Amrita Chauhan, "ELSS", The Economic Times, December 2004.
10. Sanyal Amrita Chauhan," If the price is right, go for growth", The Economic Times, January 9, 2005.
11. Shankar, V., "Retailing Mutual Funds: A consumer product model", The Hindu, July 24, 1996.
12. Team Finance Insights," If you earn, the fund manager earns", The Economic Times, September 2005.
13. Team Finance Insights, "Compute Risk", The Economic Times, September 24, 2004.
14. Team IG, "Overweight Is In", The Economic Timec, November 2004.
15. Verma J.R. and Barua, "The Ghost Who Haunts", Business Standard, June 27, 1996.
16. Verma J.R., "Misleading Investors with Impunity", The Hindu, May 22, 1996.
17. Verma J.R. and Raghunathan, "For Mutual Freedom", Business Today, May 22-June 6, 1996.
18. Verma J.R. and Raghunathan., "Trial by Bourses Unfair", Economic Times, January 8, 1996.
19. Verma J.R. and Raghunathan., " Reliance-BSE Deal - Ducking the Real Issue", Economic Times,January 5, 1996.

20. Verma J.R. and Raghunathan., " Mutual Funds at the Cross-roads", The Hindu, August 16, 1995.

21. Verma J.R. and Raghunathan., " Malegam Panel Suggestions on Accounting Norms in Prospectuses", The Hindu, August 2, 1995.

22. Verma J.R., and Barua, "How Vulture Funds Can Rescue Indian Banking", The Economic Times, July 29, 1995.

23. Vidya Shankar, S., "Mutual Funds - Emerging Trends in India", Chartered Secretary, Vol.20, No.8, 1990, 639-640.

24. Vijay Gaurav,"Mid, small caps dream in tatters", The Economic Times, June 2006.

25. Vikraman, Shaji, "Mutual Funds performance: The Criterion", Business line, February 13, 1994.

4. Research Papers

1. Chalmers, Edelen and Kadlec, "Mutual fund trading costs", Rodney L. White Center for Financial Research Working Papers, 1999.

2. Fernandes Kshama , "Evaluating index fund implementation in India", Working paper, http://www.nse-india.com/content/research/Paper66.pdf

3. Ranganathan Kavitha," A Study of Fund Selection Behaviour of Individual Investors Towards Mutual Funds - with Reference to Mumbai City", Indian Institute of Capital Markets 9th Capital Markets Conference Paper, 2006.

4. Madhusudan Jambodekar V, " Marketing Strategies of Mutual Funds - Current Practices and Future Directions", Working Paper, UTI - IIMB Centre for Capital Markets Education and Research, Bangalore,1996.

5. Panwar Sharad and Madhumathi R.,"Characteristics and performance evaluation of selected mutual funds in India", Indian Institute of Capital Markets - 9th Capital Markets Conference Paper, 2006.

6. Roy Bijan, Saiket Sovan Deb, "The conditional performance of Indian mutual funds: an empirical study", Working paper,http://papers.ssrn.com/sol3/papers.cfm?abstract_id=593723
7. Sethu, G. "Mutual Fund Puzzle", Third Capital Market Conference 1998. UTI-ICM, Navi Mumbai, December 23-24, 1999.

5. Magazines

1. Mehta Rajan Mehta,"Exchange traded funds", MutualFund Insight, Vol. 3.num 9, pgs 34-37.
2. Pandiya S., "Crash proof investing", Mutual fund Insight, Vol 3, num 10, pgs-20-24.
3. Soumendranath Lahiri, "Still bullish on equities", Mutualfund Insight, Vol 3, 2004, pp. 34-38.

6. Reports

1. Annual Reports and offer Documents of Various Mutual Funds.
2. Currency and Finance, RBI, 1987-88 to 1994-95.
3. Gupta L.C, "Indian share owners: A survey", Society for Capital Market Research and development, 1991, p.92.
4. NCAER Report 2000.
5. Report of the Committee on financial System, Government of India, 1991.
6. Report of the Social Audit Committee, Unit Trust of India, 1998.
7. Reserve Bank of India Guidelines for Mutual Funds, July 1989.
8. Securities and Exchange Board of India (Mutual Funds) Regulations, 1993.
9. UTI Report of Social Audit committee, 1994.

10. Sunder Syama, "Growth Prospects of Mutual Funds and Investor perception with special reference to Kothari Pioneer Mutual Fund", Project Report, Sri Srinivas Vidya Parishad, Andhra University, Visakhapatnam, 1998.

7. Web sites

1. www.hdfcbank.com
2. www.nse.india.com
3. www.mutualfundsindia.com
4. www.amfiindia.com
5. www.bseindia.com
6. www.sebi.gov.in.com
7. www.icicibank.com
8. www.icicipruamc.com
9. www.icfaipress.org
10. www.kotak.com
11. www.marketwatch.com
12. www.crisil.com
13. www.capitalmarket.com
14. www.businessworldindia.com
15. www.thehindubusinessline.com
16. www.indiabiznews.com
17. www.businesstoday.com
18. www.indiatoday.com
19. www.ssrn.com

Glossary

1. Association of Mutual Funds in India (AMFI)

AMFI is the trade association of mutual funds in India. AMFI represents the mutual fund industry at various policy forums, and does promotional and training.

2. Annual report

Report released by fund house once a year that details its state of affairs.

3. Annualized return

The return a fund would have generated over a year on a compounded basis. This method is the best indicator to measure the performance of a fund.

4. Asset allocation

It is the process of allocating the overall corpus to different assets like equities, bonds, real estate, derivatives etc.

5. Asset Management Company (AMC)

A Company registered with SEBI, which takes investment/divestment decisions for the mutual fund, and manages the assets of the mutual fund.

6. Balanced fund

A scheme that invests substantially in both debt and equity.

7. Benchmark

A yardstick against which the returns generated by an assets is evaluated.

8. Closed-ended fund:

A fund where investors have to commit their funds for a particular period. Closed-ended funds have to necessarily be listed on recognized stock exchanges in India, as it provides and exit route for the investor.

9. Corpus

The amount of money available with a scheme for investing. If already invested, the corpus is the current value of the scheme's portfolio.

10. Custodian

The entity that holds a mutual fund's securities on its behalf for a fee.

11. Debt funds

Schemes that invest only in debt securities with the objective of generating a steady income while preserving capital. Based on the kind, and mix, of debt securities they invest in, debt funds are broadly classified as income funds, gilt funds and liquid funds.

12. Discount/Premium to NAV

The percentage difference between the market price of a unit and its NAV. If a scheme's market price is higher than its NAV, it is said to be trading at a premium; if the price is lower, it is said to be trading at a discount. This is only applicable to closed -end scheme listed on a stock exchange.

13. Dividends

Payment made by a mutual fund to its unit holders from the income generated by it.

14. Dividend plan

An investment plan that periodically distributes the profits gained as dividends.

15. ELSS (Equity-Linked Saving Schemes)

Diversified equity funds that additionally offer a tax deduction under Section 80C on investments up to Rs. 1 lakh.

16. Equity funds

The class of schemes that invests primarily in Equity.

17. Expense ratio:

The 'expense ratio' of a scheme is its costs expressed as a percentage of its corpus, and is an indicator of how much it charges the investor.

18. Fund fact-sheet

A newsletter sent by mutual funds to its unit holders, either half-yearly or quarterly. The newsletter reviews performance of all its schemes during the reference period, give important scheme information such as portfolio details, and offers pointers on what lies ahead.

19. Fund of funds

Schemes that, instead of investing in stocks and bonds, provide the same exposure indirectly by investing in other mutual funds schemes.

20. Fund manager

The person responsible for managing a scheme's money.

21. Gilt funds

A class of debt funds that invest in government securities and treasury bills, with the objective of generating steady and regular returns while taking on modest levels of risk.

22. Government securities (G-secs)

Debt securities of tenures of over one year issued by the government. They don't carry any risk of default as it is issued by the government.

23. Growth plans

An investment plan wherein all gains are reinvested in the scheme

24. Initial Load

A charge imposed on the scheme to meet the cost related to the initial issue of the scheme. This can be charged only by closed-ended funds.

25. Interest Rate Risk

The change in the price of a debt security due to changes in the market interest rates is the interest rate risk. In the case of debt oriented mutual fund schemes, this interest rate risk affects the NAV of the fund. A rise in the interest rates leads to a fall in the price of a fixed income security.

26. Interim Dividend:

An advance installment of the dividend finally declared. The final dividend is atleast equal or more than the interim dividend. The interim dividend is fair indication of a company's profitability, during the year.

27. Load

A fee levied by a scheme on an investor at the time buying or selling units, expressed as percentage of the scheme's NAV. There are two types of load: entry load and exit load. An entry load (or a front -end load) is levied at the time of buying units, and has the effect of increasing the purchase price. An exit load (or a back -end load) is levied when unit holders sell their units, and has the effect of reducing the sale price.

28. Lock-in period

The period for which investments made in a scheme cannot be withdrawn. In mutual funds, a lock -in period of three years is applicable on equity -linked saving schemes (ELSS).

29. Market Capitalization

This represents the market value of the company. It is a product of the current market price and the number of shares outstanding.

30. New fund offer (NFO)

The maiden sale of units in a scheme through a process similar to that for new share issues. However, unlike shares, it doesn't really matter whether you buy units through an NFO or from the fund house subsequently.

31. Net asset value (NAV)

A measure of how much each unit of a scheme is worth at any point in time. A scheme's NAV is its net assets (the market value of the financial securities it owns minus whatever it owes) divided by the number of units it has issued.

32. No-load fund

A scheme that does not charge any processing fee.

33. Offer document

A detailed document that contains information pertaining to a scheme, intended to help the investor make an informed decision on whether to invest in the fund or not. It is also referred to as the prospectus.

34. Open -ended fund

A scheme investors can enter or exit at any point of time, at its then prevailing NAV. This convenience gives it the edge over closed-ended scheme, and makes it the preferred option, for mutual funds and investors alike.

35. Portfolio

The list of securities held by a scheme on a given day.

36. Redemption

When a unit holder sells the units back to the mutual fund.

37. Returns

The gain from an investment in percentage terms. In the context of mutual funds, returns are measured by changes in NAV.

38. Compounded Annual Growth Rate (CAGR)

This method calculates the returns a fund would have generated over a year. Since it breaks down performance into a unit of one year and incorporates the effect of compounding, annualized return is a better indicator of a fund's performance than a straight arithmetic average.

39. Risk - Adjusted returns

The risk incurred by a scheme to generate returns.

40. SEBI (Securities and Exchange Board of India)

The capital market regulator, also responsible for regulating the mutual fund industry.

41. Sector funds

The riskiest among equity funds, sector funds invest only in stocks of a specific industry, say, IT or pharmaceuticals.

42. Switching

Transferring from one scheme to another in a group of schemes operated by a Mutual fund, where the rules permit. A fee may or may not be charged for switching.

43. Systematic investment plan (SIP)

This is based on the concept of rupee cost averaging, SIP allows an investor to invest a pre-fixed amount in a scheme at set intervals, and derive the benefits of fluctuating share prices and NAVs. So, when the share price drops, the investor gets more units and when the NAV is high, his entire investment is valued at the existing higher level, while his cost of purchase averages out.

44. Standard deviation

Measure of volatility of the scheme's returns.

45. Treasury bills

Debt Securities of maturity less than one year issued by the government. The government tag means these bills don't carry any default risk; however, they are still susceptible to price fluctuations.

46. Trustee

Internal regulators in a mutual fund whose job is to ensure that the fund house safeguards the interests of its unit holders.

47. Unit

A unit in a mutual fund scheme means one share in the assets of a particular scheme.

48. Unitholder

A person, or entity, which holds units in a scheme.

49. Value investing

An investment style that tries to identify stocks that are undervalued to its intrinsic worth or to valuation for the industry in the market. They generally have a lower price earnings multiple but high dividend yields.

Index

D

E

F